Cybersecurity
Second Edition

Cybersecurity

Politics, Governance and Conflict in Cyberspace

Second Edition

DAMIEN VAN PUYVELDE

AARON F. BRANTLY

polity

First edition published in 2019 by Polity Press

This edition first published in 2025 by Polity Press

Polity Press
65 Bridge Street
Cambridge CB2 1UR, UK

Polity Press
111 River Street
Hoboken, NJ 07030, USA

ISBN-13: 978-1-5095-5870-4
ISBN-13: 978-1-5095-5871-1 (pb)

A catalogue record for this book is available from the British Library.

Library of Congress Control Number: 2024932242

Typeset in 11.5 on 13pt Garamond Pro
by Cheshire Typesetting Ltd, Cuddington, Cheshire
Printed and bound in Great Britain by CPI Group (UK) Ltd, Croydon

For further information on Polity, visit our website:
politybooks.com

Contents

Figures, tables and storyboxes

Figures

Tables

Storyboxes

Acknowledgments

Aaron would like to dedicate this book to his three sons, Andrew, Oliver and Daniel, who patiently waited for him to play or read books to them while he worked on various sections of it. Damien concurs and dedicates this book to his son Simon.

We would both like to thank Louise Knight who encouraged us to write and update this book. Thanks also to Inès Boxman for her valuable assistance.

We are delighted that the first edition of *Cybersecurity* encountered some success and hope the second edition continues to inspire future cybersecurity scholars and practitioners in their efforts to address the many challenges ahead.

Abbreviations

ABC	Atanasoff–Berry Computer
AI	Artificial Intelligence
ANSSI	Agence Nationale de Sécurité des Systèmes d'Information (France)
APT	advanced persistent threat
ARPA	Advanced Research Projects Agency (United States)
ARPANET	Advanced Research Projects Agency Network
BGP	Border Gateway Protocol
C2	command and control
C3	command, control and communications
CA	certificate authority
CCDCOE	Cooperative Cyber Defence Centre of Excellence (NATO)
CENTAM	Central America
CENTAS	Central Asia
CENTCOM	Central Command (United States)
CERN	European Council for Nuclear Research
CERT	Computer Emergency Response Team
CIA	Central Intelligence Agency (United States)
CIA triad	confidentiality, integrity and availability
CIS	Center for Internet Security
CISA	Cybersecurity and Infrastructure Security Agency (United States)
CISO	Chief Information Security Officer
COO	Chief Operating Officer
CPU	Central Processing Unit
CSIS	Center for Strategic and International Studies
CSTO	Collective Security Treaty Organization
CTO	Chief Technology Officer
CYOC	Cyberspace Operations Center (NATO)
DARPA	Defense Advanced Research Projects Agency (United States)
DDoS	Distributed Denial of Service

DHCP	Dynamic Host Configuration Protocol
DHS	Department of Homeland Security (United States)
DISA	Defense Information Systems Agency (United States)
DNC	Democratic National Committee (United States)
DNS	Domain Name System
DoD	Department of Defense (United States)
DoS	denial of service
DPRK	Democratic People's Republic of Korea (North Korea)
EEA	European Economic Area
EFF	Electronic Frontier Foundation
ENIAC	Electronic Numerator, Integrator, Analyzer and Computer
ENISA	European Union Agency for Cybersecurity
EPO	Entry Point Obfuscator
EU	European Union
FBI	Federal Bureau of Investigation (United States)
FCC	Federal Communications Commission (United States)
FSB	Federal Security Service (Russia)
FTP	File Transfer Protocol
GAN	generative adversarial network
Gbps	gigabits per second
GDP	Gross Domestic Product
GDPR	General Data Protection Regulation (European Union)
GPU	Graphics Processing Unit
GRU	General Staff Main Intelligence Directorate (Russia)
GUI	Graphical User Interface
GULFC	Gulf countries
HTTP	Hypertext Transfer Protocol
IAB	Internet Architecture Board
IAEA	International Atomic Energy Agency
IANA	Internet Assigned Numbers Authority
IASME	Information Assurance for Small and Medium Enterprises Consortium (United Kingdom)
IBM	International Business Machines
ICANN	Internet Corporation for Assigned Names and Numbers

IDPS	Intrusion Detection and Prevention System
IDS	Intrusion Detection System
IETF	Internet Engineering Task Force
IGF	Internet Governance Forum
IGO	intergovernmental organization
IMP	Interface Message Processor
IoT	Internet of Things
IP	Internet Protocol
IPB	intelligence preparation of the battlefield
IPS	Intrusion Prevention System
IRTF	Internet Research Task Force
ISAC	Information Sharing and Analysis Center
ISACA	Information Systems Audit and Control Association
ISAO	Information Sharing and Analysis Organization
ISO	International Organization for Standardization
ISOC	Internet Society
ISP	Internet Service Provider
ITRs	International Telecommunications Regulations
ITU	International Telecommunications Union
IXP	Internet Exchange Point
JTF	Joint Task Force
KGB	Committee for State Security (Soviet Union)
KLOC	thousand lines of code
LLM	large language model
LOIC	Low Orbit Ion Cannon
LOL	Laugh Out Loud
MAC	Media Access Control
MEA	Middle East and Africa
MENA	Middle East and North Africa
MILNET	Military Network
ML	Machine Learning
MMS	Multimedia Messaging Service
MVD	Ministry of Internal Affairs (Russia)
NAF	Northern Africa
NASA	National Aeronautics and Space Administration (United States)
NATO	North Atlantic Treaty Organization
NCCIC	National Cybersecurity and Communications Integration Center (United States)
NCMEC	National Center for Missing and Exploited

	Children (United States)
NEA	Nuclear Energy Agency
NFT	non-fungible token
NGO	non-governmental organization
NHS	National Health Service (United Kingdom)
NIPRnet	Non-classified Internet Protocol Router Network
NIST	National Institute of Standards and Technology (United States)
NOG	Network Operators' Group
NORAD	North American Aerospace Defense Command (United States)
NORSAR	Norwegian Seismic Array
NSA	National Security Agency (United States)
NSDD	National Security Decision Directive
NSF	National Science Foundation (United States)
NSFNET	National Science Foundation Network
NSI	Network Solutions Inc.
NTIA	National Telecommunications and Information Administration (United States)
OC	Oceania
OEWG	Open-Ended Working Group
OSI	Open Systems Interconnection
PC	personal computer
PII	personally identifiable information
PLA	People's Liberation Army (China)
RAT	Remote Access Trojan
RBN	Russian Business Network
RFC	Request for Comment
RIR	Regional Internet Registry
RUNET	Russian segment of the Internet
SASIA	South Asia
SCADA	Supervisory Control and Data Acquisition
SCO	Shanghai Cooperation Organization
SCS	South China Sea
SDL	security development lifecycle
SEA	South and East Asia
SEC	Securities and Exchange Commission (United States)
SIGINT	signals intelligence
SMS	Short Message/Messaging Service

SMTP	Simple Mail Transfer Protocol
SORM	System for Operative Investigative Activities (Russia)
SQL	Structured Query Language
SSA	sub-Saharan Africa
SVR	Foreign Intelligence Service (Russia)
tbps	terabits per second
TCP	Transmission Control Protocol
Telcos	telecommunications providers
TIP	Terminal Interface Processor
TLD	top-level domain
TLS/SSL	Transit Layer Security / Secure Socket Layer
Tor	The Onion Router
UDP	User Datagram Protocol
UK	United Kingdom
UN	United Nations
UN GGE	United Nations Governmental Group of Experts
URL	Uniform Resource Locator
US	United States
USCYBERCOM	United States Cyber Command
VPN	Virtual Private Network
W3C	World Wide Web Consortium
WSIS	World Summit on the Information Society
WWW	World Wide Web
XSS	cross-site scripting

Introduction

Every day, people interact with hundreds, if not thousands, of different devices, each connected to the Internet, forming a massive network of networks that has broadly become known as cyberspace. Everything from coffeepots to cars, mobile phones to grocery stores and gas stations, is increasingly connected and sharing information with the world around us. We have come to depend on this connected world in innumerable ways. We rely on the Internet to share information about our lives with friends and family, to check our bank accounts and to verify our purchases at stores.

Beyond the obvious devices we hold in our hands or interact with consciously, we depend on hundreds more that we are unaware of, but that keep us safe and facilitate modern life. Nearly every aspect of our daily lives is touched by computers and networks. Cars rely on hundreds of computer chips to manage traction control and environmental and braking systems. Connected computers at intersections manage the flow of traffic and prevent accidents. The natural resources our modern society depends on are managed by industrial control systems that regulate voltages between substations, and water pressure in city utilities. Every computer chip we come into contact with plays a role in the larger ecosystem of cyberspace. Each of these individual pieces fits within a broader puzzle that is deeply vulnerable to manipulation, misuse and error.

This book focuses on the interactions of individuals, groups and states in cyberspace, and walks the reader through the security challenges faced in an increasingly digital world. While many of the problems faced at the individual device level and in small networks are technical, the broader systemic implications of their use and misuse are inherently social and political. From relatively humble and hopeful beginnings, social scientific thought on issues related to cyberspace has been evolving for more than 70 years.[1] Debates on the technological connectedness of human society have changed from prognostications on the future to analyses of the present.[2]

Cyberspace is a unique and often perplexing environment, one referred to by the military as a domain of operations on a par with the

1

other combat domains of land, sea, air and space.[3] Cyberspace, unlike its counterpart domains, is entirely man-made and depends on physical, logical and human structures and organizations to operate. Some scholars even refer to cyberspace as a "substrate" that forms the foundation of much of modern life and permeates political, social, economic, technical and environmental sectors.[4]

Cyberspace, as a term, was first derived from a work of fiction in the 1980s and defined as a "consensual hallucination," referring to its ability to alter the perceived reality of those who engage one another through it in chat rooms or virtual environments such as Second Life and the Metaverse.[5] Its importance in popular culture was prevalent long before it was widely used, and its impact on national security policy has been significant almost from its inception. Social and cultural commentary on computers, individuals and networks and much more has often outpaced technological reality and informed discussions of the moral and ethical, legal and policy ramifications of an ever connected world.

Among the most discussed ramifications in the development of cyberspace is security. Security is not an isolated concept. Security failures in cyberspace can result in a wide range of "real-world" challenges that plague actors from individuals to states. Cybersecurity is often presented as an afterthought in the design and development of the Internet and its related technologies.[6] Although this is partially true, the lack of systemic security in cyberspace is a function of a variety of complex processes that include social, political, technical and economic considerations. Social scientific analysis of these attributes of cyberspace and associated technologies helps to examine the pieces of the puzzle and provides insights on how various outcomes occur or might be avoided.

The significance of cyberspace, and in particular security within cyberspace, to social scientists is growing every year. At present, more than half the world's population is connected in some way to cyberspace. Those who are not presently connected are expected to come online in the years to come. At the close of 2023, by some estimates, more than 450,000 new pieces of malicious software (malware) were being released daily.[7] The growth and diversity of malware spreading within cyberspace are having a substantial impact on nation states, businesses and individuals. Global anti-virus firm Symantec estimated that 978 million people in 20 countries were affected by cybercrime, equating to a total loss of approximately $172 billion or $142 per person in 2017.[8] In 2020, cybersecurity company McAfee estimated global losses from cybercrime at over $1 trillion.[9] Other malicious activities in cyberspace – such as espionage, Distributed Denial of Service (DDoS) attacks, social engineering, information operations and a host of other activities – are challenging modern societies in countless ways.

To respond to cybercrime, espionage and other malicious behavior in cyberspace, public and private actors are spending large sums of money to develop robust cybersecurity strategies, and are investing in global governance organizations and fighting for norms and other behaviors to constrain the proliferation of cybercrime, espionage and malfeasant state behavior.[10] Within the business community, technology companies are leading the fight against cybercrime through the implementation of more ubiquitous encryption within platforms, and they are fighting government policies and legal efforts to undermine encryption within their products.[11] Businesses' efforts to secure their products come with trade-offs for law-enforcement and intelligence agencies. More secure communications devices and online platforms have been used by transnational criminals and terrorist organizations to plan and engage in attacks against citizens of multiple countries.[12] Beyond the proliferation of malware for criminal activities, countless cyberattacks have targeted nation states and their critical infrastructures – including hospitals, public transit, electric and water facilities and many more. Most of these attacks were undertaken with the intent of degrading, denying, sometimes even destroying, critical national capabilities. Many states are now opting to invest substantial resources in the development of civilian and military cyber programs for both offensive and defensive purposes. International organizations such as the North Atlantic Treaty Organization (NATO) have begun outlining military responses to cyberattacks. Some countries, such as the United States, are going as far as claiming the prerogative to respond to certain cyberattacks with nuclear weapons.[13]

It is increasingly difficult to deny the immense importance and impact of cyberspace in every aspect of life in many developed and developing nations. There are huge socio-economic benefits associated with the increased development and proliferation of cyberspace into communities never before connected to the Internet. We are now able to share information with friends and family members around the world instantaneously. We can learn about other countries and cultures, engage in global commerce and support communities around the world affected by natural disasters, war or political repression in ways never before possible. The potential of cyberspace to achieve a great many benefits is limited only by the creativity of those who leverage the increasing range of technologies available to them. Yet, as cyberspace expands and becomes more vital to everyday life, the security challenges often found offline – crime, war, terrorism, cultural and political repression, among many others – must be addressed within cyberspace.

Our approach

This book is designed for readers with limited prior experience in cybersecurity, or as a refresher for those with more robust backgrounds. We introduce a variety of concepts, practical problems and core policy debates necessary to understand security in and through computer networks. Each chapter is carefully constructed to provide our readers with a comprehensive introduction to the complexities and challenges of cybersecurity in an engaging and relevant fashion. The chapters include a reader's guide presenting the bottom-line of each chapter upfront, case studies presented in storyboxes to help our readers analyze the complexity of cybersecurity in practice, as well as discussion questions to hone critical thinking skills, exercises to learn more actively about cybersecurity, and a brief list of suggested readings. Upon reading this book, readers will know the key attributes of, controversies surrounding, policies, norms and laws regarding, and challenges posed by cybersecurity, and will be well positioned to continue to advance their knowledge, should they choose to do so.

We structured this book around ten chapters designed to introduce readers to a range of concepts associated with cybersecurity. The core argument bringing these chapters together presents cyberspace as a complex socio-technical-economic domain that achieves relevance and importance through human design and manipulation. Despite its technical specificities and unique character, cyberspace is a domain of human activity and interactions. Humans created cyberspace, and use digital means to serve both beneficial and malicious purposes. The centrality of humans in cyberspace makes social scientific approaches imperative to the study of cybersecurity. An emphasis on human interactions in and through cyberspace allows us to approach cybersecurity from multiple perspectives, ranging from realism to liberalism and constructivism, as well as multiple levels of analysis from the individual to the organizational, the local to the national and international, where rising norms of governance are redefining human interactions. The interactions between the actors of cyberspace and the structure of cyberspace constitute the core of our analytical framework. Users of cyberspace have a unique opportunity to shape, and are in turn shaped by, its structure.

Chapter 1 introduces readers to the history of cyberspace, and the evolution of security and economic issues that have arisen over the years as cyberspace has grown. Chapter 2 explores what cyberspace really is and how it works by examining the basic technical functions of the domain. Most importantly, chapter 2 introduces readers to the "layers" of cyberspace as a means of making what seems to be an overwhelmingly complex environment more intellectually manageable. Chapter 3 traces the development of governance in cyberspace and examines the political tensions between different models of governance. Chapter 4 dives into the details of how cyber capabilities are developed by state and non-state actors, and how the development of these capabilities generates insecurity. Chapter 5 provides an overview of the complex national and international security implications of an evolving man-made domain that has come to pervade modern life. Chapter 6 presents the challenges posed by conflict in cyberspace, and explores how such conflict is both similar to and different from more conventional notions of war and conflict. Chapter 7 looks at how actors across all levels organize for defense and deterrence in response to a multitude of cyber threats. Chapter 8 takes a step back from state-to-state interactions and shifts the level of analysis to non-state threats associated with criminal networks and terrorist groups. Chapter 9 probes how cybersecurity and democracy, once thought to be mutually reinforcing, have become increasingly uneasy bedfellows, by examining how cyberspace can be both a tool for the enhancement of democracy and damaging to it. Finally, the book concludes by examining what the future of cyberspace has to offer with the increasingly important Internet of Things (IoT), Artificial Intelligence (AI), human–machine interactions and quantum computing.

1   The expanding scope of cybersecurity

Reader's guide

- Over the course of a century, computers evolved from a mechanical engine performing very specific tasks to a personal device serving a very wide variety of functions.

- The US military and select research centers played a key role in developing and expanding networks of networked computers to share data. In the mid-1990s, this network moved to commercial providers, which expanded access to the Internet and related services.

- The ubiquity of networked computers in the lives of billions of humans has resulted in an equally large number of vulnerabilities. The rise of cyber threats largely follows growing access to and use of computers.

- Cybersecurity is a global security issue. Insecurity in and through cyberspace concerns not only states but also non-state actors and individuals all over the world.

This chapter explores the history of cyberspace and related security concerns, from the creation of computers to the present day. The development of computers has been spurred on by human innovation, from mechanical tabulators to digital machines linked together in networks. Security concerns have played a central role in this history. The governments of the United States and the United Kingdom funded early research into computers during World War II to improve anti-aircraft defense and codebreaking. In the aftermath of World War II, the US Department of Defense (DoD) sponsored much of the early research into computing and the development of computer networks to advance US capabilities and power. This stream of government funding has allowed scientists, in government, academia and the industry, to develop computers and networking as a collaborative tool to share resources and information. Openness and transparency – two values that are essential to the scientific process – guided their work, and helped to shape the early development of what would become the Internet.

Growing access to computers spurred on a number of online communities, allowing humans to express themselves and interact in a new domain: cyberspace. Human activities such as commerce and entertainment, but also espionage and theft, found new expressions online. The 1990s witnessed a rise of cyber threats affecting all levels of society and government. Cyberspace became a cause of concern for governments, who feared that the sensitive data they kept on computers could be stolen, manipulated and potentially weaponized, to damage national defense, the economy or even the social fabric of society. As human reliance on computers has expanded, cyberspace has provided new opportunities to exert power, and to threaten the domestic and international order.

Today, cyberspace is a complex socio-technical-economic environment embraced by 5.2 billion individuals, and millions of groups and communities. All these actors benefit from the opportunities, facilitated by cyberspace, to share resources and information. Yet digital networks host an ever growing number of cyber threats, which can disrupt human activities, in the digital and physical world. Cyberspace is now a global security issue that transcends national, social and cultural boundaries. As a result, cybersecurity has begun to emerge as an important issue in the field of International Relations (IR), where researchers and practitioners debate the nature of cyber threats, and the most appropriate frameworks for mitigating them.

A brief history of the computer

The history of the computer can be traced back to nineteenth-century England, when mathematics professor Charles Babbage designed his analytical engine. Machines like the analytical engine relied on mechanical components such as levers and gears to compute complex calculations. What distinguished Babbage's machine from others – at least on paper, since his engine never came close to being built – was that it was programmable. While machines could only perform a single function, computers like Babbage's could be programmed to perform multiple functions.[1] New applications for mechanical computers emerged in the following decades. American inventor Herman Hollerith developed a method of storing information as holes punched into cards.

His machine was used to tabulate the 1890 US census.[2] The US military developed mechanical computers to improve the use of bombsights on military aircraft in the 1930s. An aimer would input parameters such as speed, altitude and direction, and the bombsight calculated the point at which to aim.[3] Human "computers" continued to direct the "program" for these machines. This dependence on humans limited the speed at which mechanical computers could support their activities.

The first generation of electronic computers emerged in the 1930s. This new technology used electric relays and switches to make calculations. The Atanasoff–Berry Computer (ABC), created by physics professor John Vincent Atanasoff and his graduate assistant Clifford Berry, is often considered to be the first electronic digital computer. The ABC was designed to solve systems of linear equations using binary numbers represented by digits such as 0 and 1. The first prototype of the ABC was built in 1939, with the final rendition weighing more than 700 pounds. The start of World War II oriented research into electronic computers. In the United States, researchers working at the Bell Laboratories developed an anti-aircraft gun director, the M-9, that could direct itself without human interaction using data fed by radar tracking. On the other side of the Atlantic, British codebreakers built another set of electronic computers, called the Colossus, to decode text generated by the Lorenz cipher, which was used by the German army to protect high-level messages. The use of these computers was characterized by a high level of secrecy, which limited any subsequent transfer of knowledge to the research and commercial sectors.[4] Storybox 1.1 presents a brief history of the ENIAC (figure 1.1), one of the first electronic general-purpose computers ever made, which is sometimes presented as the prototype from which most modern computers evolved.

Storybox 1.1 The ENIAC

In the aftermath of World War II, the US government and a group of researchers at the University of Pennsylvania completed the Electronic Numerator, Integrator, Analyzer and Computer (ENIAC). Unlike the ABC or Colossus, the ENIAC ran calculations at electronic speed, without being slowed by any mechanical parts. The ENIAC was also the first general-purpose computer, able to solve a large set of numerical problems through re-programming. Despite its versatility, this new computer was primarily used to calculate artillery firing tables, taking over the work of hundreds of humans working on missile tables.[5] The development of the ENIAC inspired several similar projects seeking to develop programmable computers that could store information.[6]

The next generation of computers emerged in 1947 and was characterized by the use of transistors, which increased their reliability.[7] This second generation was the first to be used for commercial purposes, leading, most notably, to the success of International Business Machines (IBM), a company aiming to produce computers for all. By the end of the 1950s, dozens of companies contributed to an emerging computer industry in the United States and the United Kingdom, but also in continental Europe and Japan. The development of general-purpose computers required programs to give them functionality. Research on computer programming languages (to facilitate the tasking of computers) and operating systems (to manage the flow of work of a computer), throughout the 1950s, eventually led to the distinction between hardware and software.[8] The US DoD maintained an essential role, sponsoring specific computer languages and operating systems, and indirectly driving the industry.[9] Computers remained extremely expensive,

Figure 1.1 ENIAC, *c.*1946
Source: University of Pennsylvania Archives

which limited the market for them and, by extension, their uses. By 1962, there were around 10,000 computers worldwide, most of them located in the United States.

The invention of the integrated circuit spurred the emergence of a third generation of computers. The minicomputers that arose in the mid-1960s were smaller, more powerful and more reliable. A new digital (r) evolution was taking place. Computers moved from being a government machine, to an esoteric hobby, and then, finally, to a household item. A number of inventions facilitated this evolution. Human–computer interactions improved following the introduction of multiple tiled windows on computer screens, text-editing software and the mouse.[10] New financial and manufacturing applications contributed to the emergence of a market for software and further expanded the uses of computers.[11] Developments in hardware, specifically the creation of affordable personal computers (PCs), significantly widened access to computers, inspired new uses and forged communities of practice. In 1975, Steve Wozniak and Steve Jobs announced the Apple II computer, an off-the-shelf computer targeted directly at the consumer and small businesses. A few years later, IBM introduced its first PC. At a cost of $1,565 (equivalent to $5,310 in 2023), this PC was not beyond the reach of small companies and hobbyists. The percentage of American households with computers more than doubled in the 1980s, and continued to expand exponentially in the 1990s, eventually exceeding 40%.[12] In 2014, 80% of adults in the United States, 78% in Russia, 59% in China, 55% in Brazil and (only) 11% in India had a working computer in their household.[13] In a little over half a century, government support and scientific innovation transformed the digital computer from an advanced research tool to a household item. The increasingly prominent role played by computers in modern society has opened up countless opportunities for individual pursuits.

An open network of networks

The convergence between computing and communication is a defining feature of the digital age. Networked communication over wires has existed since the telegraph (1844), and evolved with the creation of the telephone (1876) and the teletype writer (1914). These machines all rely on circuits to communicate signals, voice or written messages from one point to another. Their development led to the installation of wired connections across continents, forming vast communication networks. In the aftermath of World War II, scientists established connections between two digital computers relying on a single line of communication. If the line between these computers broke down, the communication ended. The practice of time-sharing allowed multiple users to get access to a computer simultaneously to use its processing power. Only a limited number of powerful research computers existed in the United States, and many researchers, who were far removed from their locations, sought to gain access to them.[14] Accessing computers typically required extensive organization and travel. One solution to this problem was to connect computers together as a part of a larger network. Such a network would allow users to access specific computers and data remotely, and would ensure greater reliability than a simple connection between two computers. If one computer stopped functioning properly, other computers could keep the network running.

Computer networking flourished in the United States thanks to a robust and open research culture and substantial government support.[15] Most of the support behind the development of early computer networks came from the US DoD and its Advanced Research Projects Agency (ARPA), an organization established in 1960 to fund high-risk high-gain research. ARPA was particularly keen to develop computer networking to facilitate the sharing of research findings at universities and other government-sponsored laboratories throughout the nation. In 1969, ARPA funding helped establish the first computer network and ancestor of the Internet: ARPANET. Reflecting on the role of the US military in the maturation of computer networking, national security scholar Derek Reveron notes that "there has always been an implicit national security purpose for the Internet."[16]

Networking digital computers created a new means for humans to communicate with each other. ARPANET first served as a platform for researchers to develop and refine networking technologies that linked a handful of universities and research centers. On October 29, 1969, researchers at the University of California in Los Angeles tried to log in to a computer at the Stanford Research Institute, and began typing the required "log in" command. Their computer crashed after the two first letters; the first message ever sent on the ARPANET was "lo." Figure 1.2 shows how the original ARPA network grew from 2 nodes in 1969, to 55 in 1977.[17] Each of these nodes represents a processor, which can be considered as a router that receives and sends data on the computer network. The two maps show the type of institutions hosting these nodes: research universities and institutes, national laboratories, military and intelligence agencies. The 1977 map shows the nascent complexity of a network that connected processors through both landlines and satellite connections. On the other side of the Atlantic, French and British researchers were developing similar networks (CYCLADES in France, and the Mark I project at the UK National Physical Laboratories), but funding difficulties limited their progress.[18]

In the United States, more and more universities and research centers joined or wanted to join ARPANET. To help users connect together, Vint Cerf, a researcher at Stanford University, and Robert Khan from ARPA, developed a common transmission protocol (Transmission Control Protocol or TCP) that explained how to establish a connection and transmit messages on their network. A separate protocol was then developed to couple existing networks together. This protocol, the Internet Protocol (IP), facilitated the internetworking of digital computers. The complete description of these two protocols and the rights to use them were freely available to all. Any network that wanted to join simply had to follow the Transmission Control and Internet protocols. This open access policy – inspired by the academic practice of information sharing – defined the architecture of the early Internet and allowed the network to grow in scale.[19] Information technology pioneer and former ARPA employee Barry Leiner and his colleagues explain that the early Internet was developed as "a general infrastructure on which new applications could be conceived."[20] This approach stood in stark contrast to the way in which the US DoD (still the main funder of the Internet at the time) conceived of information sharing. In the defense and national security communities, the dissemination of information tends to be tightly controlled to prevent unauthorized disclosures. An important implication of the open architecture of the Internet is that no single entity could control access to and uses of the network. While this approach spurred a tremendous growth in network users, it would also pose a number of challenges. Malicious actors soon started to use the Internet to steal resources and information, and to mislead network users.

As networking became increasingly common, its value increased and researchers developed new applications, beyond sharing machines for their processing power. Initial Internet applications focused on communication means. Researchers started posting messages and replying to each other's comments on editable pages, or bulletin boards, accessible online. In 1972, computer programmer Ray Tomlinson wrote a program for composing and reading messages, and sending them from one computer to another. As a result of Tomlinson's attempt to solve a networked communication issue, electronic mail (later known as E-Mail)

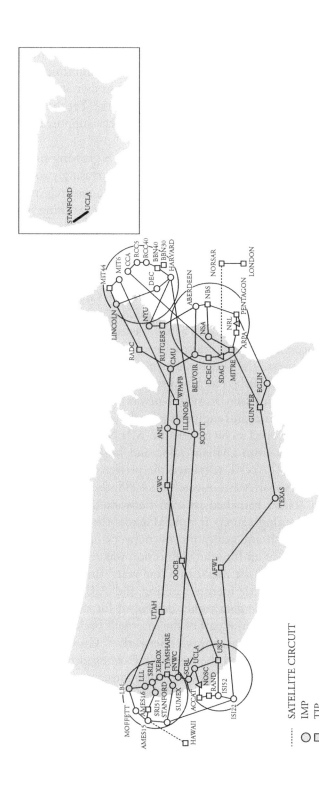

(NOTE THIS MAP DOES NOT SHOW ARPA'S EXPERIMENTAL SATELLITE CONNECTIONS) NAMES SHOWN ARE IMP NAMES, NOT (NECESSARILY) HOST NAMES

SATELLITE CIRCUIT

○ **IMP**

□ **TIP**

△ **PLURIBUS IMP**

Figure 1.2 ARPANET in December 1969 (top) and July 1977 (bottom)

Source: Frank Heart, Alex McKenzie, John McQuillian and David Walden, *ARPANET Completion Report,* Bolt, Beranek and Newman Inc., Burlington, MA, January 4, 1978, III-79-III-89

was born. Within a year, this new application generated 73 percent of all ARPANET traffic.[21] Soon the value of networked communication became clear to everyone involved, and an increasing number of universities and government agencies joined the web of networks. Yet the early Internet continued to be mostly populated by researchers, supported by investment from the US government.

The spread of personal computers in the 1980s fed a growing interest in internetworking and fostered a shift toward an increasingly social network, away from its previous principal application as a research hub. As well as a technological evolution, the growth of internetworking is a sociocultural phenomenon. These social and cultural factors differentiate the Internet from previous networks. The emergence of PC hobbyists and communities of practices focusing on computers – for example, gamers – fostered internetworking from the bottom up in the 1980s.[22] It was in this context that science fiction writer William Gibson coined the term "cyberspace." Gibson imagined cyberspace as a virtual world of data linked by computer networks and accessible through consoles.[23]

As a result of its success, the core infrastructure of the ARPANET had to expand to host new users. The network expanded beyond the United States, with new nodes established at University College London and then at the NORSAR research laboratory in Norway in 1982.[24] As more and more researchers, scientists and engineers joined the ARPANET, the military community developed its own network (MILNET) in 1983, to separate sensitive military from civilian traffic and implement stricter security requirements. ARPANET remained the preferred platform for industry, academia and government research. In 1985, the US National Science Foundation (NSF) launched its own network (NSFNET) to connect the supercomputing centers it funded across the country and promote advanced research and education on networking.[25] Any university receiving funding for an Internet connection was required to use NSFNET and provide access for users. In a few years' time NSFNET took over as the main hub for internetworking and ARPANET was decommissioned in 1990. The data routes developed for this scientific network eventually formed a major part of the Internet's backbone – the principal data routes between large computer networks.[26] Growing commercial interest in ARPANET and then NSFNET changed the nature of internetworking, transforming the research hub into a popular communication platform. In 1994, the US government decided to turn over official control of the regional backbone connections of NSFNET to private interests. Commercial Internet Service Providers (ISPs) started offering their services to individual users, who could connect online using their phone landline.[27] As the Internet expanded, commercial providers of hardware (e.g. computers and modems) and software (e.g. browsers) multiplied.

The spread of the Internet

Internetworking became mainstream in the late 1990s following the invention of the World Wide Web (WWW), which facilitated inter-personal communications in cyberspace. In 1990, a group of scientists based at the European Council for Nuclear Research (CERN) laboratory in Switzerland created a new document format to present information in a set of linked computer documents (Hypertext Transfer Protocol or HTTP). This protocol allowed users to link each document to another one through specific words, phrases or images. In 1991, these innovations spurred the creation of a new application which compiled and linked multimedia documents and made them available to any network user: the WWW. An exponential number of interlinked HTTP documents became accessible online thanks to a system that identified them: the Uniform Resource Locator (URL), colloquially known as a web address. Subsequently, researchers at the University of Illinois developed a browser software named Mosaic, which simplified public access and ability to surf the web.[28]

Internet usage expanded dramatically in the following years, spurred by the convergence of increasingly cheap and powerful computers, the multiplication of modems facilitating Internet connection through phone lines, and new browsers such as Internet Explorer and Netscape (1995).[29] At the dawn of the twenty-first century, further technological developments, such as the spread of wireless broadband technology, commonly known as Wi-Fi, and the rise of smartphones, facilitated further access to the Internet.[30] Figure 1.3 shows how the number of Internet users exploded from a few million users in the early 1990s to over 5 billion today (that is, more than two-thirds of the world population). This rapid expansion has been matched by an exponential growth in the number of websites and applications. Amazon and eBay were both established in 1995, the Chinese e-commerce giant Alibaba was founded a few years later in 1999. Together, they have reshaped the way millions of humans shop and access consumer goods. In the last two decades, the Internet has become an increasingly social space, connecting individuals online through communities of interest. American companies such as LinkedIn (2002), Facebook (2004) and Twitter (2006, X since

2023) have provided new platforms for networks of "friends" to form. The Chinese Renren Network (2005) and Russian platform VKontakte (2006) developed similar services. The advent of these social media and other online applications empowered Internet users to shape and diversify the content of the "Web 2.0."[31]

The web has now become a central part of billions of lives across the globe. In the last five years, the Internet has made the leap from a primarily terrestrial infrastructure to now having thousands of low earth orbit satellites that make Internet access anywhere, any time with low latency a real possibility around the globe. With the multiplication of social platforms and wearable technologies such as smartphones and smart watches, cyberspace is now a central arena for life in the twenty-first century. Statistics reveal that more Internet users are now located in Asia (China and India account for more than 2.93 billion users) than in Europe and North America. Today, more than 92 percent of Internet users – some 4.8 billion people – interact on social media. The evolution and spread of web-enabled technologies toward near ubiquity marks another step in the development of the Internet. "Web 3.0" will be (even) more decentralized, and will leverage emerging technologies

Number of people who used the Internet[a] in the last three months.

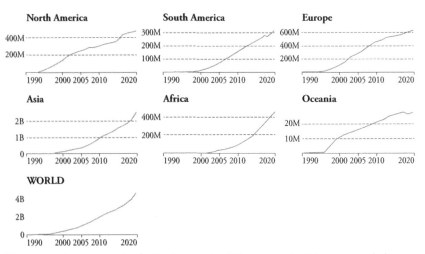

^a **Internet user:** An internet user is defined by the International Telecommunication Union as anyone who has accessed the internet from any location in the last three months. This can be from any type of device, including a computer, mobile phone, personal assistant, games machine, digital TV, and other technological devices.

Figure 1.3 Internet users since 1990, by region

Source: OurWorldinData.org based on International Telecommunications Union (ITU) and United Nations (UN) data from 2022

such as AI, augmented and virtual reality to support the emergence of a "metaverse" – a single and increasingly immersive virtual space.

The advent of the Internet has generated countless opportunities to learn from, and connect with, humans from across the globe. The borderless nature of this digital realm has opened space for millions of individuals to develop communities of interest and express their ideas and identity.

Large Internet communities have formed around common interests such as sports, cats and dogs, or environmental protection. The advent of the Internet is reshaping human lives, social bonds and politics, and challenging traditional, state-centric ideas about human interactions across the globe.[32] The increasing ubiquity of the Internet and cyberspace in the daily routines of billions of humans has resulted in an equally large number of vulnerabilities. Accidental and deliberate actions can impair or hinder everything from private interactions on social media to the functioning of entire industries, and even the security of nation states.

The rise of cyber threats

The rise of cyber threats is directly linked to the growing complexity of computers and the scope of human activities in cyberspace, from research and military affairs to economic and social activities.[33] Given that the US government played a central role in the early development of computers and computer networks, the pre-history of cyber threats is American-oriented. Michael Warner, the historian of the US Cyber Command, distinguishes four successive insights that marked the history of national cybersecurity in the United States. Early US concerns about cyber threats can be traced back to the practice of multiprogramming, which broadened access to the information stored on computers. Warner finds that Congress started expressing concerns about this practice in the 1960s when government officials realized that computers could spill sensitive data (first insight). These concerns were relatively limited in the early days of networking when the overall number of ARPANET users was in the hundreds. In 1972, US intelligence agencies tested the security of their networks and found that many sensitive databases could be accessed from a single computer. The second key insight reached by the US government was that sensitive government data could be stolen, perhaps even manipulated, from a single point of access. The threats posed by such cyber intrusion rose to a new level when computers became essential to modern weapon systems and military decision-making. The networking of computers, and the open architecture that characterized internetworking, created vulnerabilities in government and military systems which could, for example, increase the risk that adversaries would disrupt military command and control (C2) systems used for missile warning. The threat of intrusion was sufficiently serious to push President Reagan to sign a National Security Decision Directive (NSDD) warning about the risk of "interception, unauthorized electronic access, and related forms of technical exploitation" to telecommunications and automated information processing systems. The directive put the National Security Agency (NSA) in charge of monitoring all "government telecommunications systems and automated information systems."[34]

Multiple incidents confirmed growing US government concern in the following years. In 1986, a hacker penetrated sensitive systems connecting computers at the Lawrence Berkeley National Laboratory and MITRE Corporation. This remote attack relied on the ARPANET and MILNET to infiltrate dozens of computers at the Pentagon and a number of other military bases. Clifford Stoll, a systems administrator at Lawrence Berkeley Lab, first identified the attack and began to investigate its origins with the help of the Federal Bureau of Investigation (FBI) and the telecommunication company AT&T. The subsequent investigation revealed that hackers had sold the information they collected on the US networks to the Soviet Committee for State Security (the KGB). Stoll subsequently wrote a book that publicized what is often considered to be the first publicly known case of cyber espionage.[35] In 1988, a malicious code spread on the Internet and slowed thousands of computers used by US government and private organizations. This malware, nicknamed the Morris worm, demonstrated the inherent vulnerability of computer networks. The ability of cyber threats to spread across networks reinforced the need for cooperation between users. The effects of the Morris worm prompted the Defense Advanced Research Projects Agency (ARPA changed its name to DARPA in 1972) to establish a Computer Emergency Response Team (CERT) to coordinate information and responses to such computer vulnerabilities.

The public debate on cyber threats took a new turn in the early 1990s when experts started to discuss the military implications of cyberattacks. The public debate on cyber war, which we will examine in chapter 6, can be traced back to the early 1990s as analysts forecasted what war would look like in the twenty-first century.[36] At the time, cyber war was perceived as a form of information warfare, which sought to decapitate and exploit the C2 structure of the enemy forces. Cyberattacks provided new, electronic means to disrupt computer systems or corrupt the data they hosted. Computers, Warner notes, had become a weapon of war (third insight). The inclusion of computer attack in the US military arsenal would soon lead to a fourth insight: other countries may utilize computers for a similar purpose.[37]

In 1997, the US DoD ran an exercise codenamed ELIGIBLE RECEIVER, and found that a moderately sophisticated adversary could inflict considerable damage on sensitive US government networks. During this exercise, a small team of government hackers working at the NSA attacked the computer systems of multiple US military commands, gained administrative access to them, tampered with email messages, and disrupted operational systems. Government networks seemed wide open to electronic attacks. Shortly after this exercise, the US government suffered a series of real attacks that confirmed the existence of significant weaknesses. In February 1998, a series of cyberattacks targeted DoD unclassified computer networks at multiple Air Force bases, the National Aeronautics and Space Administration (NASA) and federal laboratories associated with the military. This operation, codenamed SOLAR SUNRISE, showed that the DoD detection systems were insufficient to protect government networks against unwanted cyber intrusions. Worse still, investigations into the attacks revealed that the attackers were not a foreign intelligence service, but two California teenagers who had been directed by Israeli hacker Ehud Tenenbaum.[38]

The rise of cyber threats has affected not only government networks and capabilities but also society. Originally, hackers were computer geeks motivated by curiosity and entertainment. The term "hacking" itself initially meant playing with machines, and hackers sought to demonstrate their aptitude for programming. A 1981 *New York Times* article describes how "skilled, often young, computer programmers" would "probe the defenses of a computer system, searching out the limits and the possibilities of the machine."[39] Computer industry pioneer Bill Gates, the founder of Microsoft, revealed on the BBC that he hacked into the computer system of his school as a teen so that he could attend all-girl classes.[40] Other hackers were driven by more nefarious goals. In 1981, a hacker who used the nickname Captain Zap was convicted for breaking into the computers of the telecommunications service provider AT&T and changing the company's billing system to create discounted rates during business hours.

The threat hackers posed to the corporate world, and by extension to the economy, generated increasing media coverage in the 1980s, eventually drawing the attention of legislators and entrepreneurs.[41] The

US Congress passed the Federal Computer Fraud and Abuse Act in 1986 to prohibit unauthorized access to federal computers, and traffic in computer passwords. A few years later, the Parliament of the United Kingdom passed the Computer Misuse Act in response to a 1988 court case targeting two hackers who gained unauthorized access to British Telecom's viewdata service (an early teletext network). This Act, and the growing scope of cyber threats, inspired several other countries, from Ireland to Canada, to draft legislation on cybercrime in the following years.[42]

In the 1990s, concern with cybersecurity deepened and became a security issue of societal proportions. Most of the cyber threats that are commonly known today – viruses, worms, trojans, denial of service (DoS) attacks – emerged at the same time that the Internet spread and computer networking became an increasingly prominent part of modern life. The rise of the WWW diversified the uses of the Internet and expanded the scope of cyber threats. The growth of e-commerce, for example, created new opportunities for criminals to make profit online. The possibility to make online payments also led to new types of scam relying on emails, for example. Confronted with a rise in cyber threats, the corporate world developed new answers. The computer security company McAfee was established in 1987, and released its VirusScan the same year. An anti-virus software industry developed in the following years to serve not only the government and private sectors, but also users accessing the Internet from home.[43]

Critical infrastructure and key sectors of modern society – such as agriculture, banking, healthcare, transportation, water and power – rely on computer networks that control and supervise data streams (also called SCADA systems, for 'Supervisory Control and Data Acquisition'). In 2007, the Idaho National Laboratory ran an experiment, the Aurora Generator test, demonstrating that a computer program could disrupt a diesel generator used as part of an electric grid, and cause it to explode.[44] Some experts fear that such an explosion could generate a cascading failure of an entire power grid. Growing concern about cyberattacks on critical infrastructure has pushed governments to devise strategies to protect societal reliance on cyber infrastructure. The 2003 US "National Strategy to Secure Cyberspace" noted that "threats in cyberspace have risen dramatically" and emphasized the need for public–private engagement to secure cyberspace.[45] Since critical infrastructure is privately owned in most advanced countries, working across the public–private divide is essential to ensure national cybersecurity. As such, dozens of countries have adopted a similar approach to their national cybersecurity and developed specific organizations and strategies to counter cyber threats to the public and private sectors.[46] International organizations have also become involved, seeking to facilitate the adoption of cybersecurity strategies. For instance, the ITU published a "Guide to Developing a National Cybersecurity Strategy" in tandem with corporate and multilateral partners in 2018.

A global security issue

The dawn of the twenty-first century saw the advent of increasingly sophisticated attacks and malware that spread around the world. The internationalization of cyberspace transformed cybersecurity into a global security issue. While most cyberattacks came from the United States and Europe in the 1990s, by the early 2000s they went international. In 2000, the Love Bug or "ILOVYOU" computer worm originated in the Philippines and spread across the WWW (initially relying on an email attachment). The virus overwrote files hosted by tens of millions of computers causing an estimated loss of $10 billion in work hours.[47] The Zotob worm originated in Morocco in August 2005, and caused troubles at CNN, the *New York Times*, the US Senate and the Centers for Disease Control and Prevention in the United States.[48] Research shows the increasingly global character of cyber threats. The Center for Strategic and International Studies (CSIS), a renowned think tank based in Washington, DC, has compiled a list of significant cyber incidents since 2005. While this list does not represent the whole spectrum of cyber threats, it illustrates their growing scope. The current list (2023) compiles 1,034 cyber incidents affecting government agencies, defense and high-tech companies, or economic crimes with losses of more than a million dollars. This constitutes an increase of 738 additional serious attacks over the total we reported in the first edition of this book (data up to 2018). Figure 1.4 uses CSIS data to show a rise in the number of significant cyber incidents since 2005. Figure 1.5 uses the European repository of cyber incidents (2000–23) to show the broad geographic spread of the attacks. North America, Europe and Asia host most of the victims of cyber incidents. This should come as no surprise since the penetration rate of the Internet is highest on these three continents.

In the last decade, most sophisticated threats, generally developed by well-resourced state actors, have affected computer systems across the

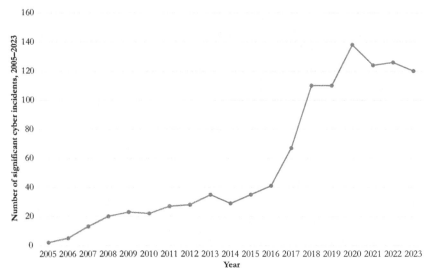

Figure 1.4 Number of significant cyber incidents by year, 2005–2023
Data source: CSIS

public–private divide. A widely consulted report released in 2011 by cybersecurity company Mandiant exposed how one of China's cyber espionage units stole "hundreds of terabytes of data from at least 141 organizations across a diverse set of industries beginning as early as 2006."[49] This advanced persistent threat (APT) targeted intellectual property – the bedrock of the modern economy – in a number of sectors, including information technology, financial services, construction and manufacturing, the chemical and energy industries, and aerospace, to name a few. Altogether, victims were located in 15 countries, ranging from the United States and Canada to Belgium, France and the United Kingdom, as well as Israel, the United Arab Emirates, India, Japan, Taiwan and South Africa. The fact that a company authored this widely discussed report further illustrates the development of a robust market for cybersecurity, which serves government as well as private-sector clients.

Given the global scope of cyberspace and cyber threats (see figure 1.5), social scientific research on cybersecurity should strive to consider cases beyond the United States. While the United States has historically played a leading role in the development of computers and internet-working, and thus continues to attract many cyberattacks, cybersecurity is truly a global security concern.

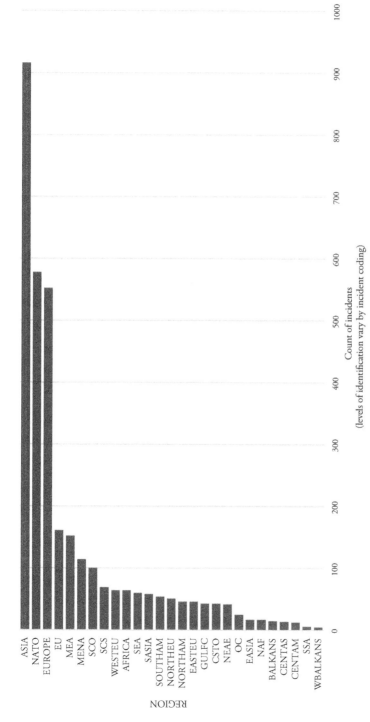

Figure 1.5 Distribution of cyber incidents by regions affected, 2000–2023

Data source: European Repository of Cyber Incidents[50]

New issues have come to the forefront of the international cyber-security debate since the first edition of this book was published in 2019. Advances in AI, including generative models, have facilitated the spread of deepfake videos and pictures that seek to manipulate vast online audiences to achieve political effects. Large language models (LLMs) such as OpenAI's ChatGPT are beginning to have a dramatic impact on cyber-space and user interactions within this evolving domain. The increasing prominence of AI in everyday life has fostered a new global gold rush, but this time it is for advanced semi-conductors. New conflicts have arisen that demonstrate the limits of cyber-enabled warfare and demonstrated the pervasive threat that cyberattacks can pose to nearly all individuals on the Internet. This book includes more than a dozen case studies and examples from different countries, as well as non-state actors, that reflect this evolving global scope.

Cybersecurity is a global problem that requires a global approach. Yet most of the physical layer of cyberspace and the governance of security threats takes place at the nation-state level, and national governments have developed the most advanced offensive and defensive capabilities in cyberspace. As a result, our analysis engages with multiple levels (individual, organizational, societal, national and global) to further our understanding of cybersecurity.

Discussion questions

1. In what ways has the development of cyberspace affected contemporary threats to cybersecurity?

2. What are the key turning points in the history of cybersecurity?

3. Read the latest CSIS list of significant cyber incidents and pick three events that caught your attention. What is the significance of these cyber incidents?

Exercise

Identify three key ways in which historical legacies continue to weigh on contemporary cybersecurity.

Additional resources

Internet history timeline, see: www.computerhistory.org/internethistory.

Paul E. Ceruzzi, *Computing: A Concise History* (Cambridge, MA: MIT Press, 2012).

Werner Herzog, "Lo and Behold: Reveries of the Connected World," video documentary (available on Netflix).

Barry M. Leiner, Vincton G. Cerf, David D. Clark et al., "The Past and Future History of the Internet," *Communications of the ACM* 40/2 (1997): 102–8.

Michael Warner, "Cybersecurity: A Pre-history," *Intelligence and National Security* 27/5 (2012): 781–99.

2 What is cyberspace?

Reader's guide

- Understanding the nature and characteristics of cyberspace provides a necessary foundation to debate about the social and political aspects of cybersecurity.

- Cyberspace is composed of three layers: physical, logical, and persona. Each of them involves a variety of actors engaged in and affected by the governance of cyberspace.

- The physical layer refers to tangible infrastructure and hardware components. It includes network cables, data centers, servers, wireless signals, etc.

- The logical layer encompasses the rules, protocols and structures that govern how data flows online.

- The persona layer pertains to the online identities and profiles that individuals and entities create and present in the digital world.

In 1983, President Reagan watched the blockbuster success *WarGames* at Camp David. The movie is a Cold War science-fiction film about a teenager, David Lightman, who hacks into a North American Aerospace Defense Command (NORAD) supercomputer, the WOPR – War Operations Plan Response – and pushes the United States to the brink of war. Nuclear Armageddon is thwarted when Lightman convinces the computer to play tic-tac-toe. The computer, leveraging AI, learns that there is no optimal outcome between two experienced players and that all possible initiations of conflict result in mutually assured destruction. WOPR then calls off the nuclear launch realizing it was in a no-win situation. The movie had a profound impact on the president, who, in a meeting with the chairman of the Joint Chiefs of Staff, questioned the plausibility of this scenario. A week later, the chairman explained to the president that not only was the plot of the science-fiction movie plausible, but reality was far worse than fiction.[1] This banal event in the history and development of cyberspace triggered an important dialogue between the US political elite and the technical community, about the implications of an increasingly connected world. The discussions of the possible ramifications of cybersecurity culminated in an NSDD (NSDD-145) on "National Policy on Telecommunications and Automated Information Systems Security." The same conversation that President Reagan started continues today in an environment that has gone from well under a million connected users in the early 1980s – most of them Americans – to more than 5.19 billion users across the world in 2023.

The previous chapter provided insights into the history and development of cyberspace to set the stage for the diverse ways in which digital technologies have come to impact humanity. Yet this cannot fully account for what cyberspace is and what it will become. The developers of IBM mainframes in the 1960s, or the designers of the navigation control systems on the Apollo missions, were not able to imagine a world in which teenagers would blithely carry mobile computers (iPhones) that are 120 million times more powerful than anything they could develop.[2] Computer pioneers could not foresee the ability of these same mobile computers to connect to nearly all of human knowledge, while still being used primarily to send emojis and watch cat and dog videos.

In tandem with substantial growth in the use of computers and networks, and increases in computing speed and information transmission, the problems first identified by a curious president after watching a science-fiction film have grown in scope and magnitude. What moved from ARPANET to NSFNET and MILNET to the Internet has now expanded to constitute an often criticized term: cyberspace. The term "cyberspace" has its etymological roots in the Greek word *kubernētēs*, meaning "to steer." However, the modern use of the word "cyber" was picked up by World War II mathematician Norbert Wiener in his 1948 book *Cybernetics: Or, Control and Communication in the Animal and the Machine*. Wiener's use of the word "cyber" is in line with the Greek definition and implies the interface and interaction of the biological and mechanical. The field of cybernetics, which he established, had strong proponents throughout academia and the government, yet the timing of this movement which sought to integrate man and machine was not matched by the then-available technology and eventually the field fell out of favor.[3]

Although cybernetics became less prominent within military and academic communities, it was picked up by science-fiction writers in the

1980s. The interplay of man and machine and the potential dystopian futures of connected societies provided ample ground for creative minds to explore. One such mind was William Gibson, who in 1984 wrote *Neuromancer*. In his work, Gibson explored the interactions of individuals within a global network, complete with AI, hackers and more. Despite the dystopian nature of the novel, the book also eloquently describes the interconnection of humans and machines, and terms this interplay "cyberspace." Gibson defines cyberspace broadly as a "consensual hallucination" – that is to say, a virtual environment in which humans engage one another and machines interactively.[4]

The term "cyberspace" expands beyond the conventional concepts of networks and encompasses both physical and virtual realities that constitute the problem set for the current volume. In the more than four decades since its use by Gibson, the word "cyber" has become a universal prefix to describe a variety of phenomena from cybercrime to cyberbullying and cyber war. The prefix "cyber" is often criticized for its universality, but the term is largely here to stay.[5] The focus in this chapter is on the function and structure of the environment encompassed by the term "cyberspace." Policy and scholarly communities are often disconnected from the technical communities that build and maintain what has come to be defined as cyberspace. Understanding the basic technical underpinnings of the environment provides students, scholars and decision-makers with a foundation upon which to engage in theoretical and policy debates.

Defining cyberspace

Before turning our attention to the structural attributes of cyberspace and how they work, it is helpful to examine some of the definitions of the term under consideration. Defining the term establishes what is and what is not under consideration. Over the course of the last 30 years, the number of definitions of cyberspace has grown substantially.[6] In this book, we use two of the more encompassing definitions of cyberspace to provide intellectual and analytical space in which to understand and evaluate a variety of complex phenomena.

In 2009, in a seminal volume on cyber power, Daniel Kuehl, a professor at the US National Defense University, defined cyberspace as "an operational domain framed by the use of electronics and the electromagnetic spectrum to create, store, modify, exchange, and exploit information via interconnected and Internetted information systems and their associated infrastructures."[7] Kuehl's expansive definition is packed with terms and concepts that begin to outline the borders of what the US DoD refers to as a domain.

First, Kuehl introduces the concept of electronics, a class of physical devices dependent on the use of electrical energy for operation.[8] Electronic devices can include toasters, circuits, telephones, computers or anything else that requires electricity to function. Second, he identifies the use of the electromagnetic spectrum, a range of frequencies and radiation, wavelengths and photonic energies.[9] The electromagnetic spectrum includes everything from WiFi and radio received on a car stereo to infrared remote controls for TVs, and much more. Third, he implies that cyberspace is neither the use of electronics nor that of the electromagnetic spectrum in isolation, but is founded on the ability to leverage both in tandem to create, store, modify, exchange and exploit information. Fourth, it is not simply the attributes of information – creation, storage, modification and exchange within a single system – but the ability to transmit information across connected systems and their associated infrastructures that constitute cyberspace. Kuehl's definition of cyberspace is a far cry from William Gibson's hallucination. He emphasizes the physical and informational nature of cyberspace, and does not address the impact or value of the information that circulates in this space. We will return to the physical nature of cyberspace later. But first it is helpful to contrast this definition with the current operational definition from the US DoD, which provides a simplified structural framework within which to conceptualize cyberspace.

Department of Defense Joint Publication 3-12, originally published in 2013, defined cyberspace as follows:

> Cyberspace consists of many different and often overlapping networks, as well as the nodes (any device or logical location with an Internet protocol address or other analogous identifier) on those networks, and the system data (such as routing tables) that support them. Cyberspace can be described in terms of three layers: physical network, logical network, and cyber-persona. The physical network layer of cyberspace is comprised of the geographic component and the physical network components. It is the medium where the data travel. The logical network layer consists of those elements of the network that are related to one another in a way that is abstracted from the physical network, i.e., the form or relationships are not tied to an individual, specific path, or node. A simple example is any Web site that is hosted on servers in multiple physical locations where all content can be accessed through a single uniform resource locator. The cyber-persona layer represents

yet a higher level of abstraction of the logical network in cyberspace; it uses the rules that apply in the logical network layer to develop a digital representation of an individual or entity identity in cyberspace. The cyber-persona layer consists of the people actually on the network.[10]

This definition of cyberspace builds on Kuehl's more physical and informational definition and adds in the concepts of logic and persona. Both definitions are helpful because they frame the possible actions and policies that can and do impact the digital domain. However useful these definitions are, they have not settled the debate on the definition of cyberspace. Researchers should always consider the uses and limits of the definition they choose. Definitions are often suited to a particular field of study. Computer scientists focus on the logical layers more intently than computer engineers, who focus on the physical layers. Policy-makers and social scientists tend to place their emphasis on the cyber-persona layer of cyberspace, and most users interact within the persona layer also. Yet the reality is that the physical, logical and persona attributes of cyberspace are deeply intertwined. How the layers interact and their value to one another form the basis of what cyberspace is. Cyberspace is a physical and virtual domain. It is the product of human creation and ingenuity. It is a domain that, while man-made, is still impacted by its interactions within other domains, such as land, sea, air and space. The remainder of this chapter breaks apart the layers of cyberspace – physical, logical and persona – to develop a more detailed understanding of its complexities.

Physical layer

Scholars of IR often study cyberspace exclusively on the logical or persona layers of cyberspace.[11] These works privilege the transnational nature of data flows made possible by computers connected into networks, and subsequent networks connected in an ever widening structure. Emphasis is largely placed on how the logical and persona layers can be manipulated with code or other forms of information. These accounts leave off the very physical and tangible nature of cyberspace – the geographic and spatial relationships that impact the way in which cyberspace functions. The physical-network layer constitutes the closest approximation to other traditional domains of interaction: air, land, sea and space. All of the physical-network layer aspects of cyberspace are located in one of these domains.

If cyberspace is the connection of billions of networked devices, then the physical unit of the network layer starts at the node itself. A node can be anything that uses electronics and the electromagnetic spectrum to store, create, modify and exchange data. A node is not the exchange of data itself, it is the physical system that makes exchange possible. For the purpose of conceptualization, nodes can be construed as any device connected to a network that has a Central Processing Unit (CPU) and would be commonly referred to as a computer. The number and types of nodes within cyberspace is diverse and grows every year. As of 2018, there were an estimated 17–19 billion devices (nodes) connected to the Internet and making up cyberspace.[12] Within this physical device structure, there are some nodes that constitute the core and some that form an ever widening periphery. Core nodes comprise servers and core routers. Servers are used for a wide variety of functions from managing and keeping track of where various nodes are within the network structure to specific network services, such as storing information, and managing various services found within the logical and cyber-persona layers of cyberspace. Routers direct packets of data around the backbone – the central nervous system for the Internet – and manage the efficiency of the network. The average speed of the core routers is around 100 gigabits per second (Gbps) with some exceeding 86 terabits per second (tbps). Either way, these routers function much faster than your typical home or business network.[13]

Core nodes are connected by backbone lines that function similarly to the central nervous system in the human body. Backbone lines are long-haul fiber-optic lines that carry bits (one of the most basic units of information used in computing) in the form of photons between core routers and servers. In the United States, these long-haul lines almost mirror the US interstate highway infrastructure system.[14] They spread out like capillaries as they enter more densely populated areas. Each branch is managed by a router that directs the flow of traffic. These capillaries of fiber lines typically connect back to the core or trunk lines at other locations to provide resilience in the face of potential network failure or network isolation of a single line. Storybox 2.1 tells a brief story of the physical nature of these lines and how vulnerable they are.

Storybox 2.1 The "spade-hacker"

On March 28, 2011, just three years after a swift and decisive war between the Republic of Georgia and the Russian Federation,

Armenia fell off the global Internet. Armenia received 90 percent of its Internet access through a series of core Internet lines that run through the Republic of Georgia. When the Internet went down, many in the region feared the worst and thought another conflict between Russia and Georgia was imminent. However, upon closer examination, the culprit was identified as a 75-year-old Georgian woman digging for copper to sell for scrap. The woman was dubbed by local news sources as "the spade-hacker."[15]

Branching away from the trunk lines, the diversity of devices increases. Regional and local ISPs for Internet access usually manage networks at the local and hyperlocal level. These providers service overlapping lines of infrastructure that include routers and switches, domain name servers (the Internet's equivalent of a phonebook) and many more nodes that make it possible for the Internet to function. Often each region of a municipality is controlled by centralized routers that connect different networks. Switches connect nodes within networks and hubs forward network traffic (packets of information) to all the nodes within a network. ISPs typically route traffic all the way to the customer or neighborhood where they use another node to manage the flow of traffic to a house and to a modem. The modem itself is then either both a modem and a Wi-Fi router or connects to a Wi-Fi router that creates a local area network for all the connected devices within a home.

Although walking around in a house using Wi-Fi might seem as though the Internet is everywhere and enveloping, the reality is that from any Wi-Fi hotspot to the hard line that feeds it back out to the global network, there is often less than 100 ft or 30 meters of physical distance. The same is true of mobile phone towers that use the electromagnetic spectrum to send and receive data from mobile devices. Although the range on these devices is substantially greater than Wi-Fi, the principle of information flowing within hard-wired networks remains the same.

Despite the lack of cables associated with Wi-Fi or mobile radios that use 4G and 5G technologies, the use of the electromagnetic spectrum is itself physical and comes in the form of radio waves, or radiation used to transmit and receive data. Whether radio waves are used to communicate between cellular towers and a mobile phone, or originate from a satellite used to broadcast the Internet from space, they are physical structures susceptible to a variety of manipulations and degradations, both natural and man-made. Figure 2.1 highlights the electromagnetic spectrum, with its different radiation types, their wavelength, approximate scale and frequency. All data that traverses the Internet, either through the air (from Wi-Fi, mobile or microwave towers) or over various types of cables (coaxial, fiber-optic), uses radiation. Typically, the higher the frequency of radiation, the more data that can be transmitted. However, the higher the frequency of radiation, the shorter the distance that data can be transmitted while still maintaining data fidelity. Some types of frequencies of radiation are better suited to certain uses than others. For instance, satellites are not capable of effectively using some radiation frequencies to transmit data because those frequencies are blocked by the Earth's atmosphere. Exceptions occur where higher-frequency data is transmitted through fiber-optic lines that direct pulses of light. Yet even fiber-optic cables must have signal repeaters installed to ensure data in the form of light can traverse long distances. In the story above, Armenia fell victim to a rogue spade on a trunk line. Wireless networks are susceptible to various forms of interference, including those beyond our planet and caused by solar flares.[16]

Despite the increasing use of satellites as orbital assets or nodes – for example through the Starlink constellation – the overwhelming majority of data in cyberspace flows through physical fiber-optic lines that traverse the oceans around the world and cross continents. Large ships lay thousands of miles of fiber lines with traffic repeaters to boost the speed and range of the signals traveling through them across the oceans and back to nodes on land. Transoceanic fiber-optic lines are vulnerable to a wide variety of hazards, including – but not limited to – sharks, which like to eat the casings around non-Kevlar wrapped fiber-optic lines;[17] earthquakes, which cause displacement or pinching of the lines; anchors dropped from ships, which on occasion sever the fiber-optic lines; and nation-state sabotage.[18]

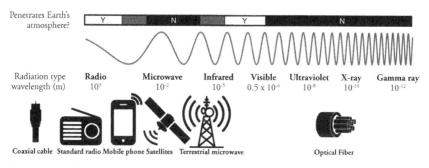

Figure 2.1 The electromagnetic spectrum

Source: Modified image created by NASA [CC BY-SA 3.0] via Wikimedia Commons

Each of the physical-network layer attributes of cyberspace – computers, modems, routers, cables, etc. – uses light and/or electricity to function. Without electricity, the physical layer of cyberspace, upon which the other two layers depend for their operation, becomes useless. A computer without electricity is a box. To reverse the argument, light and electrons used on lines can in certain instances themselves become physical instruments that degrade or damage the physical-network layer. Just as attaching a firehose to a home plumbing system will burst all the pipes in a house, running too much Internet traffic clogs the network. This can happen with DDoS attacks that overwhelm the ability of a node – usually a server – to handle requests to transfer packets of data. It can also happen when all Internet traffic within a given area is rerouted due to a cut fiber-optic line. In 2008, a ship dropped anchor and cut the FALCON cable, partially severing several nations from the Internet and causing the traffic on those lines to be rerouted.[19]

To summarize, despite a great deal of rhetoric focused on impacts occurring at the logical and persona layers of cyberspace, the domain remains tied to a deeply physical framework. Each of the physical attributes of cyberspace falls within a legal jurisdiction or within a legal framework developed through international, national or local law and regulation. These physical points are readily locatable on maps. Although cyberspace has many virtual characteristics, its underlying infrastructure is physical. From this perspective, cyberspace is not unique and many of the traditional scholarly frameworks developed to discuss politics and international relations in the physical world, from realism to constructivism, can help us understand security in cyberspace.

Logical-network layer

The logical layer of cyberspace comprises those attributes that use sets of rules or code, written instructions – often broken into categories of protocols – firmware (code that enables the hardware of a computer or device to function) and software (code that allows you to interact with and accomplish novel tasks or provide instructions to the computer). These categories break down into more nuanced structures, each with responsibility for the management and control of information within networks or on nodes. At their most basic, each of these categories is composed of a series of instructions that tell various nodes within networks how to process and transmit data. In many ways, the logical layer forms the DNA of cyberspace in that it tells physical components how to operate. Each set of instructions influences the interaction of nodes within cyberspace. At its core, the Internet functions as a packet-switched network.[20] Figure 2.2 illustrates the differences between packet- and circuit-switched networks. While circuit-switched networks require a dedicated channel of communications and can only be used for one transmission at a time, packet-switched networks route traffic through a variety of nodes within a network which both is fault tolerant and allows for multiple simultaneous transmissions. Although one of the founding myths of the Internet is that it was created to provide resilience for military communications in the event of a nuclear attack, the truth is that this resilience was initially only considered with regard to telephone or voice communications.[21] By contrast, the development of ARPANET discussed in the previous chapter was largely to facilitate decentralized usage of expensive computing resources.[22]

Packet switching describes the method by which information (packets of data) transits networks. Beyond this method, a set of rules or protocols manages the interaction of computers (nodes) that generate and transmit information in cyberspace. In the early days of ARPANET, these interactions were managed by Interface Message Processors (IMPs), steel-encased specialized computers the size of a small Volkswagen that sat in front of the computers on the network and took the data from different machines (computers) on the Internet and translated it for use. The best way to think of these is as two translators who sit with two diplomats who speak different languages. Diplomat 1 says something which is then translated by his translator into a second language. Translator 2 then translates the message from translator 1 into the language that diplomat 2 can understand. IMPs were expensive, difficult to maintain and inefficient in facilitating network communications.

The inefficiencies of the IMP were finally resolved thanks to the Transmission Control Protocol / Internet Protocol, one of the primary protocol suites for Internet operation.[23] The TCP/IP specifies how data on hosts (computers) is to be broken down into packets with information headers, as illustrated in figure 2.2. These information headers function much like the image on a puzzle box but with more specificity, and provide the ordering information for packets. These packets are subsequently transmitted with IP address information across the network. Finally, when the file that has been broken into packets, each with information headers, arrives at its final destination, it is reconstituted using the information headers as a map. If any given packet is missing or corrupted, the recipient computer can request the sending computer to resend the missing or corrupted information.

Packet-switched network

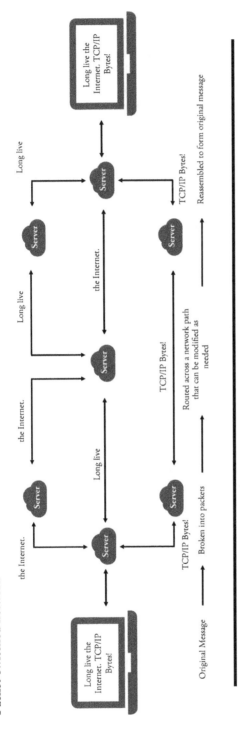

Circuit-switched network

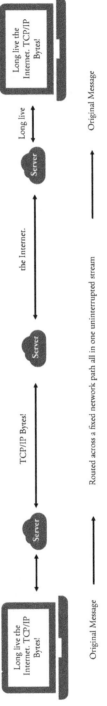

Figure 2.2 Packet-switched versus circuit-switched networks

Within cyberspace, there are a variety of protocols that set rules for how computers and networks communicate and operate. At the most basic level, protocols must address issues regarding how different data formats are exchanged, how their addresses are formatted and mapped, how information is to be efficiently routed across networks, when transmission errors occur, how to acknowledge receipt of packets, how to signal loss of information, and how information flows.[24] All of these component pieces form the basic logical rules for how cyberspace functions. Different types of services within cyberspace utilize different protocols. Some of the most common protocols include FTP (File Transfer Protocol), UDP (User Datagram Protocol), DNS (Domain Name System), TLS/SSL (Transit Layer Security / Secure Socket Layer), DHCP (Dynamic Host Configuration Protocol), SMTP (Simple Mail Transfer Protocol) and HTTP (Hypertext Transfer Protocol). There are hundreds of other protocols, some of which are proprietary and owned by patent holders, while others are public and available for general use, free of charge. Protocols operate within their own set of layers with what is known as the Open Systems Interconnection model (OSI model). The OSI model has seven layers that range from everything down to the physical-network layer in the previous section up to the highest logical layer, called the application layer. The OSI model is the primary model used by the computer science and engineering communities. Figure 2.3 shows the OSI model in comparison to the US DoD model discussed above.

Visiting websites is an example of the first two layers working together. When a user queries a website such as google.com on their computer, it sends a request which is pushed down from the browser application layer all the way to the physical layer. This initial request goes to the most efficient DNS, typically located at an individual's local ISP. This DNS server maintains a database that is regularly updated and syncs through the Internet back through various DNS servers to the Root DNS server managed by the Internet Corporation for Assigned Names and Numbers (ICANN), which will be discussed in the next chapter. This database functions in much the same way as a foreign-language dictionary does. Google.com equates to IP address 142.250.179.174. Each block in the address corresponds to a network location somewhere in the world. The DNS server sends this address back to the requesting browser which then uses the address to connect to google.com. When the Internet was first being developed, the common standard was a four-block set of numbers called an IPv4 address. There are 4,294,967,296 possible IPv4 addresses composed of 32 bits. This number of addresses has already

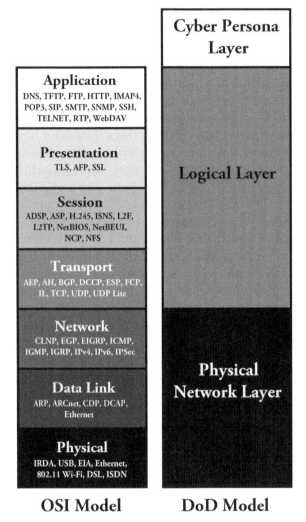

Figure 2.3 OSI and DoD models compared

been surpassed and the Internet Engineering Task Force (IETF) and its constituent bodies have begun replacing the IPv4 standard with IPv6, which contains 340,282,366,920,938,463,463,374,607,431,768,211, 456 possible addresses composed of 128 bits, giving the logical layer of cyberspace ample room to grow in the coming decades.

The logical layer of cyberspace is susceptible to a large variety of manipulations, exploitations and degradations, many of which will be examined in subsequent chapters. One example in recent years of a serious vulnerability in a protocol was the Heartbleed security bug released in 2014. Heartbleed manipulated a popular implementation of TLS called OpenSSL and allowed for attackers to intercept and reinitiate encrypted web sessions for users. For example, when a customer accesses their bank's website to check his account balance, his computer and the bank's computer connect and authenticate over OpenSSL. Heartbleed would allow an attacker to follow behind them, much like someone sneaking past a metro turnstile without paying. The hacker would not have to reinitiate the connection and would gain access to the account. Although the fundamental nature of the protocol itself was unaffected, the faulty implementation of the protocol led to potential exploitation.[25] With thousands of different protocols and implementations, the probability of vulnerabilities and exploitations of the logical layer of cyberspace remains large. Many of these protocols serve as the entry points for a variety of exploits and attacks against computers.

Beyond the logical-network layer of cyberspace used in the transmission of data between computers is the implementation of firmware and software on the computer itself. While firmware and software can engage network protocols, they can also be primarily host-based, meaning they stay on the computer. These programs are also part of the logical layer of cyberspace, although they are not necessarily involved in data transmission. Vulnerabilities (flaws in the code or its implementation) within these logical structures can have substantial ramifications. Whether it is the firmware that controls a specific piece of hardware, or software – a broader category than firmware that provides data instructions to a computer – many famous cyberattacks originate and occur somewhere in the nexus between the logical-network layer and the firmware and software. Examples of such attacks include: the 2015 Ashley Madison breach that spilled the details of more than 37 million users of a site that facilitated infidelity between people in relationships;[26] the Conficker worm, a piece of malware that provides hackers with remote access into victims' computer systems;[27] the Home Depot and Target hacks in 2013–14 that resulted in the theft of the details of more than 120 million credit cards from the point-of-sale systems.[28]

The logical layer of cyberspace defined by protocols and code, both within networks and on hosts, is extremely vulnerable to manipulation, exploitation and degradation. Minimizing such vulnerabilities is an essential part of the software development process. Software companies such as Microsoft and Accenture, and public organizations such as the US National Institute of Standards and Technology (NIST), develop manuals and tools for examining and minimizing the number of bugs (vulnerabilities) within various software programs prior to their release.[29]

As the number of lines of code used to create software increases, so too does the difficulty in auditing that code. Some experts estimate that software that does not go through a secure development lifecycle process averages between 15 and 50 bugs per 1,000 lines of code.[30] The 2018 Model Year Ford F-150 truck, for instance, had approximately 150 million lines of code, and the same model year Mercedes had more lines of code than an Airbus A380, the largest passenger plane in the world.[31] If the Ford F-150 adheres to industry standards, it has between 2.25 million and 7.5 million bugs or vulnerabilities that should be identified and patched. The diversity of the ecosystem within the logical layer of cyberspace and the speed with which that ecosystem of protocols, firmware and software evolves, combined with the challenge of eliminating vulnerabilities, make cyberspace highly susceptible to security threats.

Persona layer

The cyber-persona layer, in contrast to the physical-network and logical-network layers described above, moves the definition of cyberspace away from the technical attributes to a higher level of abstraction. In 1995, the *New Yorker* published a Peter Steiner cartoon with two dogs looking at a computer screen. The caption under the cartoon was "On the Internet, nobody knows you're a dog." In many ways, this cartoon encapsulates the nature of the persona level of cyberspace. This layer consists of the people interacting and utilizing the networks themselves. The abstraction of this level is important and well articulated in the cartoon because it serves as one of the defining generalized characteristics of cyberspace, in which the representation of any given entity can be flexible. It is often difficult to discern between various persons, entities such as businesses or corporations or even bots (computer programs designed to simulate human behaviors) online.

Cyber personas do not need to reflect actual persons and can often be hybrids or complete falsifications. In November of 2017, the *Daily Beast*, an online news publication, reported that @Jenn_Abrams – a twitter username that had garnered more than 70,000 followers, many of them from the Alt-Right movement – a strong supporter of President Donald Trump's 2016 election campaign, was a fake account run out of the Internet Research Agency in St. Petersburg, Russia.[32] Famous diplomats and celebrities argued with this twitter personality, all the while oblivious to the reality that the person with whom they were arguing was not American, was not a woman, and was not real.

Few technical discussions on cyberspace include the cyber-persona layer, yet it is in this layer where individuals operate and interact. Since cyberspace was created by and for humans, a comprehensive analysis of cyberspace requires engagement with the persona layer. By changing their persona, by masking their location, IP address or Media Access Control (MAC) address, by obfuscating their online behavior, humans are able to utilize cyberspace in ways that actors in the other domains of land, sea, air and space cannot. Spies operating outside of cyberspace can forge documents, use disguises, safe houses or other obfuscation techniques, but the degree to which they may alter their fundamental nature is constrained by physical laws. Such constraints are largely absent in cyberspace. The creation of false cyber personas has multiple uses, many of which are mundane. Entire virtual communities such as Second Life or World of Warcraft allow individuals to live out their lives virtually, playing games, socializing with others around the world and even engaging in commerce in virtual worlds.[33]

The manipulation of cyber personas can be a life-or-death matter in repressive countries around the world, and some organizations such as the National Democratic Institute, Open Technology Institute, Electronic Frontier Foundation (EFF), Reporters Without Borders, Tactical Technology Collective and others focus on building tools that enable users to more effectively hide who they are within cyberspace.[34] Programs such as Tails Boum, The Onion Router (Tor) and others use anonymization techniques to protect individuals' online personas. Interestingly, many of these programs have been developed with the support of, or within, government research organizations, such as the Naval Research Laboratories in the United States.[35] I2P, Freenet, Orbot, ASL19, Psiphon and hundreds of other platforms have been developed within open source communities around the world to facilitate anonymization. The ability to manage and control online personas is, and will continue to be, a substantial issue for journalists, human rights activists and political dissidents around the world. At this level, cyberspace is a deeply political tool, which some activists have considered to be a "liberation technology."

The ability to manipulate who, what and where individuals are in cyberspace does come with a parallel dark side. Anonymity and low probabilities of attribution allow for states to engage in espionage and attacks.[36] In cyberspace, malicious actors are able to change who and what they look like to a potential adversary or victim, and even to reroute traffic to create the impression that an attack is coming from a third-party nation, in what is called a "false flag operation."[37] Beyond nation states, other categories of actors regularly manipulate the persona layer. Criminals including paedophiles and drug traffickers, as well as terrorists, each manipulate the cyber-persona level to the detriment of their victims.[38] Many of the threats to the logical and physical layers of cyberspace originate within the persona layer.[39] Data indicate that over 95 percent of all cyberattacks that result in the compromise of computer systems succeed because of something the human user has done.[40]

Understanding cyberspace

To understand how states and non-state and individual actors interact and create cyber insecurity, it is necessary to first gain a foundational understanding of what cyberspace is and how it functions. This chapter has touched on a widely used model of cyberspace, emphasizing three overarching physical, logical and persona layers. While it is often convenient to focus on one layer at the expense of the others, together they form a synergistic entity that comprises cyberspace. Considering the complexity of these various layers can add much-needed nuance to debates on cybersecurity. Very often, war fighters, policy-makers, computer scientists, network engineers and the broader public talk across one another with limited mutual understanding. Further examining the physical, logical and human underpinnings of cyberspace breaks down communication barriers and allows for progress to be made across disciplines. Studying cybersecurity is an interdisciplinary endeavor.

Discussion questions

1. How do the various layers of cyberspace impact cybersecurity policy decisions?

2. How do the layers of cyberspace interact to create a global network that we rely on daily for work, entertainment and more?

3. Are there borders in cyberspace? What are the implications for physical borders in a virtual domain?

Exercise

Draw a map illustrating how you are connected to the physical layers of cyberspace at home, at work and in between.

Additional resources

YouTube videos by Code.org:

- "Introducing How Computers Work," https://youtu.be/Oax_6-wdslM
- "The Internet: Packets, Routing and Reliability," https://youtu.be/AydF7 b3nMto
- "The Internet: Wires, Cables & Wifi," https://youtu.be/ZhEf7e4kopM
- "What is the Internet?" https://youtu.be/Dxcc6ycZ73M

Rus Shuler, "How Does the Internet Work?" 2002, https://web.stanford.edu/cl ass/msande91si/www-spr04/readings/week1/InternetWhitepaper.htm.

3   Governing cyberspace

Reader's guide

- Given the multi-layered nature of cyberspace, a wide variety of state and non-state actors are involved in its governance.

- Multistakeholderism is an approach that brings together multiple parties (stakeholders) from various sectors to address the complex set of cyber governance issues.

- Technical governance centers on the management of the rules, standards and digital infrastructure and technologies that make up the Internet. Discussions at this level tend to focus on domain name management, Internet protocols, cybersecurity standards, etc.

- Political, social and economic governance touches upon a broad variety of questions, such as the (mis)use of online information, the prioritization of some Internet traffic, and privacy concerns.

- Efforts to establish international norms and law to govern how state and non-state actors behave in and through cyberspace are a work in progress.

Substantial governance challenges lie beyond the physical and virtual characteristics of cyberspace. This chapter emphasizes the unique governance and legal regimes within and surrounding the digital domain. Although most users do not give Internet governance even a passing thought, their daily use of the Internet and its associated technologies depends on complex regimes that form the foundation for how cyberspace functions. The World Summit on the Information Society (WSIS) defines Internet governance as "the development and application by governments, the private sector, and civil society, in their respective roles, of shared principles, norms, rules, decision-making procedures, and programs that shape the evolution and use of the Internet."[1] This definition shows the variety of actors and processes involved in the management of cyberspace. Research on the management of the Internet and the broader cyberspace often centers on the role multiple actors play. On the one hand, the notion of multistakeholderism favors a model that brings together a variety of public and private "stakeholders" – individuals or groups of interest – into a single governance regime. On the other hand, multilateralism posits that nation states are, or should be, the only important parties to governance regimes.

Governance in cyberspace dates back to the early days of ARPANET. ARPANET users posted "Request for Comment" (RFC), which became a venue for discussions on the technical and social attributes of the nascent network. The first request (RFC 1) was first published by Steve Crocker on April 7, 1969.

RFCs suggested changes and improvements to host software on the IMPs that enabled communications on the early Internet. The RFC process, which continues to this day, now includes more than 8,000 requests on nearly as many topics. Each RFC is open for comment and facilitates a decentralized governance process initiated by the original ARPANET designers.

Governance in cyberspace is a contentious and difficult issue that can be examined through various lenses. The disaggregation of governance across categories facilitates a more nuanced understanding of the contentious politics associated with the complexity of a continually evolving domain. First, cyberspace governance in its oldest form originates in its technical nature and function. A multitude of institutions and actors have a stake in how cyberspace operates and seek to influence its form and functions. Initial governance mechanisms such as the RFC system were sufficient to manage growing network complexity in its early days. As the network expanded beyond ARPA and the NSF to encompass more functions and users, it quickly became apparent that political and technical issues were arising that challenged the existing status quo.[2] Many of the early technical organizations, such as the IETF, adapted and became increasingly complex institutions tasked with managing various aspects of the Internet. Second, many of the institutions that facilitate the functional aspects of cyberspace also began to have a stake in the social and political attributes that inform not merely the technical nature of the domain, but also the implications for how individuals, groups, businesses and governments utilize the domain to achieve various outcomes. Arguments in this second category broadly balance the sovereign concerns of states against the functional concerns of engineers, the daily usage concerns of individuals, and the financial and economic concerns of firms. Third, at the highest level of abstraction and often separated from much of the Internet governance literature for practical reasons, are the laws and policies of states and international bodies in relation to their interactions within and through cyberspace. This chapter examines each of these three categories to provide the reader with a more nuanced understanding of governance in cyberspace. Although each of the issues is examined in isolation, the reality is that the three views of cyberspace are intimately intertwined and often mutually inform, reinforce or – as is often the case – contradict one another. From this perspective, the study of cyberspace, just like other domains of human activity, reflects the complexity of social interactions.

Technical governance of cyberspace

The history of governance in cyberspace is largely a technical story of innovation and adaptation to practical challenges faced in the development of a network of networks. The history of computers and computational machines dates at least to 1911 with the establishment of the Computing–Tabulating Recording Company, which would later become IBM. The conceptualization of modern governance structures on the Internet can be traced back to a more contemporary example. In 1958, Peter Samson, a freshman at MIT, stumbled across the Model Railroad Club in a room filled with model trains and an environment made of papier-mâché. The club broke down into two groups interested in working on the ever evolving project. One group focused on the user-interface of the environment and how the trains, the mountains, towns and other attributes looked and were perceived; the other group focused on how the circuits and signals under the table served to make the world above function.[3] Many of the participants in the second group would become some of the first hackers. These individuals, and the attitude of early governance on ARPANET and other similar projects, were oriented toward functional problem-solving. They adopted an engineering-centric approach focused on issues that made the visual world function.

In tracing the history of the Internet, Janet Abbate, Katie Hafner and Mark Lyon discuss the value of both working groups, and the development of the RFC process that in many ways fostered something not dissimilar from the MIT Model Railroad Club of Peter Samson.[4] Although, in the early days of ARPANET, program managers often controlled decisions over the nascent networks, they often did so following substantial consultation with engineers.

Governance efforts have been around since the very inception of the Internet. RFCs 2 and 3 introduced governance structures for how individuals involved in the network should suggest and work toward improvements.[5] RFC 3 specified the structure of RFCs, their content requirements and the initial distribution list.[6] The process was standardized with the intent of providing a forum for development.

During early development of the Internet, governance discussions focused on interoperability and efficiency, not on the core political issues that dominate more contemporary debates. Issues such as sovereignty, data localization, IP address allocations and domain names had not yet arisen in a network populated by small university and government research communities. The number of countries involved in the network grew but remained confined to liberal democracies. The primary early governance goal was not to achieve a robust governing body to solve political problems related to the network's growth and use, but the development of the network itself. To facilitate governance, RFCs served a vital role in the process of documenting and validating protocols for use within the network.

One particularly fascinating subset of governance discussions centers on the management of Internet resources. When engineers Robert Kahn and Viton Cerf began to push TCP/IP as a protocol for communications between computers, initial corporate pushback from the original network managers at the American company BBN Technologies – who managed and built early IMPs – was overcome. In the early days of ARPANET, the community of users allowed enough room for failure within engineering projects for novel protocols to be proposed, challenged and accepted or rejected on their technical merits and ability to improve the network. The best technical solutions could prevail over less efficient ones.

On March 26, 1972, Cerf and Jon Postel authored an RFC that made the first foray into the systematic management of network resources.[7] In RFC 322, the two Internet pioneers requested that all Host Technical Liaisons submit their socket numbers to the Network Measurement Group. This initial registry of numbers predates the IANA (Internet Assigned Numbers Authority), which would be established by Jon Postel in RFC 1083 in 1988 under contract from the United States DoD.[8] From 1972 until his death in 1998, for all intents and purposes, Jon Postel was the manager of all Internet names and numbers. He controlled both the registration and mapping of all website domain names (e.g. google.com or facebook.com) to Internet Protocol addresses, and the allocation of IP Addresses (e.g. 216.58.219.206 and 31.13.71.36) to all entities globally. He was also responsible for arbitrating domain name disputes, and disputes on the allocation of address space.

In 1994, the NSF subcontracted the registration of domain names to a single private company, Network Solutions Inc (NSI). This move by the NSF sparked a heated debate among states, international and national non-governmental organizations (NGOs), and within the private sector, over who should control the Internet and how. The result was a conflict often referred to as the "DNS War."[9] NSI, under contract from the NSF, was able to charge for the registration of domain names and used this money to support the costs of maintaining and running the network. The centralization of management and securement of financial resources in a US corporation was controversial. Both nation states and private businesses launched legal actions to challenge the contractual agreement and the cost of registering websites. Legal actions eventually decreased until the overall control of NSI was limited with the subsequent creation of ICANN and the expansion of domain name registrars.

In February 1998, a green paper (used for rule-making proposals) was put forward proposing the creation of a new organization, to be constituted under the National Telecommunications and Information Administration (NTIA), an agency within the US Department of Commerce. The paper, written in response to a 1997 request from President Clinton, suggested the development of a new organization capable of improving the technical management of Internet names and addresses.[10] ICANN was formally approved on September 18, 1998, and incorporated as a nonprofit under California Law 12 days later. As a nonprofit, ICANN is designed to support charitable or public purposes. Although ICANN was under contract with the NTIA, governance over domain names and IP addresses was fostered via an agreement with the IETF, the main technical organization overseeing the functioning of the Internet. In 2016, ICANN became a fully independent multistakeholder NGO when its contractual obligations to NTIA were allowed to expire.

The technical governance of the Internet, while rooted in the RFC process and still heavily dependent on RFCs, has evolved since the late 1960s. The current structure of this technical governance follows a long line of committees, sub-groups and organizations created primarily by scientists and engineers. Many of the original groups were small and technically focused. The expansion of the Internet and its increasing complexity have resulted in a present breakdown of Internet governance structures into three broad categories. The first, originating out of technical standards and development, are multistakeholder institutions. The second, originating out of the political, social, economic and societal concerns brought on by the development and expansion of the Internet, are multilateral institutions. The third category is composed of private entities such as network operators, service creators and vendors, Internet Exchange Points, and other types of businesses that build, develop, manage and utilize network infrastructures. Generally, all three groups interact within multistakeholder processes to develop and manage the core functional attributes of the Internet.

Currently, the major multistakeholder organizations that focus on the fundamental technical functions of the Internet fall under one of three broad institutional structures. The IETF, the Internet Architecture Board and the Internet Research Taskforce are part of the Internet Society and emphasize the technical function of the global Internet. The World Wide Web Consortium (W3C) manages the development of the protocols associated with the WWW – often accessed via a computer browser such as Chrome, Internet Explorer, FireFox or Safari. ICANN manages IANA and the domain name functions of the Internet. Each of these organizations is open to public membership and reserves space in their governance structures for actors of all types, while attempting not to privilege any one actor at the expense of the others. Engagement with these multistakeholder organizations is difficult due to the cost in time and expertise required to participate and exert influence.

States and private-sector organizations tend to work within and through the multistakeholder processes of the core institutions listed above. While the trend has been to work within the multistakeholder institutions currently established, many states would like to begin shifting much of the governance of the Internet away from a multistakeholder to a multilateral structure. In a multilateral structure, the needs and wants of states are negotiated and sub-state actors such as NGOs, businesses, individuals, engineers and others must seek representation via their respective state. This structure substantially weakens the influence of traditional actors over how the Internet is developed and managed.

Thus far, multistakeholder organizations, many liberal democracies and technology firms have rejected attempts to shift these core governance functions away from their current structures. Their primary argument is that exclusive state involvement in how the Internet functions would impact its ability to develop, innovate and adapt in the future. Their arguments are not without precedent. France created an independent network for online services – the Minitel – in the 1980s, Iran launched the "Halal" Internet – the National Information Network

– in 2016, North Korea has Kwangmyong ("bright light"), and Russia began deploying RuNet in 2020. While the reasoning behind these attempts to create independent networks is different, they highlight some of the fundamental political, social and economic issues that the more technical governance approaches to the Internet tend to overlook.

The political, social and economic governance of cyberspace

"Governments of the Industrial World, you weary giants of flesh and steel, I come from Cyberspace, the new home of Mind. On behalf of the future, I ask you of the past to leave us alone. You are not welcome among us. You have no sovereignty where we gather." This extract from the Declaration of the Independence of Cyberspace, authored by American poet, essayist and cyber-libertarian John Perry Barlow in 1996, served as an early rallying cry for many Internet users. However, Barlow's declaration does not account for the variety of issues that have arisen that make the absence of sovereignty in cyberspace both impractical and potentially damaging to the very ideals his declaration sought to uphold. In writing on the development and current state of Internet governance, scholar Laura DeNardis provocatively claims that there is an ongoing "global war for Internet governance."[11] Hyperbole aside, the conflict over Internet governance is one taking place across multiple venues, between and within nations. To understand why Internet governance has taken on and continues to grow in importance, it is first necessary to disaggregate some of the many issues in contention.

From the sidelines, as a user of the Internet, governance issues might seem trivial. Yet the issues in contention within the Internet are anything but trivial. The Internet – now often broadly seen as cyberspace – facilitates social, political and economic actions globally. Issues including the control over generic top-level domains (TLDs) ranging from .com and .org to .cn and .ru, and the distribution and allocation of IP addresses globally, are some challenges facing governments around the world. Countries are given control over their TLD, the .nation part of the URLs used to access and locate just about everything on the Internet. But with the expansion of TLDs into new areas such as .Amazon, .Patagonia, .wine and untold others, who should be able to control sites that arise from their use? Should the countries where the Amazon river flows or the US corporation Amazon.com be in control of a given domain? How should IP addresses – the fundamental routing numbers that make the Internet function – be distributed?

Misappropriation of these addresses or the misuse of IP addresses and domain names by one nation can have global ramifications. In 2008, in an attempt to prevent Pakistanis from accessing the videosharing site YouTube, which featured anti-Islamic videos, a Pakistani ISP was ordered to censor the site. The ISP responded by modifying the Border Gateway Protocol (BGP) for YouTube, which accidentally resulted in the global redirection of YouTube to Pakistan.[12] The provider could not deal with the amount of traffic it received as a result of this "hijacking" and many users around the world were unable to access YouTube for a couple of hours. Pakistan's YouTube mistake was not an isolated incident, but it provided an early indication that changes in domestic laws can have global ramifications.

National and regional laws can have tremendous effects on how firms may use the Internet within sovereign jurisdictions and affect users' ability to surf the web. The European General Data Protection Regulation (GDPR), which came into effect in May of 2018, is a case in point. The GDPR focuses on data rights of European citizens, but its implications are technical, political and financial, and visible at a global level due to the inherent connectivity of cyberspace and its transnational nature.[13] Laws such as the GDPR challenge the technical mechanisms that foster the efficient transmission of data and create costs for online service providers that rely on data storage servers located in nations adhering to the GDPR.

Key GDPR provisions include: the lawful, fair and transparent processing of data; the limitation of data collection, processing and storage; the provision of rights to data subjects; the requirement that data collection can only occur with clear and explicit data subject consent, and that all products must establish the principle of privacy by design. The GDPR also requires firms to conduct data protection impact assessments, prohibits them from transferring personal data outside of the European Economic Area (EEA) without first meeting established conditions, and requires many organizations to establish a position of data protection officer. Most users around the world have experienced the impact of GDPR in the form of clicking 'accept' for websites to collect cookies – small tracking scripts embedded in websites – whenever they visit a website. But GDPR has also had a significant impact on multinational technology firms. Among the most difficult rules of GDPR in its initial implementation was a requirement that firms localize all data storage so that all firms would keep data on European data subjects within the EEA. This meant developing and deploying new physical infrastructures across Europe and setting up rules within the logical layers of networks to prevent the transit of data on European subjects to third-party states outside of the EEA.

Another fascinating provision of the GDPR that is making waves in international Internet governance states "the data subject shall have the right to obtain from the controller the erasure of personal data concerning him or her without undue delay and the controller shall have the obligation to erase personal data without undue delay" (article 17). Thinking back to chapter 2, the goal of the Internet was to facilitate the transmission of data from one point to another in the most efficient way possible, with as little loss of data as possible. The original idea was to create a network that didn't forget. Article 17 establishes a means for individuals to have information stricken from the Internet – a first in the Internet governance space. However, there is a big caveat associated with the right to be forgotten. Information on an individual who exercises this right can only be removed from data services within the European Union (EU). If data on an individual extends beyond the borders of the EU, then that data is not subject to Article 17. In other words, the rule is more like geographically selective amnesia than Internet-wide data removal.

Although GDPR was written and implemented by a block of countries, its impact is being felt well beyond the EU's borders. Commentators now question why the United States and other nation states do not have similar data protection schemes in place. Within the United States, the fight over data is extremely contentious, and progress on data protection governance is finding strength in the most unlikely place: California. Home to the global Internet behemoths of Silicon Valley, the Golden State passed its own equivalent of the GDPR, the California Consumer Privacy Act. Here Internet governance devolves to a sub-national governance body with national implications. In recent years, as global Internet politics have increasingly permeated domestic politics in the United States and elsewhere, different levels of government have begun to increasingly implement restrictive laws and policies on goods and services provided in and through the Internet. Notably, with effect from January 1, 2024, the State of Montana has banned social media platform TikTok from sale and use on any device accessing the Internet in its state. How this law will be enforced and implemented will have governance implications and elevate the power of sub-national jurisdictions to regulate activities on the Internet.

Internet governance is expansive and includes a variety of challenging questions on the utilization of information, the freedom of information and many more. Some of the questions include whether smaller nations should have to pay higher Internet prices because they cannot offer symmetrical peering (data transfer) agreements with large Internet providers. Cost structures of peering agreements can and do impact potential access of impoverished nations to the modern global economy. Other questions that are addressed by Internet governance include: How should data transit between and amongst nations be managed, regulated, stored? Should traffic on the Internet be neutral, or is it acceptable to privilege some traffic at the expense of others (a question we will examine more below)? Should ISPs be required to monitor Internet traffic for illegal or immoral behaviors, or even the activities of journalists or human rights activists?[14]

States have long held jurisdiction over their territory and citizenry. International law recognizes two forms of sovereignty, de jure (legal control) and de facto (physical control), over that which occurs within their borders. The Internet challenges the sovereign rights of states. Nations have pursued increases in their sovereign rights over the Internet through a variety of fora. The ITU, a specialized UN agency, has served as one of the primary vehicles for states to press for their increased role in governing the Internet.

Internet governance at this international level rose to prominence following two UN summits entitled the WSIS, in 2003 in Geneva and 2005 in Tunis. Although organized within a multilateral organization, the UN, the summits were multistakeholder in participation and engagement. The 2003 WSIS resulted in the creation of the Working Group on Internet Governance and eventually led to the further creation of the Internet Governance Forum (IGF) as a multistakeholder body under the UN Secretary-General.

Further contention arose in 2006 with the renewal of contractual agreements between ICANN and the US Department of Commerce's NTIA. Some stakeholders expressed concern that this contract gave the United States too much influence over the Internet. To overcome these criticisms, the 2006 contract renewal opened the door for the potential internationalization of ICANN at a future, unspecified date. ICANN and its management of the DNS root zone and IANA functions ran into controversy in 2007 when a debate arose over whether to create a .xxx top-level domain. The TLD question sparked debate on the control of critical Internet resources and was central to IGF meetings held later that year in Brazil. Also, in 2006, the ITU began to more formally involve itself in discussions of Internet governance.

From 2006 to 2012, the importance of the Internet grew substantially, in tandem with marked increases in numbers of global Internet users. The role and prominence of the Internet in global journalism, protest movements and political movements in the United States and elsewhere further highlighted ways in which the Internet was not only a technical but also an inherently political domain. Decisions made about how the Internet functioned, what protocols were adopted, and how information should be treated within it became points of contention for various stakeholders.

During her tenure, US Secretary of State Hillary Clinton became instrumental in pursuing a multi-million-dollar effort to promote Internet freedom and human rights at various international conferences, and through the funding of a variety of technologies for human rights activists, journalists and dissidents around the world.[15] Secretary Clinton famously intervened with technology companies during the 2009 Green Revolution in Iran by asking social media platform Twitter (now X), used by Iranian activists, to delay a scheduled update so as to continue to provide a means for information dissemination and protest organization.[16] While these actions were seen within the Western liberal democracies as enhancing the fundamental tenets of freedom and democracy, many non-Western democracies saw these efforts as a direct attack via the newly evolving and expanding medium of cyberspace, and as a threat to their sovereignty.

In 2012 in Dubai, the ITU published the International Telecommunications Regulations (ITRs). The opening lines of the regulations affirm the sovereign rights of states, and declare the ITRs to be an effort to foster the development and harmonization of worldwide telecommunications. The opening lines of the documents establishing the ITU also emphasize the sovereign rights of states, and highlight the challenges confronted by engineers, businesses, individuals and NGOs in the face of state Internet governance efforts. As the Internet became an increasingly political tool in the 2000s, stakeholders on the Internet started to wrestle with one another for control.

The revelations orchestrated by former NSA contractor Edward Snowden about the global reach of the United States within cyberspace provided fodder for renewed calls for the internationalization of the core responsibilities associated with the Internet. Critics wondered how the United States could be trusted with the governance of key Internet assets if they were using them to spy on the world. The global outcry in response to the Snowden revelations of 2013 was swift and boosted the positions of many multilateral stakeholders, emphasizing issues such as the need for sovereignty within multilateral Internet governance frameworks and the Internet freedom agenda.

On April 14, 2014, in the wake of the Snowden revelations, ICANN and the Brazilian government organized NetMundial, a large global multistakeholder meeting on the future of Internet governance. The conference produced a non-binding document on Internet governance principles emphasizing multistakeholderism: open and participative, consensus-driven governance that is transparent, accountable, inclusive and equitable, distributed, collaborative, and emphasizes access and the lowering of barriers.[17] Controversies arose regarding the structure and organization of the permanent 25-member representative committee for governance of NetMundial when the organizing nations attempted to secure permanent representation. This attempt at buttressing multi-stakeholderism within the Internet governance agenda, while admirable, faced substantial criticism.[18]

Internet governance is one of the most rapidly evolving areas of governance globally. The continual development of technologies and the variety of state and non-state approaches to these technologies have provided a fertile testing ground for scholars and practitioners. Governance on the Internet most closely aligns with theories associated with liberal institutionalism and constructivism. Both schools of thought help to explain how and why so many divergent interests are coalescing into various organizational structures. Liberal institutionalism indicates that organizations and shared government institutions can increase and aid in the cooperation between states and thereby reduce conflicts.[19] By contrast, constructivism posits that relations between states are the result of historical or social patterns that are developed (constructed) over time rather than the result of structural or essential human or political characteristics.[20] Internet governance is characterized by both the creation of institutions and the managing of interests from very divergent social and historical contexts. These two theoretical lenses provide vantage points from which to view the role and development of Internet governance and its subsequent diffusion and impact on cyberspace.

The concept of multistakeholderism best explains the convergence of multiple actors concerned with the management of Internet resources. Mark Raymond and Laura DeNardis define multistakeholderism as "two or more classes of actors engaged in a common governance enterprise concerning issues they regard as public in nature and characterized by polyarchic authority relations constituted by procedural rules." The multiple stakeholders involved in cyberspace have established a complex and ongoing flux of governance regimes.[21] The Internet is global. Its roots are based in technical solutions that have evolved and created political, social and economic implications. The approach states take toward governance in cyberspace is often a function of their domestic regime type and position within international politics. States such as China, Russia and Iran seek multilateral solutions to governance challenges while the United States and its allies seek multistakeholder solutions.[22] This divergence of approach sets the stage for conflict, and pits organizations such as the ITU against ICANN. While the balance still largely favors multistakeholder institutions, this might not be a permanent state of affairs. Some scholars contend that the current status quo of Internet governance might lead to a fragmentation of the Internet between states that favor control through multilateral institutions and those that favor multistakeholder ones.[23]

Arguments on the free flow of information on the Internet have persisted since the network's earliest days and been a source of contention between liberal democracies and non-liberal states. Where liberal democracies are quick to distinguish between information warfare and cyber warfare, non-liberal states make no such distinction. Liberal states make the argument that cyberattacks are violations of the confidentiality, integrity or availability of networked systems or devices. From this perspective, attacks occur where there is a willful attempt to undermine the security of systems and devices to have them operate or provide access outside of intended functionality. Liberal democracies do not view the free flow of information across networks as a violation of national or international security, but rather as the proper functioning of the network and its routing protocols. They see the free flow of information across borders via the Internet as aligning with Article 19 of the Universal Declaration of Human Rights, which states: "Everyone has the right to freedom of opinion and expression; this right includes freedom to hold opinions without interference and to seek, receive and impart information and ideas through any media and regardless of frontiers."

The entire structure of the Internet from its earliest days to the present has been oriented around the free flow of data between nodes within the network. This view drives many of the fundamental engineering and architectural decisions of the multistakeholder organizations that participate in Internet governance. Yet it is this same free flow of information that is the source of consternation among non-liberal states. They view the unconstrained flow of information as a threat to their political order. To constrain this data, they go to great lengths, including the development of robust national border gateway controls such as China's "Great Firewall," Russia's RuNet, Iran's National Internet and more. These domestic Internet spaces are meant to constrain the efficiencies of the Internet and to safeguard domestic information spaces. As a result, non-liberal states are strong proponents of multilateral institutions which privilege the will of states over the multistakeholder organizations which manage much of the Internet's infrastructure.

How did the Internet spark these core arguments over multilateral vs multistakeholder governance? The answer is not simple. The infrastructure of the Internet is vast and overlapping. As a result, there are dozens of organizations that each play a role in governance. Their interactions are not as smooth as they could be, and various groups of actors often speak past one another. Table 3.1 identifies the wide number of organizations that play a role in the governance of the Internet, and the diversity of their functions.

One group of organizations that is often overlooked in topline discussions of Internet governance are ISPs. Yet ISPs and telecommunications providers (Telcos) play a major role in the governance of cyberspace. They provide for and maintain the delivery infrastructure of the Internet. In 2012, all large US ISPs committed to tackling three areas of substantial concern in cyberspace: botnets, domain name fraud and Internet route hijacking. The ability of ISPs and Telcos to address cybersecurity challenges differs significantly from country to country. Yet, as the maintainers and providers of the Internet, these actors have a substantial role to play in governance and security. Many ISPs and Telcos have joined together in both formal and informal groups called Internet Network Operators' Groups (NOGs). NOGs provide a forum within which members can discuss issues of interest and establish best practices in the implementation of protocols and new technologies. Because ISPs are often the organization 'closest' to the users of Internet infrastructure, they can play a disproportionate role in Internet governance. The role that ISPs and other service providers (e.g. cloud services) play is subject to national and supranational legal frameworks. Everything from the control of certain types of Internet traffic to the detection of criminal activities and child pornography can and does occur at the ISP level. Yet empowering ISPs to tackle these societal issues can run headlong into issues of free speech, civil liberties and more. Controlling users' data and services requires service providers to implement technologies that are likely to violate user privacy. The result is yet another Internet governance trade-off between different equities on the Internet. In the United States, ISPs are largely immune from criminal liability arising from the actions of their users as a result of Section 230 of the Communications Decency Act of 1996. Yet this rule that provides US firms with immunity for their users' behavior is not universally shared. The laws governing ISPs in other states can and do result in significant levels

Table 3.1 Major Internet governance entities

Entity	Role	Functions
Certificate authority (CA)	Issues digital certificates and certifies the ownership of a public key by the named subject of a certificate	Operations, services
Internet Architecture Board (IAB)	Oversees the technical and engineering development of the IETF and IRTF	Advice, community engagement, policy, standards, research
Internet Corporation for Assigned Names and Numbers (ICANN)	Coordinates the Internet's systems of unique identifiers, including IP addresses, Protocol Parameter Registries and TLD space	Community engagement, operations, policy, services
Internet Engineering Task Force (IETF)	Develops and promotes standards for the Internet protocols	Community engagement, policy, standards
Internet Governance Forum (IGF)	A multistakeholder open forum for debate on Internet governance issues	Advice, community engagement, policy
Internet Exchange Points (IXPs)	Provides the physical infrastructure through which ISPs and Content Delivery Networks exchange Internet traffic	Advice, operations, services
Internet Network Operators' Group	Discusses and influences matters related to Internet operations and regulation within informal fora composed of ISPs, IXPs and other stakeholders	Research
Internet Research Task Force (IRTF)	Promotes research on the evolution of the Internet, creates focused long-term research groups working on topics related to protocols, applications, architecture and technology	Operations, services
Internet Service Providers (ISPs)	An organization, public or private, that provides services for participating in, accessing or using the Internet	Operations, services
Internet Society (ISOC)	Assures the open development, evolution and use of the Internet for the benefit of all people	Community engagement, education, policy, services
Regional Internet Registries (RIRs)	Five regional Internet registries manage the allocation and registration of Internet number resources within geographic regions	Operations, policy, services
World Wide Web Consortium (W3C)	Creates standards for the World Wide Web that enable an open web platform	Standards

of censorship and surveillance. ISPs can also hold immense sway over the speed, volume and access with which users connect to the Internet. Storybox 3.1 introduces the debate on net neutrality in the United States. This debate directly concerns ISPs, which, under the principle of net neutrality, are asked to treat all data on the Internet equally.

Storybox 3.1 Net neutrality

One of the most important issues to arise in recent debates on Internet governance within the United States and many other countries around the world is the concept of net neutrality. Net neutrality is the idea that all traffic that transits the Internet should be given equal priority. Think of the Internet as a highway, where all cars with access to the road may travel at the same speed without any one car being given special privileges. In a non-neutral Internet, a priority lane is provided that allows for some cars to travel in "fast lanes" for a fee, while cars that do not pay that fee are relegated to the "slow lanes."

While some Internet firms, such as Google, Facebook, Twitter, Amazon.com and other actors with deep pockets, might be able to pay substantial sums to be provided faster access to customers, the majority of smaller Internet retailers and service and entertainment providers would be unduly slowed and therefore lose potential markets. A non-neutral Internet could privilege existing large firms at the expense of small firms that are unable to compete and new firms that are unable to break out with novel, potentially more innovative products.

In countries where net-neutrality laws have been rescinded or limited, ISPs have fragmented consumer access to specific applications or services and thereby limited their exposure to other platforms, products and services. For instance, in Portugal, a mobile phone subscriber can purchase a data plan with limited data access to the general public Internet but unlimited data access to Facebook and Snapchat.[24]

Under the administration of President Donald Trump, the United States revoked its net-neutrality rules, a move widely rebuked by most experts and industries except ISPs. The rule on the revocation of net neutrality in the United States garnered such substantial opposition that it crashed the US Federal Communications Commission public commenting service after comedian John Oliver spoke out about the proposed rule on his popular television show *Last Week Tonight*.[25] The public outcry against the government's decision also inspired satirical opposition advertisements by fast-food company Burger King.[26]

Internet governance is not only about how the Internet runs, and who controls what aspects of how it runs. The next and final section addresses legal regimes and norms of state behavior that have developed, and continue to develop, in cyberspace. Discussions about legal regimes in cyberspace emphasize concerns over behaviors of states, firms and citizens. These issues of governance typically arise through purely multilateral organizations and institutions, often with input from non-state actors such as private corporations and NGOs.

The laws and norms of cyberspace

For a variety of issues outside of cyberspace, governments have developed a robust body of international law or focused on the establishment of norms (standards of behavior) to manage the interactions between states. Although the distinction between laws and norms is in many ways arbitrary, this section focuses on the development of laws and norms pertaining to cyberspace in an effort to facilitate a more robust understanding of how states manage their interactions within this evolving domain. The scope of international law is extremely broad and extends well beyond discussions of the technical management of cyberspace. Issues such as espionage, criminal extradition and the laws of armed conflict are most often dealt with between nations in a multilateral fashion.

The establishment of the Convention on Cybercrime in 2001, and its subsequent ratification by fifty-seven nations, serves as a good starting point for discussions on international law and cyberspace. In the late 1990s, as the Internet was expanding, so too were digital crimes. The violation of digital systems and the impact of criminal activities on the confidentiality, integrity and availability of computer systems steadily rose within the international consciousness. Dozens of nations gathered in Budapest to begin devising a multilateral strategy for addressing cybercrime. The Budapest Convention on Cybercrime sought to harmonize national laws within each of the signatory countries, enhance investigative techniques and facilitate communication and cooperation.[27] The convention serves as an example of one of the first major treaties between nations to address issues arising in cyberspace.

The Convention on Cybercrime was a strong first step toward developing international consensus around issues impacting all states. Starting in 2004 and convening periodically until 2017, a United Nations Governmental Group of Experts (UN GGE) met to discuss and develop norms and laws relating to cyberspace.[28] The group released periodic reports to the UN General Assembly, providing updates on discussions and advances in the field. UN GGE discussions and reports served as the foundation for consensus upon which potential laws or norms might be established in the future. In 2020, the UN General Assembly tasked the Open-Ended Working Group (OEWG) on security of and in the use of information and communication technologies (2021–5) to further develop rules, norms and principles of responsible (cyber) behavior. By working in multilateral discussion groups, nations and non-governmental entities (stakeholders) are able to enhance their understanding of how they perceive various changes and actions in cyberspace.

Following the 2007 coordinated cyberattacks against Estonia, NATO established the Cooperative Cyber Defence Centre of Excellence (CCDCOE) in Tallinn in 2008. NATO's CCDCOE served as a central location for NATO partners to work together and address problems arising in and through cyberspace. Two of the more impactful outcomes of this effort have been the *Tallinn Manuals*, released in 2013 and 2017 and produced through a deliberative process between international lawyers and legal scholars. These manuals systematically interpret, and apply international law to, actions occurring in and through cyberspace.[29] The manuals are not legally binding and do not formally establish norms, but they are the most robust collection of legal analysis on the issues related to cyber conflict between states to date.

International interactions in cyberspace at the legal and normative levels are still in flux. Despite the lack of concrete rules of the road for states within cyberspace, general normative behaviors and legal precedents are being worked toward.[30] For countries such as the United States and many of its allies, the Law of War and many of the associated norms of international behavior still broadly apply to cyberspace.[31] Much work remains in developing norms and laws in cyberspace, but continued efforts offer the possibility of more stable interactions.[32]

One way states have sought to create more stable interactions in cyberspace is through creation of market incentives that encourage firms toward improved cybersecurity postures. Since the early 2000s, discussions have percolated through the public and private sectors over the potential utility of cyber-insurance to offset the risks associated with cyber insecurity. At its most basic, cyber-insurance is a risk protection product, designed to offset the potential financial risks associated with firm activities conducted in an Internet-connected environment. Firms that purchase cyber-insurance do so to cover the costs associated with data loss, destruction, extortion (such as ransomware), cyber-theft, hacking, DoS and other malicious activities. Just as businesses insure themselves against other forms of hazard such as fire and flood, cyber-insurance is designed to cover the costs of recovering from cyber incidents. If a firm with cyber-insurance suffers a cyber incident, it could seek compensation from their insurance provider within the constraints of its policy. One issue that has arisen in the cyber insurance market is clauses that protect the insurer against acts of cyber-warfare or cyber-espionage conducted by state actors. These are not dissimilar from exclusion clauses in more conventional insurance markets that often exclude "acts of God." Yet in cyberspace there are certain actor classes, namely states, who pose too great a risk to insure against.[33]

The creation of a new insurance marketplace, combined with the pervasive nature of malicious incidents in cyberspace, has led to calls for the creation of a policy or regulatory environment conducive to insuring companies against risk in cyberspace.[34] Strong calls for the formation of cyber-insurance markets arose first under the administration of President Obama. Yet formal pushes by the US federal government have yet to take off.[35] By March 2023, the administration of President Biden outlined a plan in the National Cybersecurity Strategy to explore whether the federal government can use national-level purchasing power to stabilize insurance markets against catastrophic risks in cyberspace.[36] By late 2023, the Federal Trade Commission began publishing a guide for small businesses on cyber-insurance.[37] Yet, despite efforts in the United States to foster robust markets around cyber-insurance, the academic evidence on the topic remains mixed.[38] There are some indications that, while cyber-insurance might help offset financial costs for firms in the short term,[39] they do little to substantially increase the security of networks and devices without substantial security vendor intervention. There remains substantial confusion about what cyber-insurance is, what its utility is for firms, and whether it improves cybersecurity. It was initially believed that the purchasing of cyber-insurance might force companies to implement certain security practices to maintain compliance with cyber-insurance vendors, yet it appears that this is often not the case. Instead, in some cases, cyber-insurance creates a moral hazard by offsetting the costs associated with poor cybersecurity practices.[40]

Efforts to recommend or even mandate cyber-insurance have also been discussed within the EU.[41] European cyber-insurance markets and mandates have also largely failed to be pushed into regulatory and policy processes. To date, most requirements pertaining to cyber-insurance in Europe and the United States are more commonly established at the contractual level between firms, or between firms and a government sponsor. Formal governance bodies, in particular the Cybersecurity and Infrastructure Security Agency (CISA), the Federal Communications Commission (FCC) and the Securities and Exchange Commission (SEC), in the United States, are discussing their potential involvement in insuring against cyber risk, but the challenges of modeling that risk undermine efforts at creating systemic insurance markets. There is little doubt that cybersecurity remains a substantial issue for governments, firms and individuals – however, the pervasiveness of risk is difficult to measure across actor classes. Governing risk in cyberspace is proving difficult due to competing market and human behavioral forces. While the concept behind cyber-insurance holds promise, the devil remains in the details of implementation. It is critical to establish governance regimes that protect firms while incentivizing them to devote adequate resources for cybersecurity. Until these issues are adequately addressed, the inclusion of formalized rules for cyber-insurance into governance practices is likely to remain elusive.

Internet governance is a complicated mess

As should be apparent, there is a substantial lack of consensus on just about every issue relating to the governance of the Internet, and cyberspace more broadly. Although this chapter divided governance between the technical multistakeholder organizations, the more multilateral international governmental organizations and laws and norms, issues of importance for the maintenance of the Internet and the interactions of states, economies, societies and individuals converge and mingle at every level and across almost all issues. As states grapple with the implications of an increasingly connected world filled with ever evolving technologies, they will attempt to safeguard their interests. Similarly, actors who invent, develop, sell and maintain the multitude of elements that make up the Internet will also press for their interests. Finally, individuals, whether alone or combined in different formations of interest groups below the state level or transnationally will press for their interests and rights in digital spaces. The competing interests across international, national, public and private sectors are likely to remain in constant tension. Internet governance is complex, messy and incredibly important to everything that touches cyberspace. The struggle over what the future of the Internet will look like is ongoing, highly political, and will continue to proceed as new technologies are developed and new policy challenges are encountered.

Discussion questions

1. Why is Internet governance important to cybersecurity?

2. What is the difference between a multilateral and a multistakeholder institution?

3. How do technical changes to the core protocols of the Internet impact policies in states?

Exercise

Write a 500-word summary of two statements released by two members of the UN Open-Ended Working Group on Information and Communication Technologies during its latest session. You can access these statements on the website of the UN Office for Disarmament Affairs (https://meetings.unoda.org/meeting/57871 /statements). Explain why you selected these two members and the extent to which their views differ.

Additional resources

Center for International Governance Innovation, "A Universal Internet in a Bordered World: Research on Fragmentation, Openness and Interoperability," www.cigionline.org/publications/universal-internetborde red-world-research-fragmentation-openness-and-interoperability.

Center for International Governance Innovation, "Who Runs the Internet? The Global Multi-stakeholder Model of Internet Governance," www. cigion line.org/publications/who-runs-internet-global-multi-stakeholdermodel-in ternet-governance.

Jovan Kurbalija, *An Introduction to Internet Governance*, 7th edn. (Geneva: DiploFoundation, 2016), www.diplomacy.edu/resources/books/introduction -internet-governance.

4   Cyber capabilities and insecurity

Reader's guide

- Malicious software (malware) is best construed as a capability rather than a weapon because it generally does not cause harm as a first-order effect.

- Cyber capabilities tend to target the confidentiality, integrity and availability of data (the so-called CIA triad). They can do so by targeting vulnerabilities in any of the three layers of cyberspace, including human psychology.

- The ability to create and utilize malware is not limited to state actors. Yet APTs require a degree of coordination and investment that experts generally associate with state actors.

- Cyber capabilities differ from kinetic ones on several important points. Despite their digital character, they can still achieve substantial "real-life" effects.

On land, soldiers use tanks, armored personnel carriers, rifles and artillery, among a variety of other weapon systems; the military deploys capabilities in the air, on the sea, and this might one day be true in space. Many of the weapon systems used in the more conventional domains of war revolve around explosives and projectiles designed to use impact or force to render harm. As states begin to leverage cyberspace for military operations, what types of weapons will they use and encounter? US military doctrine simply refers to the ability to leverage cyber means as a "cyberspace capability."[1] This chapter examines what cyberspace capabilities constitute, and how they are developed, managed, maintained and utilized by a range of actors. Examining these capabilities sheds some light on how they facilitate or obfuscate attribution, and enhance or degrade cybersecurity. As humans invest more time and resources in the development of cyber capabilities, the dynamics of cyber insecurity become more complex.

Cyber capabilities are often directed against one of three core areas associated with the security of computers and networks. These core areas are the confidentiality, integrity and availability of computers, networks and their resident data or data in transit. These three targets are collectively referred to as the CIA triad. Capabilities targeting the confidentiality of a device seek to violate the privacy of data, either in transit within networks or at rest on a computer. Capabilities targeting the integrity of computers, networks or data seek to violate the intended state of data or systems. Capabilities that target the availability of computers, networks or data seek to prevent the utilization of these devices or data when desired by the intended user. All cyberattacks, whether they take the form of espionage, sabotage or theft focus on one or more of these three attributes.

To begin, it is helpful to take a step back and reemphasize some of the core concepts from chapter 2 regarding what cyberspace is and how it works. Unlike land, air, sea and space, cyberspace constitutes a substrate that facilitates many of the weapon systems used in other domains. Cyberspace does have physical attributes in the same way as the other domains of conflict, but it is also a virtual domain with both logical and persona layers of interaction. A warfighter, spy or criminal seeking to utilize cyber capabilities to achieve an effect in cyberspace must think across and within the layers of cyberspace. Very often an attacker may use a capability to exploit one layer of the domain (e.g. a scam targeting a persona) to gain access to other layers (e.g. sensitive data hosted on a server). In many ways, the development and utilization of a cyber capability across these layers is an intellectual exercise that requires strategic, operational and tactical skills.

Historical examples of strategy help to elucidate some of the more contemporary concepts behind the development of cyberspace capabilities. During World War II, in an effort to reach the ultimate target of the Japanese home islands, General Douglas McArthur and Admiral Chester Nimitz devised an intricate "islandhopping" and "leap-frogging" strategy to stress enemy supply lines and reduce Allied casualties.[2] These hops and leaps strategically positioned Allied forces for a potential invasion of Japan. By contrast, President Kennedy in 1962 employed a quarantine (blockade) of Cuba to prevent the delivery of nuclear missiles by the Soviet Union.[3] Odysseus in Homer's *The Iliad* concocted a ploy to build a massive hollow wooden horse for the people of Troy. He and his men hid inside the horse until the unsuspecting Trojans, believing they had won the war, took the horse inside their city gates. That night the Achaeans (Greeks) climbed out of the horse, opened the gates and sacked the city.[4]

Each of these strategies approximates strategies in cyberspace. It is possible to "island-hop," "leap-frog," blockade and covertly infiltrate in the digital realm. To employ these strategies, cyber capabilities can increase or decrease in complexity in relation to the effect being sought. Average cyber capabilities are quite simple and typically constitute only about 125 lines of code,[5] while more complicated and robust malware originating from nation states can exceed more than 15,000 lines. Understanding what cyber capabilities are, and how they are developed, maintained and utilized, sheds light on the intent of those who use them, and facilitate attribution in some instances. Before delving into the development of cyber capabilities, the chapter first explains our decision to refer to cyber capabilities instead of weapons. We then provide a general taxonomy of capabilities available. Subsequent sections focus on capabilities development in different contexts, and their implications.

Cyber capabilities

This chapter refers to all forms of malware as capabilities rather than weapons. This phrasing is deliberate and part of a wider debate within the subfield of cyber conflict studies. The use of the term "weapon" implies a tool or thing designed for inflicting harm or damage, whereas a capability implies the ability or power to do something. Cyber capabilities can weaponize a target system and cause it to inflict harm, but the code itself gives the attacker (hacker) the ability to inflict that harm. This distinction is important for two main reasons. First, it positions the discussion of cyber capabilities within the framework of computer and information sciences and focuses on how code can undermine the CIA triad. Second, it helps clarify why discussions on the non-proliferation of "cyber weapons" and the promotion of a cyber "Wassenaar arrangement" (a reference to a 1996 export control regime) are difficult to articulate and implement.

There is significant disagreement between policy and technical communities over the adaptation of weapons control and dual use agreements from conventional weapons to cyber capabilities.[6] A large literature on the potential for including cyber capabilities in arms control agreements has arisen in recent years.[7] As will be examined in subsequent sections, the creation of an arms control agreement for cyber capabilities is difficult because of the nature of these capabilities; their rapid evolution, novelty, transitory nature; the capacity to obfuscate their design and development; and the ease with which they are proliferated. All the above attributes and more make discrimination between types of cyber capabilities difficult. Whether a capability rises to the level of a weapon is not readily apparent. Considering a cyber capability as a weapon can conflict with norms associated with intelligence activities and even issues associated with criminal behavior on the Internet.

Although the term "cyber weapon" is not actively used in this book, that should not diminish the potential effects or costs associated with cyber capabilities. Honing the language used to discuss cyber capabilities removes hyperbole and grounds discussions on more technical understandings of how malicious code is developed, used, and impacts systems, people and states.

The arsenal of possibilities

Many of the capabilities used for attacks, espionage or theft in cyberspace fall within a taxonomy not dissimilar from that of epidemiology or public health.[8] Software-based forms of cyber capabilities for malicious use are termed malware. Malware is a type of software designed to alter the intended purpose of a computer or its resident data. Malware falls within specific typologies of that range from viruses and worms to Trojans and rootkits.

Table 4.1 highlights various types of malware. Malware types can be used independently or combined in a multitude of different ways to achieve varying effects. Most malware is targeted to particular types of operating system (Windows, Linux or Mac OSX, Android or iOS). Certain target systems are more difficult to penetrate. As a result of varying levels of vulnerabilities, markets tend to price certain exploits more highly than others. Apple's mobile operating system (iOS) has historically been the most difficult, and by extension most expensive, system to exploit. Yet the market for exploits is constantly evolving in both cost and complexity.

Unlike in conventional conflict domains, the ability to both create and utilize many forms of malware is not limited to state actors. Actors ranging from individual hackers to criminals and terrorists can also create, reuse or purchase capabilities. There is significant variation in their capability levels. While the most complex forms of malware often originate at the state level, these capabilities rapidly disperse to lower levels of actors. Beyond the different types of malware highlighted in table 4.1, the diversity and complexity of malware vary substantially

Table 4.1 Malware types

Backdoor	Exploit within existing or installed code that allows unauthorized access to affected computers.
Bot (or botnet)	Software programs that leverage computers to engage in activities, often against the will of the computer's user or administrator.
Cryptojacking	Hacking of a computer to use its resources for the purpose of cryptocurrency mining.
Exploit	Software vulnerabilities often originating within a software "bug" that allow for unauthorized access to affected computers.
Fileless	Malware that causes files that are native to an operating system to function in unintended ways.
Hacktool	Exploitative, attacking and/or scanning tools used to penetrate and access a computer.
Mobile	Malware specifically targeting mobile operating systems.
Ransomware	Malware designed to deny a user or organization access to their files by encrypting the data on the target computer and demanding a ransom payment for a decryption key.
RATs	Remote Access Trojans allow a remote operator to control a system against the will of the system's owner.
Rootkit	Software tools that enable unauthorized access to a computer system without user knowledge.
Spyware/adware	Software that invades a computer user's privacy and transfers data to a third party.
Trojan	Non-replicating software, often installed via user interaction with hidden functions with the intent of manipulating or providing access to a computer system.
Virus	Self-replicating malicious software often hidden within a file and requiring a user to initiate infection. Viruses often attach to files enabling their spread.
Wiper	Malware that erases system data beyond recoverability.
Worm	Self-replicating malicious software that does not necessarily require any user actions.

within each type. Table 4.2 presents some additional layers of complexity that can be found within malware.

Figure 4.1 is a screen capture of a polymorphic malware sample that assesses what anti-virus programs are running on a computer in an attempt to re-encapsulate itself and avoid future detection. The increasing complexity of malware with features designed to evade common defensive measures challenges users and organizations at all levels. As

Table 4.2 Malware features

Entry Point Obfuscator (EPO)	Malware that denies forensic analysis of how malware arrived on a computer.
Metamorphic	Malware that alters its code beyond its encapsulation or encryption, designed to bypass malware detection based on pattern matching, in the same way that it might be possible one day to change the genetic make-up of a person to avoid detection.
Multi-part	Malware composed of multiple components that work together to achieve an outcome.
Multi-partite	Malware designed to infect more than one object within a system.
Polymorphic	Malware that changes its encapsulation or encryption to continuously obfuscate its appearance in order to avoid malware detection based on coding signatures, in the same way an individual might change their appearance using wigs or make-up.
Resident	Malware that resides within the active memory of a computer.
Stealth	Active concealment of presence to avoid detection.

malware displays more and more functionalities, it is used more frequently and contributes to a wider array of attacks, from espionage activities to criminal behaviors.

One of the greatest cyber capabilities available to hackers does not require digital code at all. Instead, it takes advantage of human users' vulnerability as digital targets. Many early hackers focused their efforts on human psychology and behavior. Kevin Mitnick, a famed hacker, began taking advantage of human users when he was only 16 in 1978, and continued until 1995 when he was arrested by the FBI. Mitnick had limited technical sophistication to write unique code or exploits,

```
1 Public Function Sspyg{} As Varient
2
3 Sspyg= Array {"Amazon","Anonymous","Bitdefender", "Blue Coat","Cisco
· Systems","Cloud","Data
· Center","Dedicated","ESET,spol","FireEye","Forcepoint","Fortinet","Hetz
· ner","Hosted","Hosting","LeaseWeb","Microsoft","nForce","OVH
· SAS","Proofpoint","Security","Server","Strong Technologies","Trend
· Micro","Trustwave","blackoakcomputers","mimecast",}
4
5 End Function
```

Figure 4.1 Polymorphic malware sample

but he was able to use his expert skills at social engineering to break into well-protected systems.[9] "Social engineering" refers to techniques aimed at convincing a target to reveal privileged or private information. This information can then be used to gain unauthorized access to controlled systems or services. If you have ever received an email or text message asking you to urgently click on a link, you have likely been subject to a form of social engineering called "phishing."

Considering the central place of humans in cyberspace, behavioral sciences have much to contribute to our understanding of cyber (in) security. While the technical literature on malware design and development and vulnerability identification receives substantial attention, the weakest point of most computer systems is the user (often referred to as the wet-ware).[10] Attacks including social engineering, the manipulation of information processing and human perception, cyberbullying and more, all find a place within the framework of cyber-capability development. Very often, these types of vulnerabilities can be identified as critical parts of the Cyber Kill Chain, examined later in this chapter.

There are a diversity of malicious cyber-capability types, functions and uses in cyber conflict, just as in conventional forms of conflict. In 2014, IBM estimated human error was a contributing factor in more than 95 percent of all computer security incidents.[11] Human error, arising at any level from the configuration of the physical and logical layers to human persona activities within a system, provides a robust vector for the utilization of cyber capabilities. Within this 95 percent figure, the vast majority of security incidents occur through user interaction with malicious links in emails or on websites as a result of social engineering. Other common sources of human-induced vulnerability arise due to a desire for convenience. In the early days of cybersecurity, it was difficult to convince users to adopt passwords. Apple had to change the default set-up procedures for its popular iPhone products to encourage users to put basic passcodes on their mobile devices. More recently, universities, companies, government agencies and more are requiring multifactor authentication (e.g. relying on a password and an email or text message verification as a second factor). Multifactor authentication is seen as a way to offset the risks associated with vulnerabilities within the wetware of systems: the human users. Some firms have gone so far as to put superglue into USB ports to prevent computer users from inserting USB drives into controlled systems, a notoriously effective attack vector that will be examined below.

Organizations use a variety of methods to protect their digital systems from their human users and protect against different types of manipulation or exploitation of the wetware. To combat human vulnerability, the US DoD began stripping all active HTML links from DoD emails and placed additional text in the subject line of emails originating outside of the Department stating "Non-DoD Source" in 2015. The commander of the Defense Information Systems Agency (DISA), Vice Admiral Nancy A. Norton, indicated the result of these actions has been a dramatic reduction in the number of successful penetrations of DoD networks, but not a reduction in the number of overall attempts to penetrate the network.[12]

Although the complexity and sophistication of malware continues to advance, the primary beachhead into systems and networks remains the human user. Concurrently, while human users remain vulnerable, the number of lines of code within systems continues to grow, resulting in a general increase in the number of bugs (vulnerabilities) within a given set of code. Each new bug offers a new potentially exploitable vector for an attacker. The industry average in 2012 was between 15 and 50 bugs per 1,000 lines of code (a measure known as KLOC).[13] However, this ratio is not exact, because many bugs go undiscovered. The increasing complexity and length of codes hide potential avenues through which attackers can manipulate systems and networks.

As the arsenal of cyber capabilities is growing in complexity and volume, the number of potential new vulnerabilities available to exploit grows. The relationship between new and old vulnerabilities and exploits is not linear. Cyber capabilities are developed to exploit vulnerabilities, patches that fix these vulnerabilities are released, new software and hardware platforms are deployed, and new defensive measures are developed.

The most effective way to prevent the delivery of a malware payload is to fix all known vulnerabilities as quickly as possible. Despite patching being the best way to protect systems, it is not a foolproof solution. The patching of computer systems within and across organizations is not uniform, meaning that the mere fact that a vendor releases a fix for a software vulnerability does not mean that all computers with that vulnerability are immune to potential exploits. Often individuals fail to update or patch their systems regularly, leaving them vulnerable to exploitation long after fixes have been released.

In 2017, North Korea utilized EternalBlue, an exploit developed by the NSA and subsequently stolen by the hacker group called Shadow Brokers, to create a destructive ransomware attack: WannaCry.[14] Although Microsoft released a patch for the vulnerability two months prior to its use by North Korea, millions of computers around the world had not yet implemented the patch.[15] The National Health Service

(NHS) in the United Kingdom was hit particularly hard in its electronic medical records systems and legacy systems.[16] The challenge of keeping systems up to date becomes more complex, the more specialized a system is. NHS systems, and similar systems that run critical infrastructures or large manufacturing processes, are often tailored software and hardware collections that are unable to implement generic patches without customization to prevent the fixes themselves from rendering existing systems inoperable.

Cyber capabilities for both offensive and defensive actions are in constant flux. On the defensive side, users are constantly required to update, upgrade and secure their systems and networks, changing the vulnerabilities at both the logical and physical network layers, and attempting to minimize vulnerabilities at the human persona layer. By contrast, on the offensive side, actors attempt to quickly develop, and if necessary utilize, cyber capabilities before they are no longer effective. For instance, a worm, virus or trojan developed to exploit Windows XP is unlikely to impact Windows 10. While there are similar analogies in conventional conflict, the rifle has remained a resilient tool of combat for more than 200 years and is unlikely to be defeated as an instrument of warfare anytime soon. The lifespan of malware is transitory and decreases in value as targets upgrade and patch their systems. The constraints on the arsenal of cyber capabilities impact how and why such capabilities are developed. Unlike with conventional or nuclear arms, verification that seeks to control the development, storage, dissemination and use of cyber capabilities is nearly impossible. Whereas rifles, bullets, bombs and other conventional weapons must be transported through and stored in physical space, cyber capabilities can be copied and transmitted over networks ad infinitum with little relative cost and no visibility to outside parties. While it is possible to obfuscate the observation of conventional arms, the relative challenges of detecting conventional and cyber capabilities are not comparable. The next section explores how offensive cyber capabilities are developed.

Developing offensive cyber capabilities

Developing an offensive cyber capability varies based on the effect being sought. The more complicated the effect, the more complex the development process. Criminal exploits such as ransomware are often overt and do not seek to hide their effects. Overt malware can be utilized more quickly than more complex exploits such as Flame or Buckshot

Yankee, which seek to establish remote access and pose an APT within a network or system. Both forms of malware can be damaging. Whereas ransomware attacks seek to extort victims, more covert malware exploits are often used to exfiltrate intellectual property. Both forms of attack impact individuals, businesses, critical infrastructures and governments. Researchers have identified a trend in the history of malware development, from a single developer working for a month or two to more complex teams that take much longer.[17] This trend would indicate that the aggregate level of complexity of malware is likely to increase over time.

Growing complexity is also apparent when considering cyber criminality. In Russia and Ukraine, criminals posed as reputable software manufacturers and developed software packages designed to mimic anti-virus programs in an effort to gain access to unsuspecting users.[18] Users in the United States and Europe attempting to do due diligence to protect their computers against malware purchased subscriptions to these fake anti-virus programs. These fake programs subsequently began to slowly extort the user for more money, asking for upgrades or fixes to malware, or simply provided criminals access to the user's computer. This type of attack is extremely difficult to overcome and requires a high level of due diligence from users who often lack the requisite computer skills necessary to make informed judgments.

By contrast, exploits such as fake anti-virus programs are not effective at penetrating most medium to large businesses or governments who use verified vendors. Targeting large businesses and governments requires more sophisticated capabilities that nearly always begin by targeting human users within hardened network infrastructures. These capabilities tend to be multifaceted and often require both user error and technical vulnerabilities.

The trend in malware development continues toward ever more complex organizational structures for criminal purposes, as will be examined in chapter 7. Similarly, states are relying on increasingly complex assemblages of military, civilian and proxy organizations to develop their offensive cyber capabilities. The publication of national cyber strategies and leaks to the press provide a window into the development of cyber capabilities. At present, all European countries, the United States, Canada and dozens of others have created cyber strategies, many of which include provisions for the development of offensive capabilities as well as defensive ones. These documents signal a state's intent to defend its networks, while warning potential adversaries that it too has offensive capabilities. The development of these capabilities also communicates the level of importance that states give to cyberspace and its potential impact on security.

The rest of this section examines two different directions in the development and use of cyber capabilities: the development of criminal networks, and powerful state-sponsored cyber actors.

Criminal cyber-capability development

Within the criminal world, the Russian Business Network (RBN) is one of the most famous – or infamous – organizations. Throughout the mid-2000s, the RBN both developed and provided a variety of services for criminal activities in cyberspace.[19] At its peak, it is estimated that the RBN was earning over $150 million per year.[20] Criminal activities within the RBN infrastructure were as diverse as child pornography, phishing, spam and malware distribution.[21] The RBN is also famous for providing resources for patriotic Russian hackers to launch DDoS and cross-site scripting attacks against government websites in the Republic of Georgia, both during and prior to Russia's 2008 invasion of South Ossetia and Abkhazia.[22] The RBN denies its complicity with criminal activities, but forensic data indicate a sophisticated web of connections between ISPs and BGPs designed to obfuscate traffic and facilitate criminal activities.[23] The RBN spanned more than 24 networks and utilized dozens of different malware varieties.[24] Collective organizations such as the RBN allow for the consolidated development of malware within ecosystems conducive to criminal behaviors. The organizational structure of the RBN, while centralized in its root infrastructure, was highly decentralized in the development and utilization of malware. The RBN's efforts were entirely profit seeking, although it was susceptible to state influence by the Russian Federation. Current research on the status of the RBN has largely fallen by the wayside as Russian intelligence services – such as the Foreign Intelligence Service, the SVR (Sluzhba Vneshney Razvedki), and the General Staff Main Intelligence Directorate, the GRU (Glavnoye Razvedyvatel'noye Upravleniye) – have risen in prominence. Russian criminal hacking networks are thought to be still quite prolific, but by most accounts the RBN as an independent entity no longer exists.[25] The story of the RBN demonstrates, in part, a process of state co-optation: the use of non-state actors for state purposes while it is convenient to the state, and the eventual subsumption of those actors into state-managed organizations at some future point. This co-optation of sub-state or criminal actors by the state is most common in authoritarian states. Iran and China have also sought to incorporate cyber criminality into state capabilities. The processes of co-optation vary from state to state, yet the result is largely the same: increasingly powerful state cyber capabilities.

The RBN is by no means unique. There are a plethora of criminal organizations, ranging from Mexican drug cartels to individual criminal hackers, who both generate novel exploits and utilize existing malware through available libraries such as Metasploit. Cyber capabilities added a dimension to criminal theft that has in many ways made criminal behavior easier in terms of time and energy, and less risky for the perpetrator. Whereas a bank robber used to have to leverage the threat of violence to compel a teller to hand over money, a modern bank robber accesses the financial information of the bank via the Internet through anonymous routing services such as Virtual Private Networks (VPNs) or Tor, to steal substantially more money in less time, with greater anonymity.

State cyber-capability development and proliferation

The efforts of the RBN and similar criminal enterprises, while organized, are less focused on specific targets and are not centrally controlled. By contrast, the People's Liberation Army (PLA) Unit 61398, a military hacking unit accused by the US Department of Justice of engaging in substantial intellectual property theft from US commercial firms, is centrally organized, funded and controlled.[26] In 2013, Mandiant (now FireEye) released a comprehensive report detailing the espionage efforts of this unit.[27] PLA Unit 61398 constitutes a highly organized military unit within the 2nd Bureau of the 3rd department of the PLA General Staff.[28] Analysts estimate this unit compromised more than 141 companies across 20 industries as of 2013.[29] Mandiant deemed the unit APT1 (Advanced Persistent Threat 1) because of its immense reach and scale. APT1 maintained persistent access on target systems in excess of 1,764 days.[30] The unit leveraged more than 40 different malware families or subtypes of the cyber capabilities identified above. Each of the targets selected was exploited for intelligence gain. Unit 61398 must have had substantial staffing and resources with annualized budgets to stage such an operation. Mandiant assesses that the unit had been in existence since at least 2006 and had stolen in excess of 6.5 terabytes of data (for comparison, the US Library of Congress is composed in its entirety of 15 terabytes).[31] The scale and organizational complexity of Unit 61398 far outpaces that of the RBN. While the RBN was profit seeking, Unit 61398 was focused on national security and economic espionage.

Externalities associated with the proliferating nature of cyber capabilities include a diffusion of malware away from state actors down to sub-state and criminal elements. Robust malware libraries are available both through open-source collections and through profit-seeking ventures. The diffuse nature of mid- to low-tier cyber capabilities has facilitated criminal activities in and through cyberspace. The malware and skills that facilitate espionage are equally relevant to the theft of information from corporate databases, which is often initiated via emails leveraging social engineering. Cybersecurity breaches in the private sector have resulted in the availability of personally identifiable information (PII) markets, resulting in credit card fraud and identity theft.

The production and distribution of malware are not entirely democratized, with many of the most complex malware types remaining at the state level, due to the time and specificity required for their creation. However, the volume of malware available below the state level fosters strategic challenges for economies around the globe. The creation of malware by states, criminal organizations, corporations such as the Hacking Team, and individuals indicates an increasingly contested and potentially risky environment.

There is no single approach to developing effective malware and each actor, state or criminal must tailor their efforts to the resources available to them and the targets they seek to attack or exploit. Similarly, there are dozens of different software development models used globally in the development of software for commercial and non-commercial use. Like conventional software, many forms of malware are iterative – meaning that each subsequent version of a software improves upon prior versions. Malware packages often start out small and slowly expand to address new vulnerabilities that can then be exploited. Although each new attack might be given a new name, the malware that underlies each attack may have been used in previous attacks in part or in whole. For instance, the 2015 attack on Ukraine's electric grid was the third iteration of that malware family over the previous decade.

Identifying vulnerabilities that can be exploited by different types of malware is a time-consuming and expensive process. At the lowest levels, penetration testing targets individual components of applications or systems to determine or find vulnerabilities that can be exploited. Basic forms of penetration testing can be automated. However, automation is not a sure-fire way to find vulnerabilities. On a larger scale, firms and nation states can hire or outsource penetration testing. More eyes on more systems are likely to identify more vulnerabilities. Yet another way to build cyber capabilities is to leverage existing software repositories, many of which are developed by researchers or sold on the dark web. Countries or actors with limited resources might turn towards this reuse approach as a more cost-effective means of developing cyber capabilities. Capabilities secured this way are unlikely to be useful against other nation states but might be very effective against non-state actors and groups.

Once vulnerabilities are discovered, it is often a matter of making changes to existing malware families to exploit these newly discovered vulnerabilities. The result is that a "payload" of malware (the data that is transmitted) might be relatively similar across cyberattacks while the delivery vehicle might be quite different. As examined above, the delivery mechanism of a cyber capability can often be extremely difficult to detect.

As a means of assessing the general processes for developing malware, US defense company Lockheed Martin created the "Cyber Kill Chain," a useful model for examining how actors develop and utilize offensive cyber capabilities. Table 4.3 provides a detailed walk through the Cyber Kill Chain.

The Cyber Kill Chain provides a good procedural model for how offensive cyber activities are undertaken, but it does not explicitly outline what resources, skills, strategies, operations and tactics are needed to both develop and utilize cyberspace capabilities for offensive actions. Criminal organizations such as the RBN are likely to do the minimum *reconnaissance* necessary to prepare for a cyber operation. If they are engaged in spamming or other forms of social engineering, they might conduct a basic search on the Internet or write emails that are generic enough to work for dozens of individuals. By contrast, Unit 61398 probably engages in substantial reconnaissance of its targets. It leverages all-source intelligence to develop a picture of a target and assesses which vulnerabilities are most likely to be successfully exploited. Reconnaissance activities for both criminal and state organizations are ongoing, but we can reasonably assume that states devote substantially more resources to understanding a target to develop tailored malware and ensure success. The RBN and similar criminal organizations are more likely to engage in criminal activities that yield greater profits by attacking more broadly and with fewer upfront costs devoted to reconnaissance.

In the *weaponization* phase of the Kill Chain, both criminal and state actors take the information or intelligence gained from the

Table 4.3 The Cyber Kill Chain[32]

Step 1: Reconnaissance	The attacker gathers information on the target before the actual attack starts. He can do it by looking for publicly available information on the Internet.
Step 2: Weaponization	The attacker uses an exploit and creates a malicious payload to send to the victim. This step happens on the attacker's side, without contact with the victim.
Step 3: Delivery	The attacker sends the malicious payload to the victim by email or other means, which represents one of many intrusion methods the attacker can use.
Step 4: Exploitation	The attacker gains access to the victim via a software, hardware or human vulnerability.
Step 5: Installation	Installing malware on the infected computer is relevant only if the attacker used malware as part of the attack, and even when there is malware involved, the installation is a point in time within a much more elaborate attack process that takes months to operate.
Step 6: Command and control (C2)	The attacker creates or maintains a command and control channel in order to continue to operate his internal assets remotely. This step is relatively generic and relevant throughout the attack, not only when malware is installed.
Step 7: Action on objectives	The attacker performs the steps to achieve his actual goals inside the victim's network. This is the elaborate active attack process that takes months, and thousands of small steps, in order to achieve.

reconnaissance phase and begin the process of creating a payload that can be delivered to the target. As in the island-hopping strategy, states are likely to want payloads to be delivered to specific targets, and therefore more carefully craft weaponized code. Criminal organizations seeking profit do not need to expend time or money on highly specialized targeting and therefore can avoid such strategies to focus on the exploit requiring the least effort.

The craft with which code is weaponized can provide substantial forensic clues as to its authorship. Many states are beholden to international law, and their weaponized code attempts to conform to these legal standards. For instance, the Stuxnet worm that attacked Iran's nuclear enrichment facilities appears to have been written in close consultation with lawyers.[33] The code targeted specific configurations of Siemens controllers that were designed to manage centrifuge arrays in specific configurations known through International Atomic Energy Agency

(IAEA) reporting to have been used in Iranian nuclear enrichment processes. The code also verified the date on the systems to ensure that it was operating within its specified timeframe. How code is weaponized and what its constraints and limitations are can and often do provide indications regarding the actor who developed the code, and the strategy and tactics it employed. The weaponization phase often requires expertise well beyond that of hackers, and can necessitate engineers, physicists or a variety of technical, legal and policy specialists. Stealing data might not be that difficult, but changing the enrichment levels of a centrifuge array will probably require a nuclear engineer.[34]

Once code has been weaponized, its *delivery* can be as simple as emailing an infected PDF or Microsoft Word file to an unsuspecting recipient, or it can involve leaving dozens of infected USB drives outside of a US military facility in Iraq, as was the case for Buckshot Yankee.[35] Delivery techniques can be direct or indirect; they can be complex or remarkably simple. Delivery methods are predicated on the target(s) being sought after, and the capabilities of the attacker to leverage a diverse set of delivery tactics. Sometimes, as in the case of the Natanz nuclear facility in Iran, a human insider, either knowingly or unknowingly, transports the malicious code into a facility. At times, it is possible to draw targets out so that they go onto a specific website or an IP address – this approach is known as a wateringhole attack. In Ukraine, the Russian military has used cellular tower spoofing to hijack soldiers' mobile communications and send infected attachments purporting to be from family or friends, via Multimedia Messaging Service (MMS) or Short Message/Messaging Service (SMS).[36]

Delivering a weapon often requires access into the system being targeted. This access constitutes the exploitation phase of an attack. At its most basic, *exploitation* is the culmination of the delivery phase of an attack and links delivery and installation as well as subsequent functions within the Kill Chain. Exploitation can target any of the three layers of cyberspace. Exploitations of the physical network and logical network layers often require the use of a 0-Day (a previously undiscovered or unpatched). Exploitation at the human persona layer often involves social engineering a human user to click on a link or visit a website. The overwhelming majority of exploits occur through human interactions. Kevin Mitnick, one of the most famous hackers of the 1990s, was moderately skilled on the technical side but excelled at social engineering. He was arrested by the FBI in 1995 and charged with computer hacking and wire fraud.[37] Social engineering remains one of the most effective means of exploitation. This is largely due to the human nature of cyberspace, but also to the substantial investments most organizations put into defensive tools to secure the more technical attributes of networks and systems.

Following the delivery and exploitation of a target, malware frequently needs to be installed. If malware is being *installed*, then it must be directed against systems it can infect. Malware designed to run on Windows is unlikely to work on machines running MacOS or Linux. Even within specific versions of operating systems, malware must account for updates and patches so that it can be installed and function as intended. Not all cyberattacks require installation. DDoS attacks can overwhelm an adversary's ability to handle large volumes of traffic without installation. This was the case with the Mirai DDoS attacks in 2016, which disabled a major DNS that provided services to companies such as Netflix, GitHub, Twitter, Reddit and Airbnb.[38] The installation phase can be difficult and, if improperly done, might alert system users or network administrators, or trigger system defenses such as anti-virus software or intrusion detection and prevention systems (IDPSs). If these defenses identify a malware, they will seek to limit its potential effects. The installation of malware can trigger prompts to users or administrators that might alert them to the attackers' intentions or degrade system resources temporarily so as to indicate that a system's functioning state is changed. Indications of installation must be managed for an attack to be successful. Crafting malware for successful installation often requires in-depth knowledge of how systems are managed and what privileges various user accounts have with systems and networks, to overcome cyber defenses.

Attacks that seek to gain a foothold – in a similar way to the island-hopping strategy – often require C2 capabilities. Some attacks can be run from a single C2 server, or, for instance, Unit 61398 attackers established 937 C2 servers spread across 849 IP addresses in 13 countries.[39] The resources available to the attacker and the attributes of the target itself determine the development and maintenance of C2 for the purpose of attacking an adversary. Criminal organizations are unlikely to have the capability to manage large-scale C2 in the same way a state might, but with moderate resources they can still achieve robust C2. More complex C2 facilitates increasingly robust and resilient offensive cyber actions. However, the establishment of C2 is resource intensive and can require substantial time and coordination. C2 capabilities are typically established in advance of malware installation. First, if malware needs to be directly installed by the attacker, C2 establishes the communications link that allows for installation. Second, if malware is self-propagating or user-installed, and exfiltrates data or executes commands at the direction of the attacker, it requires a place to call home for directions or the reception of data. The management of C2 over time is difficult and can expose an attack if done improperly.

One early case that has become legend is the tale of Clifford Stoll's tracking of KGB-funded hacker Markus Hess as he stole information from Lawrence Berkeley National Laboratory.[40] C2 requires the transmission of data from one system to another. Anomalies in traffic usage, where the data originates and where it goes, and even the electrical consumption of devices can raise red flags among systems administrators. Clifford Stoll worked as a system administrator at the Lawrence Berkeley National Laboratory when he traced a $0.75 accounting error to the unauthorized use of 9 seconds of laboratory computer time. Stoll eventually realized that a hacker had acquired access to the Laboratory system, and contacted intelligence and law-enforcement agencies. His meticulous forensic analysis resulted in a surprising find, a KGB penetration. His investigation illustrates the difficulty of maintaining long-term presence on a target system.

To achieve such a presence on a target system requires substantial C2 capabilities. Often, C2 capabilities are routed through proxy states or organizations to obfuscate their origin or intention and to prevent attribution. In the case of DDoS attacks, C2 can function like a conductor of an orchestra, calling on different bots (infected computers) within its network to launch an attack at different times, or using all of them simultaneously.

Finally, after all the previous steps have been implemented, the last step in the development and utilization of an offensive cyber capability is an *action on objectives*. In this final stage of the Cyber Kill Chain, effects are actuated. Actions span a spectrum from exploitation and exfiltration of data, passwords or other credentials, to the manipulation of data to violate its integrity within a system, the degradation of a system to slow it down or minimize its efficiency, and the destruction of the system or device it is running. The majority of offensive cyber actions focus on the theft (exploitation and exfiltration) of data. Both the RBN's criminal endeavors and those of Unit 61398 were primarily interested in the theft of data. While the RBN sought profit, Unit 61398 sought intelligence for both national security and national economic gain. The majority of malware seeks to steal data for profit or intelligence, but new forms of malware such as CryptoLocker are now being used for extortion, via the threat of data destruction and the degradation of systems. Whereas previous attacks made money from the data itself, by engaging in credit card fraud and identity theft, attacks using CryptoLocker extort the computer's or system's owner to pay a fee to unlock their data. In sum, cyber actions can take multiple forms and be used to achieve different objectives. Unlike many conventional weapons – such as bullets or bombs – which result in first-order effects, the impact of cyber capabilities is necessarily indirect.

The effects and characteristics of cyber capabilities

Bullets fired from a gun achieve first-order effects through their impact with a given target. Bombs dropped from a plane cause first-order effects through their explosive blasts. Beyond the theft of data for espionage or criminal purposes, there are few first-order effects achieved through offensive cyber operations. The apparent absence of first-order effects is one of the main reasons why some scholars have been reluctant to use the expression "cyber war." Below is a comparison of eight key attributes of cyber capabilities and kinetic weapons. Understanding these attributes helps decision-makers choose the most applicable tool in a given situation.

First, effects in cyberspace differ in their key characteristics from kinetic effects. Kinetic weapons privilege direct effects over indirect effects; by contrast, cyberattacks privilege indirect effects, or what Herb Lin refers to as second-hand third-order effects.[41] The second attribute is that of reversibility. The effects of most kinetic weapons are difficult and often costly to reverse. It takes time to rebuild an area that has been destroyed by a bomb, to heal from a gunshot wound. Cyberattacks are in many cases reversible with limited cost to either the attacker or the target, particularly within short time horizons. For instance, a CryptoLocker attack on a victim can be reversed if the victim pays a fee to the hacker, thereby releasing (decrypting) the data. Third, cyber capabilities are often costly to research and develop, but inexpensive to maintain. Kinetic weapons, however, have costs extending from research and development through procurement and maintenance. Once an exploit is available for a given vulnerability, it will remain effective until that vulnerability is patched. Fourth, kinetic weapons often are limited in both number and complexity based on the wealth of a state, whereas the capacity to build cyber weapons can be relatively democratized as the resources (i.e. coding skills, hardware and software) necessary for their creation are widespread and inexpensive. Fifth, the intelligence requirements necessary for successful deployment of both cyber and kinetic weapons are high. Both types of weapon require strategic intelligence to understand the adversary's capabilities. The utilization of both types of weapon also requires substantial intelligence preparation of the battlefield (IPB). Sixth, both kinetic and cyber capabilities involve uncertainties in planning and execution – however, the process of conducting battle damage assessments after use can be very complex in the case of cyber capabilities, in contrast to kinetic weapons. Since cyber effects are indirect, it is often difficult to discern whether the cause of a problem with a computer is the result of a cyberattack, an error or some other malfunction. In 2016–17, when North Korea experienced a series of ballistic missile test failures, some observers hinted that these failures might be the result of US "left of launch" cyberattacks against the missiles themselves. However, as noted by David Sanger, while many "cyber experts" claimed these test failures were due to cyberattacks, aeronautical engineers specializing in missiles indicated that the probable source of the failure was mechanical and not cyber related.[42]

Seventh – and often overlooked – is the returnability of cyber capabilities upon use. Once a bomb explodes or a bullet is fired, it generally cannot be re-exploded or re-fired. A cyber capability once used, if not properly deleted from the target system, can be forensically reconstituted and repurposed as a new capability for the adversary or other actors who might gain access to the code or vulnerabilities it exploited. The returnability of cyber capabilities against the attacker or other actors eliminates the concept of fire and forget. In cyberspace, if you fire, you also need to protect your own systems against the weapon being used. Eighth, proliferation is a challenge for both kinetic weapons and cyber capabilities. However, transporting tanks, bombs, missiles and even guns is substantially more difficult than emailing or file-transferring malicious software with the click of a mouse. Tracking, maintaining security of and accounting for an arsenal of cyber capabilities over time poses substantial challenges to many states, as evidenced by the NSA's loss of numerous exploits to the hacker group the Shadow Brokers. Table 4.4 provides an overview of the major differences between kinetic and cyber capabilities.

Although characteristics diverge between kinetic and cyber capabilities, substantial effects can be achieved by both. Both types of capabilities are capable of achieving violence either against large populations or targeted against individuals.[43] The predictability of effects achieved through kinetic weapons remains more easily understood by policy-makers, warfighters and criminals. And, although effects of cyber capabilities are difficult to assess in the current forms of use, this might

Table 4.4 Kinetic versus cyber capabilities

Kinetic capabilities	Cyber capabilities
Direct effects	Indirect effects
Difficult and costly to reverse	More easily reversible / transitory
Costly to maintain	Easy to maintain
Costly to develop Substantial intelligence requirements	Relatively easy to develop Substantial intelligence requirements
Relatively simple damage assessment	Very complex damage assessment
Not returnable	Returnable
Physical burden of proliferation	Easy proliferation

not always be the case as new weapons are developed and more and more systems connect to cyberspace and increase the potential for violence. The continued development of ever more advanced cyber capabilities is likely to create new effects that might more closely approximate those of kinetic weapons. While, in the near term, prognostications of a "cyber Pearl Harbor" remain unfulfilled, as the number and importance of computers and cyberspace expand, the effects that are able to be achieved in and through cyberspace with cyber capabilities are likely to increase.[44]

Returning to cyber capabilities

As discussed at the beginning of the chapter, there remains a substantial debate within the field of international relations as to whether cyber capabilities constitute a weapon at all. While Lucas Kello identifies cyber capabilities as "virtual weapons," other scholars – such as Thomas Rid, Erik Gartzke and Jon Lindsay – push back on the application of the term "weapon."[45] This chapter deliberately uses the muted term "cyber capability" as opposed to a more aggressive term – "cyber weapon." Removing hyperbole from the debate allows us to focus on what it is that states and criminal actors seek to achieve via cyber means and how they go about doing so. There is often a desire to leverage common terminology across domains – however, as was seen in 2016, the use of conventional language to describe "cyber bombs" hitting the Islamic State is not really applicable. Talking about "cyber bombs" obfuscates the true nature of cyber capabilities and their inherent complexity, and establishes false impressions of their effect.[46] Cyber capabilities are just that: capabilities. They can be developed, used and discarded and are wholly dependent on the target and objectives being sought. In cyberspace, unlike in conventional war, one cyber capability does not necessarily equate to another in the same way that one bullet is similar to other bullets. The organization, planning and management of capabilities in cyberspace have proven difficult. The continued expansion of cyberspace provides ample room for the development of new forms of capabilities in the years to come.

A continued focus on malware and the vulnerabilities of systems and networks often overlooks the largest security gap associated with cyber capabilities: the human user. The single greatest vulnerability a hacker, state or criminal can target is the user of a system. While the emphasis of this chapter was on the development of capabilities in terms of malware, one of the most successful capabilities hackers deploy is a thorough understanding of human psychology. Social engineering against a user can substantially ease the technical requirements necessary for the development of most other cyber capabilities.

Discussion questions

1. Is malware a weapon or a capability? Discuss.

2. Are cyber capabilities developed by states or by criminal actors more dangerous? Why?

3. How does Lockheed's "Cyber Kill Chain" help in understanding cyberattacks?

Exercise

Use the Security Planner (https://securityplanner.consumerrepor ts.org) to develop your personalized plan to keep your sensitive-information data secure. Discuss your results with at least one other student or colleague. Which recommendations are helpful, and how likely are you to adopt them?

Additional resources

Robert Belk and Matthew Noyes, "On the Use of Offensive Cyber Capabilities: A Policy Analysis on Offensive US Cyber Policy," *Belfer Center*, March 20, 2012, www.belfercenter.org/sites/default/files/files/publication/cybersecur ity-pae-belk-noyes.pdf.

Dennis Distler, "Malware Analysis: An Introduction," *SANS Institute InfoSec Reading Room*, February 12, 2008, at www.sans.org/white-papers/2103.

Emily Goldman and John Arquilla, *Cyber Analogies* (Monterrey, CA: Naval Postgraduate School, 2014), https://calhoun.nps.edu/bitstream/handle/10945/40037/NPS-DA-14-001.pdf.

5   Cybersecurity and strategy

Reader's guide

- Cybersecurity strategy seeks to identify *ways* in which decision-makers can use all the *means* available to them to achieve security *objectives* in and through cyberspace.

- Cyber power is the ability to exert influence in and from cyberspace. This form of power is closely linked to other more traditional diplomatic, informational, military and economic instruments.

- Cyber strategies have proliferated at the national and international level in the past decade. This proliferation is a sign that the field is maturing as a policy area.

- National differences can explain variation of cyber strategies. Despite significant differences, cyber strategies all seek to address problems of coordination linked to the extensive nature of cyberspace.

Cybersecurity is a complex endeavor, involving millions of actors and billions of devices. Cyberspace permeates so much of the critical social, economic and military infrastructure of modern nations that it forms a foundational substrate upon which national security relies. This chapter focuses on national and international efforts to achieve cybersecurity, and the continuing relevance of state actors in cyberspace. Although non-state actors – such as hackers, criminal organizations, nonprofit organizations and companies – affect cybersecurity, states have unparalleled authority, legitimacy, expertise and access to resources.[1] Governmental and societal reliance on information technology infrastructure inevitably creates vulnerabilities that public authorities seek to mitigate. National decision-makers, and the processes they follow, shape cyberspace and the interactions that take place within it.

The need for national and international cybersecurity is now widely recognized, and the debate on the ends, ways and means necessary to achieve this condition has attracted increasing public and scholarly attention in the last decade.[2] This chapter first considers how states can leverage key instruments of power to support their national security in and through cyberspace. The networked nature of cyberspace requires national cybersecurity to span multiple divides between public and private, and local, national and international organizations. The second section zooms in on the role of cyber diplomacy, an emerging set of practices and themes in the literature. Subsequent sections examine the national cybersecurity strategies of three major powers: China, Russia and the United States. All three emphasize the need to coordinate multiple actors and approaches to security in and through the digital realm. We conclude that, despite significant differences in national cyber strategies, nation states face a number of common challenges to achieving national cybersecurity.

Cyber power, national security and strategy

National security can be understood both in the objective sense of physical safety, and in a more subjective way, as the protection of national values.[3] While the physical safety of nations poses similar challenges across the globe, variation in national interests and values – specifically between liberal democracies and authoritarian regimes – produces different approaches in the pursuit of national security.

To maintain national security, governments wield power. In its simplest form, power is the ability to influence others. This ability rests on economic, demographic, political and sociocultural resources, among others. States use a variety of instruments – diplomacy, information, military and economic capabilities (also known as DIME) – to leverage these resources and pursue goals they believe will have a positive impact on their regime or population. In democracies, governments are elected to formulate national interests through policy objectives and strategies that translate into action.[4] They sometimes opt to wield hard power, using or threatening to use military operations and economic sanctions to force other actors to change their behavior. At the softer end of the spectrum, policy-makers use information and diplomacy to influence actors through persuasion. One of the core challenges confronting high-level decision-makers is to effectively combine hard- and soft-power resources – what Joseph Nye calls a smart-power strategy – to achieve national security objectives.[5] Much of the contemporary debate about national cybersecurity explores how to leverage specific cyber capabilities to contribute to such a strategy.

The concept of cyber power provides a useful basis for discussing the role of cyber capabilities in the context of national security policy. Strategist John Sheldon defines cyber power as "the ability, in peace, crisis, and war to exert prompt and sustained influence in and from cyberspace."[6] With the distinction between "in" and "from" cyberspace, Sheldon suggests that cyber operations establish influence beyond cyberspace, in the physical world. For Daniel Kuehl, another strategist, cyber power is a dimension of the informational instrument of power that "links to, supports, and enables the creation and exercise of the other instruments" to create advantages and influence events.[7] Cyberspace is inherently linked to the economic performance of major nations. Digital goods and services accounted for 10.3 percent of the US economy in 2021 and over 39.8 percent of the Chinese Gross Domestic Product (GDP).[8] States also leverage cyber capabilities as a means of influencing opinions throughout the world and, increasingly, to exert military force. Cyber capabilities have come to permeate all elements of national power.

During the Cold War era, the information element of national power was focused on strategic communications and propaganda, two types of information-based influence operations meant to affect the perceptions and attitude of specific audiences. With the advent of cyberspace, the information domain has expanded significantly. All sorts of state and non-state actors can leverage cyberspace to advance their interests in and through the digital world. The Internet is sometimes referred to as the "great equalizer," reflecting the way in which easy access to cyberspace empowers actors that do not traditionally wield significant informational influence. In a realm where both state and non-state actors play a prominent role, power cannot simply be exerted over others to influence them, but must also be utilized co-operatively.[9] Wielding power in cyberspace and achieving national cybersecurity require public–private and international cooperation.

Leveraging instruments of power in a coordinated manner is essential to achieve national objectives. Strategy seeks to achieve such coordination by aligning ends (objectives), ways (courses of action) and means (resources). In practice, it often entails the creation of a policy document that identifies the actions necessary to achieve national objectives within a particular domain of interaction. Thus a national cyber strategy seeks to connect elements of cyber power in the pursuit of national objectives. One of the earliest definitions of what constitutes a national cybersecurity strategy was outlined in *Cyberpower and National Security* by Franklin Kramer, Stuart Starr and Larry Wentz. The authors defined national cybersecurity strategy as "the development and employment of strategic capabilities to operate in cyberspace, integrated and coordinated with the other operational domains, to achieve or support the achievement of objectives across the elements of national power in support of national security strategy."[10] Achieving national cybersecurity requires the development of human, technological and organizational resources and procedures that contribute to specific national objectives.[11] A specific cybersecurity strategy at the national level will frequently be paired with strategies across different levels of government. For instance, the United States releases strategies at the national level, and at departmental levels to include strategies for the Departments of Defense, Homeland Security and the intelligence community (Office of the Director of National Intelligence). These documents often provide additional nuances relevant to the form and function of particular organizations within government. Beyond the departmental or ministerial level, national cybersecurity strategies often fall within a constellation of affiliated strategies that address issues ranging from economic development in online environments to dealing with AI and more.

National strategies vary. They can be broad and encompassing, or narrow and focused. Some strategies are aspirational guides, while others are more grounded in current capabilities. Nearly all strategies respond to and sometimes seek to anticipate the state of and changes in both domestic and international political environments. As perceived adversary behavior changes, national strategies are often tailored to address new challenges and threats. Frequently, strategies address concerns that arise and attempt to lay out a path toward alleviating those concerns. At times they include justifications for why some objectives, ways and means were chosen rather than others. This in turn signals a state's understanding of the strategic environment to other states and serves to minimize information asymmetries. National strategies also serve as a guide for domestic actors to follow: they identify issues that need to be addressed and broadly how to address them.

A range of factors explain why (cybersecurity) strategies vary. States pursue different interests and objectives and follow different strategies to translate their resources into desirable outcomes. Proponents of strategic culture argue that states formulate national assumptions – based on their political, cultural, philosophical and cognitive characteristics – that limit the options they consider. Cultural legacies brought by different organizations can also play a role in framing issues and evaluating policy options.[12] These elements, as well as bureaucratic preferences and legal constraints, can be expected to produce national styles and preferences that shape the way nations use their cyber power.[13] However, analysts need to be careful not to make extreme generalizations that would seek to predict state behavior based solely on national circumstances and legacies.[14] While domestic factors are important in understanding national cybersecurity, a number of other influences – such as the structure of the international system and the particular characteristics of cyberspace – pose similar security challenges to decision-makers across the world.

When we step back and look at more states in the international system, the act of formulating a national cybersecurity strategy becomes increasingly complex. Many states must take into consideration not only their domestic bureaucratic structures and cultures but also those of international or supranational governmental organizations of which they are either members or signatories. From this perspective, formulating a national cybersecurity strategy for member states of the EU is more complex than for a state such as the United States or South Korea. In February 2023, the European Union Agency for Cybersecurity (ENISA) released policy guidance in a formalized document entitled: "A Governance Framework for National Cybersecurity Strategies."[15] At present, ENISA analysis does not find full conformity across all EU member states. Moreover, a survey of national cybersecurity strategies represented in table 5.1 below illustrates the multiplication, and sometimes also the fragmentation, of strategies at the domestic level. Each of the years next to the state represents a new national strategy, often either fully overwriting previous strategies or augmenting the overall national strategy of a state.

EU member states must take into consideration issues pertaining to domestic capacity including governmental authorities, agencies, and governance regimes within their own country. They must also have clear chains of command and coherent frameworks to liaise with private sector partners. At the supranational level, the EU also seeks to harmonize governance and legal frameworks. States must also adhere to considerations pertaining to human rights both at the EU and broader European levels. The range of issues listed here and many others force states to think comprehensively about how they develop and implement cybersecurity strategies. Synchronization across member states is important and helps to foster consistency in laws, policies, regulations, practices, and procedures across member states.

If compliance with European guidance was not complicated enough, many of these same states must also adhere to NATO's strategic concept.

Table 5.1 National cybersecurity strategies of European Union member states

Country	Adoption year of strategy
Austria	2012, 2013, 2013, 2021
Belgium	2016, 2019, 2021
Bulgaria	2011, 2016, 2016, 2017, 2018, 2018, 2019, 2020
Croatia	2007, 2014, 2015, 2017
Cyprus	2012, 2020
Czechia	2011, 2014, 2015, 2015, 2017, 2018, 2020, 2021, 2021
Denmark	2018, 2018, 2018, 2019, 2019
Estonia	2017, 2017, 2018, 2018, 2018, 2019, 2021
Finland	2012, 2013, 2017, 2020, 2020, 2021
France	2013, 2015, 2017, 2017, 2018, 2019, 2019
Germany	2009, 2014, 2015, 2016, 2016, 2021, 2021
Greece	2018, 2018
Hungary	2012, 2013, 2013, 2014
Ireland	2015, 2018, 2019, 2019
Italy	2013, 2013, 2015, 2017, 2017, 2017, 2018, 2019, 2020, 2021, 2021, 2022, 2022
Latvia	2013, 2013, 2015, 2016, 2019
Lithuania	2014, 2016, 2017, 2017, 2018
Luxembourg	2014, 2018, 2018, 2018, 2021
Malta	2016, 2021
Netherlands	2017, 2018, 2018, 2018, 2018, 2019, 2019
Poland	2014, 2015, 2017, 2018, 2019
Portugal	2013, 2013, 2013, 2018, 2019
Romania	2013, 2015, 2018, 2021
Slovakia	2015, 2015, 2016, 2021
Slovenia	2016, 2018, 2019, 2020, 2020
Spain	2017, 2019
Sweden	2015, 2015, 2017

Source: CCDCOE 2023; authors

This document defines the challenges faced by the North Atlantic alliance and its member states and outlines the principal military and political tasks necessary for the alliance to address these challenges. NATO, through its CCDCOE, formerly used to publish a guide on developing a national cyber strategy for member states. Since 2016, the CCDCOE has been working with the ITU to enhance the latter's national cybersecurity strategy framework. The ITU publishes guidance on the formulation and publication of national cybersecurity strategies. This guide, however, does not impose any specific requirements on states and instead serves as a framework upon which national cybersecurity strategies might be based.

The creation of a strategy document for national cybersecurity is complex. It requires coordinating with a multitude of actors, often across domestic and international levels. A great deal of time and effort is put forth in articulating national strategies. Yet, at the end of the day, each of these strategies is generally considered to be temporary, a work in progress that must periodically adapt to changes in the strategic environment.

Cyber diplomacy

Closely related to the creation of national cyber strategies are the diplomatic efforts that states undertake to shape and shift norms and behaviors of allies and adversaries in cyberspace. Most of these efforts fall within the Internet governance frameworks discussed in chapter 3. Many of the technical debates pertaining to cyberspace are solved through both multistakeholder and multilateral fora, including ICANN, IETF, IAB, ITU, W3C and other similar organizations. States often send both diplomatic and private-sector representatives who push for their particular domestic and international interests. These fora have seen heated debates over the years that contend with everything from Internet resource allocation, peering agreements, data transit rights, patent and copyright enforcement, to freedom of information, including free speech and security issues.

At times, security issues arising in cyberspace extend beyond established Internet governance organizations and frameworks. Cybercrime, examined in chapter 8, is one such area. In areas that fall outside of established diplomatic lines of effort, states often undertake bilateral or multilateral efforts, frequently in tandem with advice and support for NGOs and intergovernmental organizations. One such example is the Budapest Convention on Cybercrime of the Council of Europe which brought together 68 parties, 23 aspirant signatories and multiple observers to the convention. The convention, which was initially signed in 2001, outlines a framework for states to cooperate on issues pertaining to cybercrime. Much of the agreement focuses on defining what cybercrime is, and how states should address it both domestically and when crimes occur transnationally. It might be surprising that much of the convention focuses on definitions, but the goal is to establish a mutually agreed starting point from which nations can work together to address common challenges. In addition, the convention establishes procedures for states to work together to investigate and prosecute perpetrators of cybercrime.

The Budapest Convention is widely considered to be a success in cyber diplomacy. Yet many states have not signed it, disapproving of the issues it addresses and the way in which it addresses them. Furthermore, the convention does not address a range of issues pertaining to warfare, intelligence and common understandings of sovereignty. Many of these issues have been addressed, albeit with limited success, via the UN GGE process. Since 2004 there have been six meetings of the GGE. These meetings brought together different groupings of nations to develop shared norms for cyber conduct within the broader context of international security. The idea behind the GGE process is to initiate dialogue on issues of importance between states and to have them move toward consensus on subsets of broader issues pertaining to security. Of the six meetings, four (2010, 2013, 2015 and 2021) have produced consensus reports submitted to the UN General Assembly. The 2004 and 2016–17 rounds did not achieve consensus and thus no report could be issued to the General Assembly.

Let us zoom in on cyber diplomats at the national level. In the United States, the Bureau of Cyberspace and Digital Policy within the Department of State is typically charged with participating in and negotiating the US position within the GGE. The Bureau relies on professional diplomats well versed in international security issues pertaining to cyberspace. The United States also seeks to develop multilateral understandings of norms in cyberspace outside of conventional international governmental organizations. As recently as 2022, the United States convened states to focus on the future of the Internet. The result was a "Declaration for the Future of the Internet" signed by over 40 states. This declaration outlined shared goals including: the protection of human rights and the fundamental freedoms of all people; the promotion of the free flow of information; the advancement of inclusive and affordable access to benefit all economically; the enhancement of transit and privacy; and adherence to multistakeholder models of Internet governance.[16]

Frequently, diplomatic efforts in cyberspace are incorporated into the texts of national cybersecurity strategies through phrases such as "working or coordinating with partners and allies." At other times, cyber diplomacy can take place through more informal processes outside the direct oversight of states. One such example that has a profound impact, not only on cyber diplomacy but on shaping national cyber-security strategies, has been the *Tallinn Manual* process run out of NATO's CCDCOE and edited by Professor Michael Schmitt. *The Tallinn Manual 1.0* (2009–13) and *The Tallinn Manual 2.0* (2013–17) brought together international legal scholars to examine the applicability of international law to cyber warfare and cyber operations, respectively. Although these two volumes are non-binding and do not constitute formal diplomatic processes, the resulting manuals have helped to inform international debates and diplomatic efforts pertaining to cyber-security. The CCDCOE is currently coordinating the process for a *Tallin Manual 3.0*.

The above discussions have focused on the formation of national cybersecurity strategies within the constraints of domestic and international political environments. A discussion of the rise and importance of diplomatic efforts further nuances the understanding and positioning of national cybersecurity strategies within the international system. Yet, in practice, what do state cyber strategies actually look like and what are the objectives, ways and means they propose? The following sections emphasize the national approaches to cyber power and security favored by the three powerful nations in cyberspace: China, Russia and the United States. These sections emphasize a number of differences, but also some commonalities in the way these major powers guide and organize their actions in and through cyberspace.

China: controlling information

The development of the modern Chinese state and its emergence as a great power in cyberspace was not preordained. In the 1990s, China, while rapidly developing, lacked sufficient human and technical capacity in information communications technologies. This lack of endogenous capacity was confronted head on in a 1998 book written by two Chinese PLA colonels, entitled *Unrestricted Warfare*.[17] In their book, Colonels Liang Qiao and Wang Xiansui proposed a new way of challenging potential adversaries without engaging in direct confrontation. To achieve this strategy, and exploit the rapidly evolving technological landscape, China began implementing an ambitious program of technological development. In 2000, then-General Secretary of the Communist Party Jiang Zemin gave a series of seminal speeches in which he established the trajectory of China's information society and outlined a strategy to transform China into an advanced cyber power.[18]

These intentions were formally outlined in a 14-year plan that emphasized the priorities of a resurgent China in cyberspace. In tandem with developing the educational facilities and pushing for students to enter into information technology careers, the plan established the necessity of developing both internal controls on information and the capacity to exploit the information vulnerabilities of other states. More than 20 years later, China is technologically advanced and often dominates the quest for high-performance computing and AI. The nation currently benefits from a booming economy, and hosts close to a quarter of the global Internet population. Consequently, the Internet is an important enabler – and also a possible source of vulnerabilities – in the emergence of China as a great power.[19]

The authoritarian nature of the Chinese regime shapes its conception of cybersecurity and use of cyber power. At the domestic level, China has sought to control the flow of external information into the national sphere, to exert sovereignty over its society. For the Chinese government, Internet threats are not only technical but also informational. While various democratic nations, such as the United States and Sweden, monitor Internet traffic in and out of their country, China filters out unwanted content.[20] To control information, Chinese authorities have developed a "golden shield," colloquially known as the Great Firewall of China. The Ministry of Public Security defines the boundaries of this wall, providing censorship guidelines that must be followed by ISPs and citizens alike. The Chinese Internet police relies on a combination of legislation, technologies and human workforce to enforce censorship and shut down websites, delete or redirect information and arrest dissident bloggers.[21]

This effort to censor the Internet aims to limit the influence of Western media and other news sources, which are seen as subversive tools that threaten the stability of the regime.[22] Chinese "netizens" do not have access to a number of foreign websites and applications, such as Facebook and Google Maps. Service providers are also forced to block access to websites presenting information on "subversive" movements and ideologies, such as the teachings of the Dalai Lama. In principle, Chinese censorship aims to limit separatism, terrorism and extremism. Chinese authorities have implemented substantial digital controls and practice significant surveillance on ethnic minority populations, including Uighur Muslims. In practice, critics point out that information control also limits freedom of expression. In a detailed study of Chinese social media, Gary King and his colleagues found that Chinese censorship does not seek to systematically suppress government criticism on social media but attempts to "reduce the probability of collective action," such as protests.[23]

The Chinese government's ability to control Internet traffic on its territory provides a useful tool against external attacks. The government could shut off domestic access to the Internet in an effort to prevent major cyberattacks. However, experts have questioned the impermeability of the Great Firewall, noting that some activists have managed to bypass it.[24] Researchers have questioned the extent to which China is well equipped to confront technical and economic threats at home. The widespread use of pirate software in China creates vulnerabilities as their users do not automatically get access to security upgrades and patches.[25] Further concerns exist about the extent to which cyberspace has facilitated the development of a black-market economy, over which the government has limited control.[26]

At the international level, China is both a source and a target of cyber insecurity. Historically, the Chinese government believed that it could not match the United States in conventional assets and therefore sought to develop asymmetric means to wield informational power. This asymmetric approach sought to turn the technical superiority of adversaries into a liability.

China has tended to focus its efforts on cyber espionage and the theft of intellectual property in order to develop an informational advantage across the fields of economics, military affairs, politics and technology, and to weaken the operational efficiency of its adversaries.[27] Recent years have seen these efforts come to fruition with the development of advanced weapon systems including fifth-generation jet fighters and advanced anti-ship missile technologies.[28] This focus on information gathering is consistent with the Chinese strategy of pre-emption and "informationized war." The Chinese military wants to anticipate threats and act early to gain the initiative. This pre-emptive approach requires preparation and mobilization in peacetime, including the recruitment of a wide pool of talented personnel, as well as the continuous testing of adversaries' networks to uncover their strengths and vulnerabilities and signal intrusion capabilities. The information gathered through reconnaissance and espionage efforts can then be utilized to deceive or entice an opponent and adopt an appropriate strategy that will lead to the greatest gains.[29]

China is often decried in the West for its confrontational cyber posture and efforts to penetrate Western computer systems for military and economic gain. In the last two decades, a number of major cyber operations originating from China – from Titan Rain to APT1

– stole sensitive information from Western governments and industries. However, the extent to which Chinese-led APTs have translated into economic and military gains is unclear.

While these operations reflect an active stance, they might not be as aggressive as is commonly perceived. Some analysts argue that they reveal China's concerns about adversaries' efforts to penetrate its own government and private-sector systems.[30] Chinese authors writing about cyber warfare emphasize the role of the United States in driving cyber insecurity, and the need for China to develop cyber capabilities to maintain its sovereignty and protect itself from US destabilization.[31] For Valeriano, Jensen and Maness, Chinese cyber behavior reflects a desire to achieve balance with the United States and maintain power in Asia.[32] These concerns would explain why Beijing engages in cyber espionage and information manipulation rather than cyber degradation.

National cybersecurity in China is spread across multiple organizations. Jon Lindsay emphasizes the complex networks of overlapping committees and groups making decisions under the banner of the Chinese one-party government.[33] This institutional fragmentation has limited Chinese abilities to foster strong cybersecurity across the public–private divide, and weakened critical infrastructure protection. The PLA has invested significantly in its cyber warfare capabilities, both offensive and defensive. The responsibility for cyber operations in the Chinese military is generally attributed to the PLA General Staff's 3rd Department, which holds responsibilities for signals intelligence (SIGINT) and seems to play a primarily defensive role. The Chinese General Staff Department 418th Research Institute and its Unit 61539 are generally considered to be the Chinese Cyber Command. A number of other cyber units are co-located with civilian entities, specifically universities and schools.[34] Following a military reform launched in 2016, many of these units have been reorganized under a Strategic Support Force.

Chinese cyber operations also rely on entities and individuals that are not officially acting on behalf of the government and not directly tied to the PLA, allowing the government to formally deny any involvement and responsibility. Following Mao Zedong's notion of mobilizing popular support to wage a protracted struggle, Beijing has fostered the development of cyber militias and "patriotic hackers" organized in networks around the PLA and contributing to the development of Chinese cyber power.[35] According to some recent research, these militias bring together from 8 to 10 million individuals and primarily serve a defensive role.[36] The extent to which the PLA will effectively leverage and merge these disparate cyber capabilities remains to be seen.

Russia's holistic approach

Russia maintains a holistic approach to cybersecurity that considers strategic interactions across all the elements of power.[37] This approach is well suited to the all-encompassing nature of computer networks in modern societies. At the domestic level, Russian authorities have sought to control the flow of information and data in cyberspace to maintain national sovereignty. Following Tsarist and communist precedents, the government maintains a strong degree of state control on information to protect its regime and keep the loyalty of its people in check. Prior to the collapse of the Soviet Union, the KGB installed a System for Operative Investigative Activities (SORM) at network junction points around the country. This system of devices has since evolved and now provides the FSB, Russia's Federal Security Service, with unprecedented surveillance capabilities on Russian networks.[38] Russia has not built a Great Firewall, but the government supervises the media to make sure they promote patriotic values and traditions.[39]

Russian officials are particularly concerned with the influence of the Western information society and way of life. To limit Western influence and maintain its sovereignty, Russia has expressed a desire to develop an independent Internet and create its own domain name system that would limit external influences.[40] Russian law requires ISPs to host data belonging to Russian persons and entities on the Russian territory (to limit surveillance from other countries).[41] Beyond these technical measures, the Russian government has supported the development of a Russian ecosystem of Internet services, including the Russian social networking service Vkontakte and the Russian search engine Yandex. The executive branch of government leverages this Russian segment of the Internet (also known as RUNET) as an instrument of power, both at home and abroad, to pursue Russian sovereignty.[42] RUNET provides Moscow with a tool to support a distinct digital subculture and influence former Soviet states such as Georgia and Ukraine.

Since its invasion of Ukraine on February 24, 2022, the Russian Federation has substantially tightened control over its domestic Internet.[43] It has effectively banned Russian people's access to a range of Western media platforms such as Facebook and Instagram.[44] Russian authorities intensely surveil domestic platforms and Internet spaces and frequently charge individuals with crimes against the state for sharing non-state-sanctioned information in online or public spaces.[45] Russia has also rerouted Internet traffic away from the global Internet in areas that it occupies in Ukraine.[46]

At the international level, Russia leverages cyberspace as an asymmetric means to engage with an adversary (the West) that is stronger in other elements (economy, military). Here, Russian use of cyber operations to project power and sow chaos contrasts with the more defensive outlook of Chinese cyber strategy. In Russia, cyber operations are construed as a form of information warfare that seeks to disrupt enemy civil–military facilities and systems, leadership, troops and populations.[47] Russian doctrine attributes great importance to the role of public perception and seeks to exploit psychological and cognitive factors as a part of a broader informational struggle. The aim is to manipulate the adversary's picture of reality, interfere with its decision-making process and influence its society to produce favorable conditions. The Russians use "reflexive control" to convey "to a partner or an opponent specially prepared information to incline him to voluntarily make the predetermined decision desired by the initiator of the action."[48]

In this context, cyber operations might seek to affect enemy information gathering and analysis, and manipulate the information disseminated in mass media and online. Such operations can be used to disorganize the structure of a society, distort public consciousness and affect elites and citizens alike. For example, Russian military movements in Eastern Ukraine were accompanied by DDoS attacks disrupting computer systems in Kyiv. Sowing such confusion can help to buy time in the initial stages of a conflict and thicken the fog of war.[49] Since 2016, Russian efforts to interfere in democratic elections across Western countries have become increasingly apparent. Russia has used cyber operations to gather protected information, alter some of its content and leak selected documents online to influence electorates. Russian trolls have used social media to foment societal tensions in the West, instill chaos and reinforce its position on the international scene. These actions have sent strong signals that Russia is a capable and dangerous cyber actor, but their overall utility as an instrument of power remains debatable.[50] Storybox 5.1 discusses Russian interference in the presidential elections in the United States (2016) and France (2017) to exemplify the Russian use and limits of cyber operations as an informational instrument of power.

Storybox 5.1 Russian interferences: hit and miss

According to a declassified US intelligence community report, President Vladimir Putin ordered an influence campaign targeting the 2016 US presidential election.[51] This campaign sought to undermine public faith in the US democratic process and harm the electability of Secretary Clinton (initially a candidate for the Democratic Party presidential primaries). The Russian campaign relied on a messaging strategy that blended covert intelligence operations, mostly through cyber activity, with overt efforts by the Russian government, state-funded media and social media users to delegitimize Clinton's candidacy. Russian military intelligence (the GRU) used online persona Guccifer 2.0 and the website DCLeaks.com to release data obtained through cyber operations to selected media outlets.

The crux of the operations relied on the GRU's ability to penetrate Democratic National Committee (DNC) networks from summer 2015 to 2016. Russian hackers compromised the personal email accounts of Democratic Party officials and stole large volumes of data. The US intelligence community assesses that the Russian services consider their cyber-enabled disclosure operation to be a "qualified success" because of its impact on public discussion in the United States.[52] Experts expect Russia to continue its propaganda and disinformation campaign to further exacerbate social and political fissures in the United States, and beyond.[53] This operation also served domestic purposes, drawing the Russian public's attention to flawed aspects of democratic institutions.[54]

∗ ∗ ∗

In contrast to the success of its interferences in the 2016 US election, Russian efforts to influence the French presidential election of 2017 failed to divide French society and affect outcomes. One key aspect of the Russian campaign in France was the leaking of information that had been captured from then-candidate Emmanuel Macron's presidential campaign. The Macron leaks were a combination of real emails and forgeries released a few hours before the final vote on the second tour of this election.

Research on the failure of this operation to influence the French elections highlights a combination of structural factors and anticipatory measures. At the structural level, the two-round system of the French presidential elections makes it more difficult to identify potential candidates well ahead of the elections. The second round also provides an opportunity for the population to shift their support to a mainstream candidate. In this case, the mainstream candidate Emmanuel Macron faced a candidate for the extreme right party Rassemblement National. The quality of the French media environment, specifically the marginal role of tabloids and alternative websites, further limited the impact of the Macron leaks. In addition, the establishment of an independent administrative authority in charge of the integrity of the elections encouraged traditional media not to exploit the Macron leaks.[55]

The French government and presidential candidates had the opportunity to learn from Russian influence operations in the United States, as well as similar efforts in the Netherlands and the United Kingdom. The French national cybersecurity agency (ANSSI) organized workshops to train political parties, and warned Macron about a potential attack. The Macron campaign team compartmentalized information and communicated only face to face on the most sensitive issues. They talked publicly about hacking attempts against them and even forged emails and fake documents to confuse the hackers with irrelevant information. These measures undermined the validity of the leaked documents and made the population doubt the authenticity of the material.[56]

Responsibility for Russian national cybersecurity falls on the FSB and its SIGINT unit, the Ministry of Internal Affairs (MVD) and the SVR. The FSB and MVD are responsible for monitoring online information on extremist groups, for example. When doing so, they rely on national service providers and the companies at the basis of RUNET. Russian national cybersecurity relies on the synergy between the Russian security services and its business sector, both of which cooperate to purge RUNET of unwanted content.[57]

The Russian government has developed an ambivalent relationship with cyber criminals. The government tolerates, and sometimes encourages, hackers when they target adversaries. Reliance on hackers allowed Russia to maintain some distance from the well-coordinated cyberattacks that targeted Estonia in 2007 and Georgia in 2008, and to deny any responsibility. This reliance on hackers can be linked to the close ties between the Russian government and broader criminal networks.[58] Western analysts argue that the Russian government deliberately lets hacktivists and cyber criminals operate from its territory to "erode the boundaries of organized violence" and wage influence without resorting to open conflict.[59] The extent to which criminal organizations such as the RBN are driven and coordinated by government entities is not clear, but they certainly seem to enjoy a degree of immunity.[60] Scholar Nikolas Gvodsev concludes that Russia's hackers might have struck a bargain with the government whereby they will be left alone – perhaps even politically protected – as long as they do not target the state and its key interests. This Russian strategy is not without risks, as criminals could, one day, turn against their political protectors.[61]

The United States: a pro-active cyber power

The United States is one of the most connected nations in the world – its economy, civilian infrastructure and government services are all highly dependent on cyberspace. Unlike China and Russia, the United States actively defends and promotes freedoms – specifically, freedom of speech – in cyberspace. The technological dependency and openness of the United States have created significant vulnerabilities that its adversaries have sought to exploit. The number of significant cyberattacks on the United States has required the government to adopt a very active stance on national cybersecurity and spawned the creation of a number of organizations and policies designed to enhance national cyber defense and resilience.

The US government has published dozens of strategic documents reflecting the growing importance of cyber power and national cybersecurity. Cyberspace emerged as a distinct national security policy area during the presidency of Bill Clinton when the White House established a structure to coordinate efforts across the public–private divide to "eliminate any significant vulnerability to both physical and cyber attacks on our critical infrastructure."[62] Since then, a variety of defense, military and national security strategies have identified cyber threats to critical infrastructure and services as a pressing national security threat.[63] The US approach emphasizes the importance of international alliances, specifically NATO, in deterring shared threats and promoting stability in and through cyberspace.[64] The transatlantic alliance has been one of the main pillars supporting the development of strong and resilient cyber defense and cooperative cybersecurity in the West. The US government has embraced cyberspace as an instrument of soft and hard power. The 2011 International Strategy for Cyberspace proposed the promotion of US values throughout cyberspace, including fundamental freedoms, privacy and respect for property. To achieve these objectives, the strategy sought to leverage defense, diplomacy and development. China and Russia consider US support for an open cyber environment, and specifically the spread of US-backed social media and Internet technologies such as Tor, as an effort to interfere in their domestic affairs. Some US cyber operations have more directly interfered in other countries' affairs. In a famous case of cyberattack discussed in the next chapter, the United States successfully deployed a computer worm to sabotage Iranian nuclear centrifuges.

In a government that traditionally divides responsibilities between multiple departments and across society, coordinating national cyber-security policy and implementation presents a significant challenge. Critics note that the division of labor that characterizes American society limits the US ability to anticipate and respond to problems in a timely and coherent way.[65] To counter cyber threats, the US government has developed a number of platforms, such as Information Sharing and Analysis Organizations (ISAOs) and Information Sharing and Analysis Centers (ISACs) to promote common security standards, share information and coordinate threat assessments and responses across the public–private divide. However, these efforts remain limited by issues of privacy and trust between government and private-sector organizations.[66] Nearly six years after the first edition of this book, experts continue to question the extent to which the private sector is willing and ready to communicate with government entities about vulnerabilities. Equally, some government agencies remain reluctant to systematically share sensitive information with outsiders.[67] Problems of public–private coordination are less apparent in China and Russia where the public authority of government is more sweeping and evident.

Responsibility for cybersecurity and related incidents is broadly divided into domestic and foreign responsibilities. The US Department of Homeland Security (DHS) is responsible for protecting critical infrastructure at home, from both physical and cyber threats. In 2018 it created a dedicated organization called CISA, which had a sweeping $2.9 billion budget for 2023 and works on a range of domestic national cybersecurity initiatives. CISA houses the National Cybersecurity and Communications Integration Center (NCCIC) which runs its operations, the US CERT, its Industrial Control Systems Cyber Emergency Response Team and the National Coordinating Center for Communications. The domestic role of DHS in cyberspace has grown substantially, particularly since the establishment of CISA. By contrast, the Department of Justice, acting through the FBI, is the lead federal agency for threat response and law enforcement activities.[68] Both departments are expected to effectively coordinate their activities within their respective lines of effort, but the extent to which they do so in practice is not clear. Since 2009, the US has established a Cyber Command (USCYBERCOM), which brings together all components of the US military that work on cyber threats. USCYBERCOM was elevated to an independent unified command in 2018 under the direction of General Paul Nakasone, putting it on par with other warfighting commands and confirming the growing importance of digital combat. In May of 2018, USCYBERCOM reached full operational capability when the last of its 133 national mission teams became certified.

The latest Cyber Command "vision" points out that America faces competitors who are deliberately operating at a level below armed aggression. This strategy has become known as the Defend Forward – Persistent Engagement strategy and was developed by a team of scholars in residence at the US Cyber Command as a counter to the perceived failures of deterrence in and through cyberspace.[69] The document highlights a desire to target adversaries' weaknesses, imposing costs on them so that they are forced to shift their resources to defense. Until August 2018, classified US Presidential Policy Directive imposed severe limitations on when, how and by whom offensive cyber operations could be authorized. In the summer of 2018, then-President Trump reportedly revised the standing direction and loosened the requirement that all offensive cyber operations required presidential approval.

In their analysis of US cyber strategy, Valeriano, Jensen and Maness present the United States as a "sophisticated" cyber power.[70] They argue that the notion of the precision strike has shaped the conduct of US cyber operations. Cyber capabilities are used to "infiltrate command networks, often through counterintelligence honeypots, and paralyze them at an opportune moment."[71] This approach utilizes cyber capabilities to gain information superiority, identify specific targets and develop a sophisticated method to strike precisely and in a timely manner.

To stop or limit attacks by adversaries, the United States has sought to adopt a whole-of-government approach and liaise with partners across government, industry and academia.[72] US strategy recognizes the need for better alignment with the private sector, including ISPs and security companies. Other Western governments have faced similar coordination challenges and developed similar approaches. American allies such as South Korea and France have also established a Cyber Command (respectively in 2009 and 2016). The United Kingdom established a National Cyber Security Centre in 2016.[73] Governments increasingly coordinate their cybersecurity efforts through both bilateral and multilateral cooperation agreements.[74] As of November 2023, more than 84 countries had national cybersecurity strategy documents, each addressing the nuances and challenges, as well as interpretations, of the operating environment in and through cyberspace. A number of international organizations, including the African Union, the Association of Southeast Asian Nations, the EU and the UN, have set up working groups and developed strategies to coordinate national efforts to improve cybersecurity.[75]

More recently, the United States has developed cyber-adjacent strategies that have global strategic implications. Under President Biden, the United States has sought to use its economic might to severely alter the global market for semiconductors. In October 2022, the US Department of Commerce released a series of new export controls on advanced computing and semiconductor manufacturing items.[76] Several months later, the Biden administration further strengthened these rules to prevent advanced microchip manufacturers from selling microchips or using funds from the US government in ways that might benefit China.[77] The administration paired these rules with legislation passed in August 2022 to promote the domestic manufacture and research of semiconductors (also known as the CHIPS Act).[78] Finally, the US issued a National Artificial Intelligence Research and Development Strategic Plan to guide the country toward the future of cutting-edge technology.[79] While the US has long dominated the development and production of advanced computer chips, authorities are increasingly concerned about losing this edge. In a widely acclaimed book, economic historian Chris Miller dubs the "fight" to control this critical technology a "chip war."[80]

The US is undertaking these actions at a time when advances in AI are making headlines daily around the world. From LLMs such as ChaptGPT, to self-driving vehicles, automated weapon systems, and advances in health technology, the Biden administration is attempting to constrain the technological advances of one of its principal adversaries. It can do this because, although most of the manufacturers of advanced semiconductor equipment and fabrication centers are not in the United States, the technologies that they use contain many components that are US-based and these firms are heavily reliant on US markets and systems. The current US strategy seeks to balance carrots and sticks. The rules limiting the global sale of semiconductors to China entail heavy penalties, while the CHIPS Act offers strong incentives for foreign firms to onshore the manufacturing of semiconductors to the US. As semiconductor manufacturing has advanced, the global market has been left with few firms capable of producing increasingly complex chips. For example, Dutch company ASML has been caught by the economic might of the US government and forcibly incentivized not to engage in sales of advanced semiconductor manufacturing equipment to China.[81]

As we can see, the US strategies associated with cybersecurity are inclusive of nearly all aspects of national power identified above and seek to positively position the US and its allies in an increasingly contentious space in the years to come.

Common lenses and challenges

The dynamics of national cybersecurity can be understood through the canon of international relations. In the realist tradition, cyberspace is an extension of the Hobbesian worldview in which states pursue their national interests by maximizing power. Chris Demchak and Peter Dombrowski argue that cyberspace, a man-made domain, cannot escape the "Westphalian world of virtual borders and national cyber commands."[82] In the digital realm, states strive to ensure their citizens' online safety, and the economic well-being of their nation. They also exert their power in cyberspace and push to assert national policies both at home and abroad. From this perspective, nation states are exerting their monopoly over the legitimate means of control of cyberspace. State control is apparent when governments require ISPs to share data with them and to filter out traffic. At the international level, Chinese APTs, the US cyber operation against Iranian centrifuges, and the Russian efforts to interfere with democratic elections in Western countries, all suggest that states are wielding power in cyberspace. As such, classic IR debates about coercion, deterrence, escalation and alliance are increasingly central to the discussions surrounding cybersecurity in social science.

Following a liberal internationalist tradition, some scholars have started to explore the emergence of international norms of behavior in cyberspace.[83] Nation states are growing increasingly interdependent and have much to lose from overt conflict in cyberspace. Evidence suggests that state-on-state cyberattacks and governments' efforts to control their domestic cyberspace have been tempered by the interdependencies of an increasingly globalized world.[84] Consequently, most governments want some degree of international cooperation. However, divergences over the governance of cyberspace highlighted in chapter 3 show that different models – some more supranational than others – continue to coexist. These national differences can be explained by domestic factors such as regime type, and political and strategic culture.

Despite differences in national approaches to cybersecurity, most cyber powers confront common challenges in cyberspace. China, Russia and the United States all struggle to control and manage the various actors involved in cyberspace. These common challenges explain why nations that wield cyber power against each other cooperate on specific cybersecurity issues, such as the theft of banking information.[85] The rapid evolution of connected information technologies – from malicious codes to new applications to the IoT – and AI challenges governments' desire to control cyberspace domestically, and provides opportunities to wield power on a global stage. National cybersecurity is inherently transnational, and therefore requires the interaction of a plethora of different actors, only some of which have the resources and authority to coordinate effective responses.

Discussion questions

1. What are the pros and cons of considering (some) cyber capabilities as a type of weapon?

2. Contrast and compare the American, Chinese and Russian approaches to national cybersecurity.

3. How is the tension between centralization and decentralization visible in the organization of cybersecurity strategy?

Exercise

Pick a recent document in the CCDCOE's list of national security and defense strategies (https://ccdcoe.org/library/strategy-and -governance). Does the strategy identify how it will leverage the four elements of power (diplomacy, information, military, economy)? Does it focus on only some of these elements or identify an even broader range of instruments?

Additional resources

Center for Strategic and International Studies, Cybersecurity and Cyberwarfare, Preliminary Assessment of National Doctrine and Organization, 2011, www.unidir.org/files/publications/pdfs/cybersecurity-and-cyberwarfare-preliminary-assessment-of-national-doctrine-and-organization-380.pdf.

Franklin D. Kramer, Stuart H. Starr and Larry K. Wentz (eds.), *Cyberpower and National Security* (Washington, DC: National Defense University, 2009).

NATO Cooperative Cyber Defence Centre of Excellence, "Cyber Security Strategy Documents," October 18, 2018, https://ccdcoe.org/cybersecurity-strategy-documents.html.

Brandon Valeriano, Benjamin Jensen and Ryan C. Maness, *Cyber Strategy: The Evolving Character of Power and Coercion* (Oxford University Press, 2018).

6   From cyber war to cyber conflict

Reader's guide

- Scholarly characterization of conflict in cyberspace has moved away from early debates on cyber war, to focus on cyber conflict and competition. Using these terms carefully is important to draw valid diagnostics and helpful policy prescriptions.

- Cyberspace plays an increasingly prominent role in enabling and supporting military tactics, operations and strategy.

- The effects of cyberattacks on international security remain relatively limited when compared to more kinetic capabilities. Bits and bytes cannot conquer territories.

- States use cyber operations to compete with each other below the threshold of armed conflict.

Early IR scholarship on cybersecurity has been characterized by arguments about the forms, uses and effects of cyber warfare. Human history has seen the boundaries of the battlefield expand through technological transformations that continually redefine what it means to go to war, from land to sea, from air to outer space, and now to cyberspace. Since the early 1990s, security experts and media pundits have prophesied the dangers of cyber war, yet in the last decade a growing number of researchers have expressed skepticism. While the academic debate between the prophets and skeptics has remained contentious, militaries around the world have expanded their operations in and through cyberspace. People may not be directly killed by bits and bytes, but they can be harmed by those instruments of modern society that rely on cyberspace and its associated technologies. Understanding how states might leverage potential effects in and through cyberspace in times of war and conflict, and how cyber operations change the character of war, is important to policy-makers, military planners and students of cybersecurity.

War in the fifth domain

The long history of war and its near-continuous impact on human lives across the millennia have characterized the history of international relations, as scholars attempt to address ever important questions on the causes of war and peace. From this perspective, it seems logical that, when confronted with a "new" domain, researchers should attempt to understand the occurrence of a new form of conflict and the conditions for peace. But what is cyber war? How different is it from war in other domains? Defining cyber war is crucial if we are to understand it, not least because of the economic, political and societal implications of waging war.

The spectrum of conflict in cyberspace encompasses everything from bullying and criminal activity to espionage and sabotage. At the violent end of the scale, cyberattacks can threaten critical infrastructure, economies, property and the well-being of citizens. There is no question that significant cyberattacks and incidents threaten national security, but this does not necessarily mean that they qualify as an act of war. Law scholar Michael Schmitt has argued that, thus far, cyberattacks have not been sufficiently organized, intense or destructive to constitute acts of war.[1] The US government holds that a cyberattack would have to "proximately result in death, injury or significant destruction" to qualify as an act of war.[2] However, the (proximate) effects of cyberattacks are not always clear. In practice, the current threshold set by international law is open to interpretation and is likely to evolve.

Since the beginning of the twenty-first century, thousands of NATO soldiers have fought in Afghanistan, Iraq and Syria without their countries being in a formal state of war. Many countries use force through military means without formally declaring war. Cyber war is no different.[3] A number of government officials and pundits have claimed that the United States is fighting a cyber war. However, legally speaking, this is not the case. Researchers have criticized the hysteria that surrounds the discourse on cyber war, with some even suggesting it to be impossible in practice.[4]

War is a political process through which groups of individuals threaten harm to influence an adversary. War – and, by extension, cyber war – will always be an instrument of politics. Although the political nature of war is constant, the conduct of war or warfare – typically through military operations – has evolved over time.[5] In the traditional understanding, two or more countries would go to war and their soldiers would confront each other on a battlefield using swords, bows, guns, gas, bombs, etc. With the advent of cyberspace, the belligerents and the type of engagements characterizing war now permeate across the three layers of cyberspace. Cyberspace has expanded the character and characteristics of war without affecting its inherently political and physical nature.

Cyber war is coming!

Most of the debate on cyber war is about its characteristics, and the extent to which cyberspace is transforming the conduct of war – or, more specifically, whether cyberspace is prompting fundamental changes in warfare. The notions of violence and force, which are often used to define war and warfare, are less apparent in cyberspace than in the physical world.[6] Thus, scholars have debated the form and effects of cyber war.

In the early 1990s, security researchers started considering the implications of the information technology revolution on the conduct of war. Experts debated the occurrence of a revolution in military affairs that would radically change the character of war.[7] In this context, two RAND Corporation scientists, John Arquilla and David Ronfeldt, published a scholarly article entitled "Cyberwar Is Coming!" in 1993. In their article, Arquilla and Ronfeldt argued that the information revolution was altering not just the character of conflict – that is to say, the specific ways in which a conflict is waged (e.g. parties involved, terrain, technologies, etc.) – but also the nature of conflict, spurring a need for new military structures, doctrines and strategies. They introduced two original concepts to think about these new conditions: netwar and cyber war. The concept of netwar emphasized "societal-level ideational conflicts waged in part through internetted modes of communication."[8] They defined cyber war as military operations seeking to disrupt or destroy information and communication systems. Cyber war, the researchers noted, "is about organizations as much as technology. It implies new man–machine interfaces that amplify man's capabilities."[9] Reflecting on the implications of cyber war, Arquilla and Ronfeldt identified a number of puzzles that would capture the attention of researchers two decades later. What would cyber war look like? What would be the roles of and the relationship between offense and defense in cyber war? Could cyber victory be attained without destruction?

Increasingly complex communications and information infrastructures captivated the attention of American strategists and policy-makers for the next decade and beyond. But the key concept that drove the debate on the evolving character(istics) of war continued to be that of a revolution in military affairs, and not cyber war. For the proponents of the revolution in military affairs, new technology was enabling information to flow more freely from the battlefield to the headquarters and vice versa, leading to more network-centric forms of warfare.[10] While the advent of cyberspace certainly led to new efficiencies at the organizational level and evolving military structures and practices, few authors today would make the case that these changes qualify as a revolution in military affairs.[11]

In the mid-2000s, a number of cyberattacks drew extensive media coverage and prompted some experts to ask whether cyber war was (finally) emerging as a threat. In April 2007, a series of cyberattacks targeted Estonia following growing tension with Russia over the relocation of a World War II statue of a Soviet soldier from the center to the outskirts of Tallinn. Waves of spam and automated online requests swamped Estonian servers, taking down dozens of websites and online services. The DoS attack affected government services, newspapers and broadcasters, as well as banking services, causing millions of dollars of losses.[12] Though Estonia could not technically prove beyond a doubt who was behind the attacks, the government, leveraging substantial circumstantial data, pointed to its neighbor Russia, and called on NATO for support. In an ensuing debate, international experts agreed that Russia was the most likely culprit, though direct responsibility could not be formally established. Were the attacks on Estonia an act of cyber war? For John Arquilla, these attacks qualify as a kind of "low-intensity war," in which the use of military force was applied selectively and with restraint to influence an enemy.[13] Yet most experts find it difficult to conceive of a war in the absence of casualties and physical damage to property. In another notable case that took place a few months later, Israeli forces are suspected of using a cyberattack (Operation Orchard) to temporarily deactivate the Syrian air defense network. This attack allowed the Israeli air force to conduct a successful airstrike on a suspected nuclear reactor in northern Syria.[14] For cybersecurity expert Gary McGraw, this attack is a case of cyber war "because the link to a kinetic effect is clear – a completely destroyed Syrian facility."[15] However, the Israeli airstrike caused this kinetic effect, and not the cyberattack.

The growing number of cyberattacks and intrusions worldwide, including against the United States, fueled the imagination of some American experts, keen to warn about the dangers of cyber war. In their book entitled *Cyber War*, Richard Clarke, a former special advisor on cybersecurity to the president, and Robert Knake, a former National

Security Council staffer, imagined a scenario in which devastating cyberattacks would induce power blackouts, collapse air traffic control systems, and cause train and subway derailments and refinery and gas explosions leading to several thousand deaths.[16] This vastly exaggerated scenario was reminiscent of the "electronic Pearl Harbor," which experts had warned against as early as 1991.[17] This expression was then popularized by Secretary of Defense Leon Panetta in a 2012 speech:

> The most destructive scenarios involve cyber actors launching several attacks on our critical infrastructure at one time, in combination with a physical attack on our country. Attackers could also seek to disable or degrade critical military systems and communication networks. The collective result of these kinds of attacks could be a cyber Pearl Harbor; an attack that would cause physical destruction and the loss of life. In fact, it would paralyze and shock the nation and create a new, profound sense of vulnerability.[18]

Media and CEOs of cybersecurity companies also used the expression "cyber Pearl Harbor" – and others like "cybergeddon" – to attract readers and clients.[19] Skeptical observers have repeatedly pointed out that these scenarios have not materialized. But the hysteria around cyber war remained, it shaped the early scholarly debate on the topic and continues to drive some reporting on cybersecurity incidents.

Will cyber war take place?

In a widely read article, political scientist Thomas Rid argues that "Cyber War Will Not Take Place."[20] Rid examines examples of cyberattacks to raise a number of definitional questions that framed the early debate on cyberspace and international security. He argues that all politically motivated cyberattacks are not war but sophisticated versions of sabotage, espionage and subversion. To support his argument, Rid carefully (some might say narrowly) defines cyber war. According to him, "any act of war has to have the potential to be lethal; it has to be instrumental; and it has to be political."[21] Following this definition, not a single cyber offense identified in the debate on cyber war would constitute an act of war on its own.

First, the lethality of cyberattacks is never direct; neither is it essential to the success of cyberattacks. It is conceivable that a cyberattack could cause a train to crash, or an electricity grid to stop working. Following these events, people could be killed or military units could be rendered defenseless. However, in practice, "no cyber offense has ever injured a person" and cyberattacks "need not be violent to be effective."[22] Second, Rid finds that most uses of cyber power are minimally – if at all – instrumental. The cyberspace component of an attack is rarely sufficient or central in forcing adversaries to change their behavior. Distributed Denial of Service (DDoS) attacks, for example, can limit a government's ability to communicate but won't force it to sue for peace. Third, Rid points out that political attribution of cyberattacks is rare. Though a cyberattack might be political, in the absence of attribution, the attack is depoliticized. Rid concludes that cyber war will not take place as long as cyberattacks continue to be characterized by the absence of violence, unclear goals and no political attribution.

Other types of activities seem to dominate the spectrum of conflict in cyberspace: crime, espionage, subversion and sabotage. None of these activities fulfills the three criteria Rid identifies. Cybercrime is apolitical, and criminals conceal their identity to protect themselves. Cyber espionage seeks to penetrate an adversary's system to extract sensitive information. Its purpose is not directly political – rather, it seeks to gather information to inform policies and politics. Cyber subversion is political because it seeks to erode social bonds and trust in collective entities. However, cyberspace is a platform to reach out to an audience, but not the target of subversion. Finally, cyber sabotage – the deliberate attempt to weaken or destroy an economic or military system – is instrumental. However, its nature is predominantly technical, and its targets are material things, not humans. Saboteurs can also avoid attribution and open violence.[23] Storybox 6.1 tells the story of the Stuxnet worm, a famous case of cyber sabotage – or cybotage – that dominated the early discussions on cyber war.

Storybox 6.1 Cybotage: from Stuxnet to Shamoon

In June 2010, computer security analysts working for Belarus company VirusBlokAda discovered a worm that intentionally targeted industrial equipment and software in a number of countries.[24] The malware used a previously unknown, or zero day, vulnerability to spread on computers via USB sticks. The malware, dubbed Stuxnet (a combination of the file names .stub and .MrxNext.sys) was designed to target a specific type of program used in industrial control systems that drive motors and switches. Further analysis revealed that the malicious code was highly sophisticated, using not one but four zero-day exploits as well as fraudulent certificates, and that Iran was the center of the infection. The malware had been specifically designed to covertly inject commands and sabotage industrial controllers used in the Natanz nuclear facility in Iran.[25]

Starting in 2008, Stuxnet generated small adjustments, manipulating the speed at which nuclear centrifuges in Natanz were spinning, to prompt them to break down. The attack reportedly took out nearly 1,000 of the 5,000 or so centrifuges Iran was using at the time to purify uranium. All the while, the computers controlling the centrifuges showed no sign of these physical changes and Iranian scientists thought they were confronting random breakdowns. Since the Iranian control system was air-gapped, nobody suspected a cyber-attack. But the worm was likely transported via a thumb drive onto the air-gapped network and eventually spread beyond after an Iranian engineer connected his computer to the centrifuges and back to the Internet. Stuxnet was eventually discovered after infecting thousands of machines throughout the world.

Reporters subsequently revealed that the attack was a joint operation between the US and Israeli intelligence services, codenamed "Olympic Games."[26] The two countries developed a new type of sabotage – some would even say a military-grade cyber weapon. Interestingly, Stuxnet had multiple built-in safeguards to prevent it from damaging non-targeted systems, which led many observers to comment that the malware looked as though it had been verified by lawyers before deployment.[27] In many ways it was the controls built into the code that led to its attribution to Israel and the United States. Although there were also some surprising features hidden in the code (so-called Easter eggs) that further supported this attribution.

Stuxnet was a tipping point in the debate on cyber conflict. This worm demonstrated that an offensive cyber operation could target and compromise a remote system to cause physical damage across international boundaries. Despite the damage Stuxnet inflicted on Iranian centrifuges, the Iranian nuclear program only experienced a temporary setback as a result of the covert operation.

In war and conflict, the adversary also has a say in how the fight is conducted. There is substantial evidence that the Stuxnet worm acted as a wake-up call for Iran to invigorate its own offensive cyber program. In an ironic twist, it appears that Iran created a new malware type that was remarkably similar to a malware included within the Olympic Games operation.[28] The malware, called Shamoon, penetrated Saudi Aramco computers and began to delete files on those systems using a "Wiper" module. Within hours, nearly 30,000 Windows-based machines were impacted by the malware.[29] The attack crippled Saudi Aramco's business. During the hack, the perpetrators also taunted Saudi Aramco employees and management by sharing proof that they still maintained access to the company's networks. It took the company two weeks to reconstitute their networks and recover from the attack. In the intervening time, the Saudi Arabian Oil Group bought most of the world's supply of hard drives (around 50,000 drives at one time) to replace those damaged in the attack.[30] This recovery effort alone seems to have impacted the global price of hard drives from September 2012 until January 2013.[31]

While there is a broad consensus on the need to distinguish between war, crime, sabotage, espionage and subversion, Rid's claim that cyber war will not take place, and his focus on lethality as a criterion for war, have been more controversial.[32] In a response to Rid, John Stone argues that cyberattacks can be understood as acts of war. He reminds us that Clausewitz defined war as "an act of physical force" and argues that Rid conflates force, violence and lethality. Force is the capacity to cause physical damage to humans but also to objects. Force should not be conflated with lethality, or the ability to kill somebody. For Stone, "all wars involve force, but force does not necessarily imply violence – particularly if violence implies lethality."[33] From this perspective, acts of war do not need to kill humans – they can generate a large amount of violence by targeting the manufacturing capabilities of an enemy, for instance. Stone concludes that cyberattacks, particularly cyber sabotage, could constitute an act of war. However, the debate on cyber war remains unsettled. If Rid set the threshold for cyber war too high, Stone might have set it too low. Brandon Valeriano and Ryan Maness have criticized Stone's position, pointing out that "without violence, injury, and death, the term [war] loses much of its meaning and implication."[34]

When considering what exactly cyber war is, researchers have provided a significant contribution to the broader debate on the evolving character and nature of war. Overall, the debate on cyber war demonstrates how fuzzy and subjective a concept war can be. The use of the prefix "cyber" – denoting the use of computer network attacks to wage war – also has its limits. In the most extreme scenarios, where a cyberattack would end several thousand lives and disrupt the lives of millions of others, "cyber" becomes superfluous. A cyberattack of such a scale would lead to war, not cyber war.[35]

From cyber war to cyber conflict

Most IR scholars have moved beyond the hype. Myriam Dunn Cavelty was one of the first scholars to systematically criticize the hyperbole around cyber war. In her 2008 book on cybersecurity, she uses securitization theory to reveal the socially constructed nature of cyber threats in the US discourse.[36] Other approaches now appear to be more fruitful. John Sheldon, for example, focuses on cyber power, which he defines as "a form of influence in and from cyberspace."[37] Brandon Valeriano and Ryan Maness have emphasized the needs for systematic and theoretically informed empirical research to counter the cyber hype. They have used available data on cyber incidents and disputes to explore the significance of cyber conflict, which they define as "the use of computational technologies in cyberspace for malevolent and destructive purposes in order to impact, change, or modify diplomatic and military interactions among entities."[38] From this perspective, cyber war is only one possibility in the broader spectrum of cyber conflict. Their study of state rivalry in cyberspace, based on a database of incidents running from 2001 to 2011, shows that "the actual magnitude and pace of attacks do not match the popular perception."[39] So far, the fear of cyberattacks is greater than the damage they have caused. Their research supports the more moderate view that states have demonstrated restraint in their use of cyberattacks, mostly because of the potential for blowback, replication and collateral damage.[40] Yet new cases of cyberattacks challenge the moderate view. Storybox 6.2 examines attacks on the Ukrainian energy grid in 2015 and 2016, which suggest that some of the cyber doom scenarios might not be as far-fetched as the most skeptical voices in the debate initially thought.

Storybox 6.2 Ukrainian blackouts

Since the Ukrainian revolution of 2014, which overthrew Kremlin-backed President Viktor Yanukovych, Russia has become increasingly aggressive toward its neighbor to the west. Following the revolution, Russia annexed the Crimean Peninsula, and launched a series of skirmishes in the eastern region of Donbas. Russian operations in Ukraine have also taken place in cyberspace, targeting multiple sectors of Ukrainian society – banking and finance, health, media, military, politics, transportation, etc. These attacks have allowed Russia to perfect its approach to cyber warfare and test Western resolve.[41]

In December 2015, some 225,000 Ukrainians were left without electricity when hackers disabled 15 electricity substations and back-up power supplies. The attackers first conducted a phishing attack to lodge an all-purpose trojan known as BlackEnergy in the computer systems of specific Ukrainian power companies. They eventually gained access to industrial control software used to operate key equipment, and unloaded another code, named KillDisk, for destruction. The 2015 Ukrainian blackout lasted a few hours, until engineers manually switched the power on again. A year later, another attack took down a larger transmission station in Kyiv for an hour. This second attack demonstrated more sophistication, using a piece of malware, "CrashOverride," that had been tailored specifically to sabotage the energy grid.

Cybersecurity analysts believe that the same group of hackers – Sandworm – conducted the 2015 and 2016 attacks, and have expressed concern over this group's ability to refine its attacks and attempt to infiltrate US systems.[42] Most of the clues they have found, regarding these attacks as well as the possible motives, clearly point toward Russia.

Moderate voices recognize that the Internet will be a theatre of future conflict and that new cases may challenge their position. Yet they doubt that cyberattacks could decide the outcome of a conflict. First, cyberattacks remain limited because cyberspace is inherently linked to the physical world. Stuxnet, the most dramatic example of cyber sabotage that is publicly known, probably required a human using a flash drive to bypass the air gap protecting Iranian nuclear centrifuge systems. Second, cyberattacks are often limited in duration and have more readily reversible effects than conventional kinetic attacks. Stuxnet delayed but did not destroy capabilities, and the Ukrainian blackouts only lasted a few hours. Finally, cyberattacks do not destabilize international relations, because states exercise restraint in their use of cyber power. The risk, for Valeriano and Maness, is that governments' excessive concern with cyber war will limit freedoms and innovation on and through the Internet.[43]

Another strand of research explores the potential motives behind cyber war to question its existence. For Erik Gartzke, the debate on cyber war has focused too much on means of cyberattacks (capabilities) and their outcomes (destruction and lethality), and not enough on the motives of those who are able to act.[44] Why would a state use cyberattacks to target an adversary? Force is traditionally used to punish, to conquer and to compel enemies to do things. Gartzke finds that most of the actors who are capable of harming their adversaries – online or elsewhere – do not do so, because they have insufficient reason to do so. Like Valeriano and Maness, he finds that cyberattacks on their own do not pose a threat that is significant enough to affect the political decisions of a sovereign nation. While cyberattacks might inflict costs on an adversary – for example, by shutting down the electricity grid of a country – this damage can be fixed, and there would be no long-lasting harm that could cause a shift in the balance of power.[45]

While researchers have pointed out that the anonymous nature of cyberattacks is a problem for defenders who might not be able to directly attribute them,[46] Gartzke adds that the absence of attribution is problematic for attackers. Why would an adversary attack and remain anonymous? Anonymity might protect an attacker from retribution but would also prevent him from getting credit for the attack. From the point of view of the victim, there can be no surrender if there is no attribution.[47] The attacker must then necessarily conclude that cyberattacks cannot achieve much without being associated with more conventional kinetic forms of military violence, where attribution is less problematic. In this context, cyberattacks are likely to remain a secondary tool, behind the use of conventional kinetic forces able to inflict unacceptable harm on an adversary.[48]

At a conceptual level, Gartzke's argument reinforces the point that what is distinctive about cyberspace, as a domain of operation, is that it is connected to all the other domains of military operation. This finding suggests that cyber power will most benefit well-established or strong military powers such as China, Russia and the United States, which can most effectively rely on their superior military power.[49] Indeed, most of the case studies of effective cyber operations discussed in the literature – including in this book – tend to focus on these countries. Cyber power should not be considered as an isolated instrument but in conjunction with other forms of warfare. Storybox 6.3 shows how Russia embraced a holistic use of cyberattacks during its 2008 conflict with neighboring Georgia.

Storybox 6.3 Leveraging cyberattacks: the Russo-Georgian war of 2008

In August 2008, Russia launched a series of large-scale overt cyberattacks to augment its on-the-ground military operation in Georgia.

A number of patriotic citizen hackers launched DDoS attacks and defaced select websites belonging to dozens of government, news and financial institutions. As much as 35 percent of Georgia's Internet networks were affected. The networks used to launch the DDoS attacks, and the Georgian efforts to defend itself in cyberspace, spread far beyond the Russo-Georgian border, involving cyber infrastructure in over 60 countries.[50]

The cyber campaign against Georgia was carefully planned and closely coordinated with Russian military progress on the ground. The attacks diminished the Georgian government's ability to respond and communicate while Russian tanks were moving into South Ossetia in the early days of the campaign. This denial opened space for Russia to make gains at the strategic level and disseminate propaganda that pinned responsibility for the conflict on Georgia. These cyberattacks were not essential to the Russian intervention but they provided "marginal improvements to military effectiveness."[51]

The Russo-Georgian war was the first time in history that a cyberattack was so closely synchronized with a conventional military campaign.[52] Reflecting on how Russia leveraged cyberattacks to augment on-the-ground operations, John Arquilla concluded, in a nod to his 1993 article with David Ronfeldt, "Cyberwar Is Already upon Us."[53] More measured voices have used this case to discuss the use of cyber power in war, rather than cyber war. Russia effectively mobilized the cyber power provided by patriotic citizens and hacker communities, limiting the ability of Georgia and the international community to attribute the cyberattacks to Russia, and to respond to them.[54] Though these attacks succeeded in limiting Georgia's ability to communicate, at the strategic level, Russian propaganda eventually failed to generate international consensus on Moscow's version of the events.

Cyberspace and military operations

In the last decades, advanced militaries across the world have developed institutions and doctrines to better integrate cyber power into military operations. The US government established a Cyber Command in 2009, and the United Kingdom a Joint Forces Cyber Group in 2013 to plan and coordinate cyber warfare operations. Since 2017, the Commandement de la cyberdéfense leads French military operations in cyberspace. The Chinese PLA's equivalent is the Strategic Support Force.

Military operations in cyberspace can occur in various contexts, ranging from peacetime to high-intensity warfare. Peter Dombrowsky and Chris Demchak point out that cyberspace has "added layers of complexity to existing tactics and operations, and become increasingly influential in the strategic calculus of several major powers in the international system."[55] Cyber operations employ cyberspace capabilities to achieve objectives in and through cyberspace. Cyberspace is both a means and a target for militaries to exert power. Actions "in" cyberspace seek to deny or even manipulate an adversary's use of information systems and networks. The military also operates "through" cyberspace on a routine basis, using computers to support commanders' decisions. Core military functions such as C2 and logistical support rely on cyberspace to integrate, synchronize and direct operations at digital speeds. The network-centric character of modern militaries creates vulnerabilities that need to be defended.[56]

The US military distinguishes between offensive and defensive cyberspace operations. Offensive operations seek to disrupt the adversary's operations to deny them access to information systems, to deceive or manipulate adversaries, to degrade their capacity, or to destroy their computers or computer networks and applications. Defensive operations seek to detect, analyze and mitigate threats to computer networks, to preserve the ability to utilize cyberspace capabilities and to protect data, networks and systems.[57] Defensive operations can actively seek to jam or disrupt enemy offensive capabilities, or be more passive and block attacks. The distinction between offensive and defensive operations is useful, and provides a fruitful way to link military operations to strategic debates about the relationship and balance between offensive and defensive capabilities. However, this dichotomy has also been criticized for being too US-centric and overlooking alternative conceptions of cyberspace operations based on resilience, for instance.[58]

The use of the term "operations" should not obscure the fact that cyberspace capabilities affect all the levels of war, from tactics to operations and strategy. At the tactical level, cyberattacks are planned and code manipulations achieve specific military objectives. Storybox 6.4 examines the recent tactical use of cyber operations during the February 2022 Russian invasion of Ukraine. This storybox highlights both the capabilities available and the constraints on them. At the operational level, personnel are trained, and resources are acquired and allocated to facilitate the implementation of the strategy at the tactical level. The strategic level establishes ideas and coordinates the elements of power – diplomacy, information, military, economy, etc. – to achieve national, and sometimes multinational, objectives.[59]

Storybox 6.4 AcidRain: taking down Ukraine's satellite communications

On February 24, 2022, the Russian Federation initiated a full-scale invasion of Ukraine. In the hours prior to the ground invasion, the Russian Federation launched a coordinated cyberattack against the principal satellite communications provider for the Ukrainian Armed Forces, the Viasat KA-SAT network. By the time the ground invasion of Ukraine had commenced, its satellite communications systems were inoperable.[60] The attack turned out to be relatively unsophisticated in nature and did not include any new or advanced zero-day vulnerabilities.[61] Instead, the operation targeted the VPN software used by Viasat.[62] The malware used to penetrate the KA-SAT network was dubbed AcidRain and attributed to the Russian Federation through a variety of linguistic markers within the code, including ethnic slurs directed against Ukrainians.[63] The malware itself was relatively simple and constituted a brute force attack against the targeted systems followed by the insertion of a wiper malware that began the process of erasing the device's memory and file systems.[64] The primary target within the KA-SAT network was the land-based modems that established communications with the orbiting satellites. The result of the attack was that these modems were wiped and unable to facilitate communication without rewriting the software on the systems. Although the attack did impact the back-up communication systems of the Ukrainian Armed Forces, it did not seriously impede the primary means of communication used by Ukraine to organize its defense.[65] Instead, however, the spillover costs of the attack did have a substantial impact on Ukrainian partner nations – in particular, the civilian energy-generation infrastructure of wind turbines in Germany, of which approximately 6,000 lost communication with their operators.[66]

The attack demonstrates the tactical limits of cyber capabilities during military operations.[67] Although the attack was successful, its impact was minimal according to Ukrainian government sources. Its impact was offset by systemic resiliency in communications infrastructure. The attack did not undermine the ability of Ukrainian soldiers to use secure radios, Internet or mobile infrastructures, and had absolutely no impact on their ability to conduct military operations using drones such as the Bayraktar TB2, a drone carrying guided missiles, that was of critical importance to Ukraine early in the war. These other systems used alternative forms of communication that allowed the Ukrainian military to mount a robust national defense.

Although many scholars, pundits and even some security experts claimed the hack indicated the start of a new phase of "cyber war," the reality was more mundane and illustrates the importance of basic cybersecurity and resilience in military operations. What the attack does show is the potential for cyber operations to be an enabler or a force multiplier of actions in times of conflict.

At all these levels, cyberspace capabilities are increasingly integrated with other domains. Since cyberspace underpins all other warfighting domains, it is best approached in a combined or integrated way. The American military talks about joint operations and multi-domain battle. Militaries across the world are learning to combine cyberspace capabilities with land, sea, air and space capabilities, and maneuver across all domains to maximize battlefield opportunities.[68] The Russo-Georgian war of 2008 is an example of cross-domain military operation, in which Russia leveraged cyberspace for a specific informational purpose along with more traditional maneuvers on land.

Cyber and nuclear capabilities

In the years since the first edition of this volume was published, a few scholars have begun to examine the intersection of cybersecurity and nuclear security. Nuclear capabilities have long been a core issue for international security, and related debates have played a central role in the study of strategy and security. From this perspective, it should not come as a surprise that scholars have increasingly raised concern about the possibility an adversary would use cyber capabilities to interfere with nuclear weapons or power-generation infrastructures. Though the probability of this scenario appears to be low, its impact could be devastating. Analyses of these risks tend to focus on several key attributes of nuclear security, including the security of command, control and communications (C3) systems, security of nuclear weapons themselves, the security of the platforms used to transport and deliver nuclear weapons,[69] and nuclear energy infrastructure.[70] Much of the discussion on nuclear weapons relating to C3, delivery systems or weapons revolves around challenges posed by the increasing complexity of the weapons and systems of delivery. Scholars rightfully point out that, as the modernization of these weapons and the systems used to control or manage their deployment are updated, they are likely to be increasingly imbued with digital artifacts – microprocessors, sensors, radios and more – that are vulnerable to manipulation. They also accurately identify a range of fundamental challenges associated with technological advances in civilian and military contexts.

Technologies used to control, deliver, or even communicate to users of, weapon systems are themselves increasingly interwoven into aspects of modern cyberspace. The inclusion of sensitive technologies raises the possibility for something going catastrophically wrong. Could state hackers potentially break into one of these systems and undermine the ability of a nuclear power to use its nuclear forces? Could they potentially initiate or trigger a launch by manipulating sensors? Well-documented histories of near-misses and failures associated with these weapon systems raise a range of additional concerns. For example, prior to upgrading them with new digital technologies, the technologies associated with nuclear weapons were expected to last decades. What happens when software vendors go out of business or no longer support operating systems for nuclear weapons or their C3 infrastructures? These are serious issues that are being raised and considered within governments.

Closely associated with concerns pertaining to nuclear weapons are those related to civilian infrastructures. As nuclear power facilities upgrade their systems, they become increasingly complex and by extension are likely to have more potential vulnerabilities. Such facilities could become targets of state and non-state actors, and warrant appropriate regulatory oversight to ensure security. Yet because there is limited public transparency on issues pertaining to cybersecurity at nuclear facilities or related to nuclear weapons, there remains a great deal of concern about potential deliberate or accidental issues that might arise. When both groups of problems are contextualized within the broader topic of war or conflict, the level of concern only grows.

Strategic competition in cyberspace

Taking stock of major changes in the international environment, several experts now write about strategic competition to characterize interactions between major states or groups of states in the international system. In their study on the topic, Mazarr, Frederick and Crane develop a four-point framework to assess competition between major powers, focused on: (1) the overall context for the competition; (2) national power and competitiveness; (3) international position and influence; and (4) bilateral competitions.[71] Each of these attributes has a variety of elements and indicators, ranging from geopolitical and social interests to core national interests and economic posture and engagement. The result is a reframing of war and conflict away from hard assertions of power, which aligns well to the overall direction taken by recent debates on cyberconflict. When all the evidence is presented, the effects of offensive cyber operations do not appear to rise to the level of violence necessary to meet the threshold for armed conflict.

Yet if cyber war is not taking place, then what is happening? How should we characterize states hacking into one another's critical infrastructures, manipulating elections, stealing information – degrading, disrupting or even damaging one another in and through cyberspace? For Michael Fischerkeller, Emily Goldman and Richard Harknett, countries are involved in a strategic competition with one another in cyberspace.[72] They define strategic competition in cyberspace as those activities of states within a bounded space of competition in which they seek to gain positional advantages relative to other states in the international system. This competition is defined by continuous tacitly agreed-upon engagement between competitors. States, developing an increasingly robust understanding of the upper bounds of interactions in cyberspace, have settled into persistent competitive interactions through shaping operations. The environment, cyberspace, encourages states to seek out opportunities to exploit weaknesses below the level of armed conflict in an adversary's networks. These operations can be, and are often, quite painful and can include everything from acts of subterfuge such as Stuxnet and BlackEnergy, to enabling campaigns such as in the stories we presented on the Russo-Georgian War and AcidRain, to intelligence operations designed to undermine potential adversary advantages in other domains of conflict. Independently, these actions do not constitute acts of armed aggression under international law.

For Fischerkeller and colleagues, states act persistently, with the intent to exploit adversaries to foster changes in perceived conditions of security and insecurity.[73] The strategic environment forces states to interact through what they term cyber "faits accomplis."[74] A cyber fait accompli is defined as "a limited unilateral gain at the target's expense where that gain is retained when the target is unaware of the loss or is unable or unwilling to respond."[75] The conceptualization of cyberspace as an environment of strategic competition is not new and dates back more than 20 years to Greg Rattray's work examining strategic warfare in cyberspace.[76] Yet, in the intervening time, the bounds of the environment occurring below the generally accepted level of armed conflict, and the limited escalatory potential of actions in cyberspace to spiral out of control and across domains of conflict, have become clearer.

The United States has settled strongly behind the concept of strategic competition. As a result, and as we showed in chapter 5, it has revisited its national security strategies with the understanding that interactions in cyberspace are competitive and all adversary actions must be consistently contested through a defend forward posture. It is unclear whether adversaries and allies agree on this formulation. At present the vast majority of case data available supports the notion that interactions in cyberspace are competitive in nature, non-escalatory, and not seen as constituting acts of war or armed aggression.[77]

Conclusion

The debate on cyber war has been essential to helping establish cybersecurity in the field of IR. Early scholarship on the subject has sought to define the key terms that follow the prefix "cyber": war, warfare and operations, among others. The doomsday scenarios imagined by the first prophets of cyber war have not come to fruition, but they did have real-life consequences, triggering concern and reactions from policy-makers. For the more moderate or skeptical voices in the debate, cyber hype has led to poor investments. The US government has devoted vast resources to develop military cyber capabilities. Yet critics note that cybercrime, not cyber war, is the most prominent threat facing Western societies. Many scholars and policy-makers have increasingly turned away from the term "cyber war" in favor of the term "cyber conflict." Although both terms are very similar, the notion of cyber conflict does not carry with it the emotional and legal baggage that is often associated with war. Yet, even as many shift to new terms to describe what is going on in cyberspace as conflict rather than war, terminology is changing yet again to focus on competition. From a US perspective, defining interactions in cyberspace as competition opens up new avenues for the DoD to try new tactics such as defend forward, without having to invoke terms of war or conflict. As a result, US Cyber Command is able to engage perceived adversaries in ways not possible under previous threat framing. Whether this shift from war to conflict and now increasingly to competition will prove valuable – both descriptively and prescriptively – to the US and its allies remains to be seen.

Among the broader issues discussed above was a belief that cyberspace somehow had revolutionized military affairs. There is now a broad scholarly consensus that this has not happened. Bits and bytes are not taking out tanks on the battlefields in Ukraine or conquering territories through devastating attacks on critical infrastructure. Although the cyber Pearl Harbor debate appears only in the rear-view mirror, the debate on how cyberspace capabilities are transforming militaries remains open. There is no question that military institutions and doctrines have had to be adapted – if not created – to better take into account the emergence of a fifth domain of war. This domain presents some unique characteristics – for example, its man-made character – but has not fundamentally altered the nature of war. Cyberspace operations remain inherently linked and limited by humans, politics, culture and the fog of war. They should not be approached on a stand-alone basis, but in combination with other domains of warfare and human activity. The next chapter will explore how pre-existing concepts of deterrence, bargaining, the arms race and escalation, to name but a few, can help us understand national cybersecurity.

Discussion questions

1. What are the differences between cyber war, conflict and competition? Discuss the implications of these terminological choices.

2. Do you agree with Rid's statement that "Cyber war will not take place?"

3. To what extent is cyberspace transforming military affairs?

Exercise

Draw an escalation ladder of cyberattacks from the least to the most (politically) violent type of operation you can think of. Think about the criteria you use to place specific examples on your ladder of escalation.

Additional resources

Michael P. Fischerkeller, Emily O. Goldman and Richard J. Harknett, *Cyber Persistence Theory: Redefining National Security in Cyberspace* (Oxford University Press, 2022).

Ralph Langner (March 2011), "Cracking Stuxnet, a 21st-Century Cyber Weapon," TED Talk, www.ted.com/talks/ralph_langner_cracking_stuxnet _a_21st_century_cyberweapon.

Thomas Rid, *Cyber War Will Not Take Place* (London: Hurst, 2013).

Brandon Valeriano and Ryan C. Maness, *Cyber War versus Cyber Realities: Cyber Conflict in the International System* (New York: Oxford University Press, 2015), ch. 2.

7　Organizing deterrence and defense in cyberspace

Reader's guide

- Deterrence and defense in cyberspace have largely failed to prevent and dissuade adversaries from attacking networks and the computers within them. This does not mean that they are pointless, just that they are not perfect.

- Deterrence by denial seeks to impose costs on potential adversaries by increasing the level of difficulty associated with attacking computers and networks through any of the three layers of cyberspace.

- Deterrence by punishment seeks to dissuade potential adversaries by signaling that the costs of a cyberattack will outweigh its perceived benefits. Establishing credible punishment for cyberattacks is challenging.

- State and sub-state organizations have institutionalized cyber defense. The rise of "cyber commands" signals capacity for cyber defense and offense, thus contributing to a more credible security posture.

Cyberspace presents substantial security challenges requiring state and non-state actors, public and private entities, to engage in defensive actions to ensure the confidentiality, integrity and availability (CIA triad) of data and the systems that use and depend upon data for their intended functioning. While much of the defensive nature of cyberspace revolves around the development of ever more sophisticated technical devices and software programs, there remains a robust need for states to implement a "mosaic" of deterrence strategies, ranging from deterrence by denial to deterrence by punishment, to organize their cyber defense.[1] Technical solutions, combined with policies intended to deter adversaries from engaging in undesired behaviors and actions, form the bulwark behind which actors organize to protect cyberspace.

Fundamental cybersecurity begins with an understanding of how to maintain and defend a network or system (computer) against error and malicious actors who either directly or indirectly target the pillars of the CIA triad. Beyond the maintenance and defense of systems and networks, cyber actors across all levels of jurisdiction find it increasingly necessary to identify ways to impose costs on malicious actors. Imposing costs can occur in a variety of ways, through acts of punishment or denial, and can occur within or across domains of interaction (meaning they can occur in cyberspace and in the physical world).

Defense and deterrence in cyberspace are about weighing costs and benefits, risks and rewards, in an attempt to find a balance where the defender state, company, organization, school, individual or any actor in between is able to achieve their goals and objectives. Defense in cyberspace is unique and tailored. Although certain practices span actors and levels, there is no single solution to the challenges present within cyberspace. Many states and non-state actors develop detailed strategies to shore up their cyber defense, but these plans inevitably clash with reality. Military theorist Carl von Clausewitz used the term "friction" to "distinguish real war from war on paper."[2] In recent years, the United States has adopted this terminology and pursued "cyber friction" to continuously contest adversary behaviors and frustrate their plans in and through cyberspace.

This chapter examines the concepts of cyber defense and deterrence, first by discussing micro-level policies and technologies to defend networks, computer systems and users in cyberspace, and second by evaluating the applicability and current status of deterrence strategies and policies being used by different levels of government. Cyber defense and deterrence both center on the goal of preventing the unintended use of cyberspace and its components. Understanding the challenges confronting cyber defense and deterrence, and the many ways different actors attempt to address them, provides perspective and illustrates why organizing for defense in cyberspace is and will remain difficult.

Technical cyber defense and deterrence by denial

Cyber defense and deterrence by denial form two sides of the same coin. Together, they technically, financially and psychologically impose costs on potential adversaries by increasing the level of difficulty associated with penetrating computers and networks. The three layers of cyberspace – physical, logical and persona – provide a useful roadmap for thinking about cyber defense and deterrence. When focusing on cyber defense using technical solutions, the emphasis is on designing or reinforcing systems, networks and their users against errors, both intentional and unintentional, as well as deliberate acts of malfeasance, at every step along the way from an individual computer system to a complex network. Defense is the balancing of costs and benefits over time. There is no such thing as perfect defense in cyberspace. All defense is based on the choices and needs of the users or organizations who own a system or network. Every choice has costs, both financially and functionally.

Cyber defense starts early. Even before the component parts of a computer system are developed, its designers are forced to make choices that impact its future security. The more complicated the design of hardware, in particular the CPU and Graphics Processing Unit (GPU), the fewer the number of potential manufacturers, and the more difficult an eventual CPU will be to validate and assess for errors. Complexity can be the enemy of security because it can hide accidental and deliberate errors. At the physical level of cyberspace, each processor, hard-drive, memory component and so on, throughout the computer, adds complexity. Controlling or restricting the development and manufacturing of, and access to, some services and products can facilitate security, not least by limiting or constraining adversary access to key technologies.

After the initial design of hardware components, firms must decide where to source their component parts. In a process known as supply chain management, firms make decisions about where and how to manufacture the component pieces – that is to say, both the hardware and software – of a computer system. Supply chain security is so important in the manufacture and distribution of products that the United States released a "National Strategy on Global Supply Chain Management," which encourages firms to assess and mitigate related risks.[3] Many countries now impose requirements on manufacturers related to where and how various computer systems are developed, as well as the chain of custody that tracks components within computer systems between their initial manufacture and their eventual delivery to government clients. Detailed sourcing requirements for computer system components are time consuming and expensive. Such requirements are imposed to prevent the injection of deliberate vulnerabilities into products prior to their delivery.

A broad range of external factors affect the logistics of combining these components within a supply chain to build integrated machines, from geopolitics to weather and even viruses. The COVID-19 pandemic illustrated some of the fundamental constraints associated with hardware supply chains. The pandemic slowed global chip production and sales, resulting in substantial delays in the manufacture of thousands of goods dependent on microprocessors. The result was a vulnerability not in the code, or the hardware, but in the manufacture of the component pieces of cyberspace and its associated connected technologies.

The physical components of the systems being delivered are only part of the production process for an end user. A computer system comprised only of its physical parts is little more than a box of plastic, silicon and metals. To operate a computer system requires software that directs the functioning of the physical components. There are multiple layers of software that operate on each computer system. Most consumers interact with their computers via a Graphics User Interface (GUI) operating system, such as Mac OS, Windows 11, Linux, iOS or Android. These operating systems are immensely complicated computer programs comprising millions of lines of code developed in dozens of countries around the world. To mitigate errors – both deliberate and accidental – within code, the firms and collectives (in the case of Linux) who develop software are encouraged to use what is called a "security development lifecycle" (SDL). SDL is a process used to reduce maintenance costs and increase the reliability of software. This process encourages developers to systematically plan, design, code, test and maintain the software they produce. This process is known as security by design. Security by design has not been the standard of development for many devices and services associated with rapid advances in technology associated with the Internet. The IoT has been notorious for its lack of security in the design process. Using a process such as SDL reorients the development of software and places security at the forefront rather than as an afterthought. While security by design does not eliminate risk, it substantially reduces risk across software ecosystems. Security by design frontloads costs associated with cybersecurity and minimizes post-sale and post-deployment security costs. Software products that fail to use an SDL are much more susceptible to vulnerabilities and therefore have weaker defenses.

For most users, from individuals to small and medium-sized firms, the process of security development for their devices ends prior to their delivery. Computer systems are delivered with hardware and software components ready for end-user configuration, and further optional security measures such as anti-virus software, firewalls or similar end-user strategies are based on their specific needs and requirements. However, for militaries and governments, the delivery of products starts a second defensive process of hardware and software verification. The more sensitive the use of a product, the more this product is scrutinized before deployment. Government organizations such as the US Army take the verification of their systems, even non-sensitive systems like the Non-classified Internet Protocol Router Network (NIPRnet) very seriously, and request the source code for the operating systems of computers they allow on their network. The Army then heavily modifies and reduces the functionality of many attributes of these operating systems in an effort to further alleviate potential vulnerabilities. Moreover, many governments, firms and even universities limit how, and what, devices are allowed to connect to their computer networks, in what is referred to as network access control. Some organizations even limit which software programs are permitted on end-user systems.

Each of the actions above attempts to minimize potential vulnerabilities prior to the initial use of a computer system or network. Despite all these efforts, all computers remain vulnerable to a variety of exploitations at every level. In the case of Spectre and Meltdown, hardware vulnerabilities identified in Intel chips (CPUs) enabled hackers to access data and information on computer systems.[4] Software vulnerabilities known as zero-days (vulnerabilities not previously identified) reside within every software program on every computer. The more complex the computer hardware and the more complex the computer software, the higher the risk of vulnerability. Developing complex systems without robust SDLs results in an overwhelming mix of defensive challenges prior to a computer's initial use.

After initial product delivery and configuration by an end user, defensive cyberspace actions shift to the protection of individual computer systems (host-based defense), groupings of computer systems within a computer network (networked-based defense) and efforts to prevent human users from deliberately or inadvertently introducing weaknesses into either a computer system or network (human user defense). For each of these types of action, both technical and policy measures seek to minimize potential vulnerabilities and enhance defense. No single policy or technical solution provides sufficient defense to prevent all attacks. Rather, a combination of defensive technical and policy measures are typically implemented to reduce the likelihood and subsequent impact of an attack. Moreover, all defensive solutions are specific to the peculiarities of the computer systems, networks and users being protected. However, some policy and technical solutions, such as password protection of computers, are generally applicable across use cases.

There are multiple approaches to cyber defense. Many are industry specific or entail requirements rooted in regulatory policies at the national and regional levels. Other frameworks are rooted in professional and standards organizations. Table 7.1 presents several of these cybersecurity frameworks.

Table 7.1 Cybersecurity frameworks overview[5]

Framework	Governing body	Brief description
ISO IEC 27001 / ISO 27002	International Organization for Standardization (ISO)	The ISO 27001 framework sets international guidelines for establishing information security management systems, emphasizing a risk-based approach to safeguard business information systems against potential threats
NIST Cybersecurity Framework	National Institute of Standards and Technology (NIST, US)	Developed in response to the US Presidential Executive Order 13636, the NIST Cybersecurity Framework aims to fortify the security of vital national infrastructure, shielding it from internal and external dangers
IASME Cyber Assurance Standard	Information Assurance for Small and Medium Enterprises Consortium (IASME, UK)	The IASME standard targets small to medium-sized businesses, providing assurance that they have achieved recognized cybersecurity, privacy and data protection measures
System and Organization Controls (SOC 2)	American Institute of Certified Public Accountants (AICPA)	SOC 2 helps organizations that handle sensitive customer data on cloud platforms to uphold stringent security protocols
CIS Critical Security Control v8	Center for Internet Security	The Center for Internet Security (CIS) has established the CIS v8 framework, comprising 18 concrete cybersecurity steps designed to bolster the security protocols across various organizations
NIST 800-53 Cybersecurity Framework	NIST	The NIST 800-53 publication by NIST guides federal agencies in implementing robust cybersecurity measures
COBIT (Control Objectives for Information and Related Technologies)	Information Systems Audit and Control Association (ISACA)	COBIT is a framework for information technology management and governance. It is based on a set of five core principles and is aligned to other frameworks and standards
COSO (Committee of Sponsoring Organizations)	COSO	COSO's framework empowers organizations to detect and manage cybersecurity threats through a structured set of 17 requirements spread across five domains: control environment, risk assessment, control activities, information and communication, and monitoring

Table 7.1 (*cont.*)

Framework	Governing body	Brief description
TC CYBER	Technical Committee on Cybersecurity Framework	The framework established by TC CYBER, which stands for the Technical Committee on Cyber Security, was crafted to enhance the telecommunication standards throughout nations in the European regions
HITRUST CSF (Control Security Framework)	Health Information Trust Alliance (HITRUST)	The HITRUST cybersecurity framework outlines a range of strategies for bolstering security. It is specifically designed to resolve the unique IT security challenges confronted by healthcare sector organizations
CISQ	Consortium for IT Software Quality	CISQ sets benchmarks for software developers to ensure that both in-progress and completed software programs are secure and reliable
Ten Steps to Cybersecurity	UK Department for Business	The UK Department for Business's "Ten Steps to Cybersecurity" initiative educates business leaders on cybersecurity threats and prevention strategies for enterprise growth and development
FedRAMP	Federal Risk and Authorization Management Program, USA	FedRAMP offers a standardized framework for US federal agencies to assess and manage cybersecurity risks for infrastructure and cloud services
HIPAA	Health Insurance Portability and Accountability Act, USA	HIPAA provides comprehensive rules for healthcare organizations to protect patient and employee health information securely
GDPR	General Data Protection Regulation, EU	The General Data Protection Regulation (GDPR) represents a contemporary framework established to protect the personal data of individuals within the European Union
FISMA	Federal Information Systems Management Act, USA	The Federal Information Systems Management Act (FISMA) provides a cybersecurity framework tailored for federal agencies, detailing essential security requisites which these agencies can implement to strengthen their cybersecurity defenses
NY DFS	New York Department of Financial Services, NY State	The NY DFS delivers a cybersecurity framework for financial entities operating within New York, and NERC CIP (below) lays out security measures for safeguarding North America's critical energy infrastructure

Table 7.1 (*cont.*)

Framework	Governing body	Brief description
NERC CIP	North American Electric Reliability Corporation Critical Infrastructure Protection	The Critical Infrastructure Protection (CIP) standards from the North American Electric Reliability Corporation (NERC) constitute a cybersecurity framework aimed at safeguarding vital infrastructure and assets
SCAP	Security Content Automation Protocol	The Security Content Automation Protocol (SCAP) is a regulatory standard that provides security specifications to unify the communication among various security products and tools
ANSI	American National Standards Institute	The framework from the American National Standards Institute (ANSI) includes a set of standards, informative guidelines, and technical documents that detail the processes for setting up and upkeeping Industrial Automation and Control Systems (IACS)

The broad range of frameworks presented in table 7.1 can give the impression that cyberspace is very closely regulated. However, the implementation and use of these frameworks depends on a series of trade-offs in time, money, accessibility and more. Some frameworks are compulsory, while others are voluntary. Some frameworks are designed to overlap with others, often because their scope differs. GDPR, for instance, is an overarching legal and regulatory framework that is mandated in the EU, yet most organizations will also adhere to one or more of the other frameworks.

The implementation of these frameworks frequently requires coordination between various levels of leadership across an organization. Many organizations have a Chief Technology Officer (CTO) and more specialized Chief Information Security Officer (CISO). Both these individuals will interact with other leaders such as a Chief Operating Officer (COO) to agree to a particular security framework and oversee its implementation. The process of implementation requires leadership and organizational buy-in or it will fail. One of the most common sources of cyber insecurity arises out of organizational failures to adequately implement one of the above cybersecurity frameworks. These frameworks are meant to reduce aggregate risk but they do not eliminate all risk. Often the reduction of certain risk types or categories is privileged over that of others. Selecting the most applicable cybersecurity framework can have important implications for an organization's overall cybersecurity. It can also serve as a prerequisite for contemporary risk-offset strategies such as cyber insurance.

One of the most widely used risk frameworks globally is outlined in a series of publications by the US NIST, known as the NIST 800 series. The NIST 800 series of publications provides templates for the development of cyber defense that can be tailored across organization types. Many organizations and governments across the world use these publications as a guide. These publications document best practices and outline how and why organizations should establish certain policy mechanisms to bolster cyber defenses and reduce vulnerabilities. For example, the NIST 800 series presents best practices on password security and network access controls, encryption standards and configurations of networks. Altogether, there are more than 207 unique publications in the NIST 800 series, and further specific documentation relevant to critical infrastructures, e-commerce and cloud computing in the NIST 500 and the NIST 1800 series is also available.

Beyond policy mechanisms highlighted in the NIST publications, hundreds of firms specialize in cyber defense. Cybersecurity companies such as Trellix (formerly FireEye), Mandiant, CrowdStrike and many more offer technical solutions that reside on computer systems (host-based defense) or on networks (network-based defense). Host-based defensive measures on computer systems include everything from anti-virus software and firewalls, such as Windows Defender, to access controls such as passwords and biometric identification. Each new defensive measure on a computer system can make it more resistant to cyberattacks – however, host-based defensive measures are not without trade-offs. Anti-virus scanners can consume the processing power of computers making them run slower. Passwords and biometrics can limit the number of people who can use a computer, making it more difficult to share expensive devices within families or organizations. Firewalls can inadvertently block traffic or programs that a user wants to use. Implemented properly, host-based defensive measures can enhance the security of a computer system without imposing too many costs on the functionality of the system itself. In the near future, usernames and passwords are likely to be a thing of the past. Major software developers and services such as Google and Apple are in the process of moving to a new type of login credential called passkeys. Passkeys are a unique digital key stored in an encrypted format on a device instead of in the servers of a third party or company. These keys leverage cryptography to remain secure and rely on biometric sensors, a PIN or a pattern to ensure their rightful owner uses them. Because they are considered more secure, passkeys are likely to overtake two-factor authentication and password combinations.

Patch management is one of the most important host-based defensive measures. Many software vendors release "patches" – updates to software that fix bugs (vulnerabilities) or improve the functionality of software. Microsoft historically released patches regularly on what it referred to as "Patch Tuesday." As new vulnerabilities are discovered, the vendor attempts to quickly find solutions to these vulnerabilities. Once a solution is developed, it pushes these to the end user. In most instances, end users are required to install these patches. Users often ignore these updates and, as a result, their computer system remains vulnerable over time. A failure to install released patches substantially increases the risk of compromise because, once a patch is released, malicious actors can learn about the vulnerability the patch seeks to mitigate. Thus, while installing a patch increases defenses in cyberspace, a failure to do so does not merely maintain the previous level of risk, but actually results in an increased risk and therefore a weakened defense.

Not all actors are able to immediately install released patches on their computer systems or networks. Some actors, particularly those who use specialized computer systems – such as electronic medical records systems in hospitals, or critical infrastructure providers – utilize custom versions of common software. Therefore, a power company such as Duke Energy might not have Windows 10 installed, but instead have Duke Energy Windows 10. A patch installed on customized software platforms, particularly those involved in critical infrastructure, can result in incompatibilities of existing software and hardware components and result in substantial damage. The release of a new patch results in a rapid race to implement the patch in such a way that it is compatible within each unique operating environment. The process of patch customization can take days, weeks and even months. During this period, the unpatched systems remain vulnerable to a publicly known vulnerability.

The goal of network defense is to protect not just a single computer system but many systems all within a network. There are two broad types of network defense: internal and perimeter. Internal network defense seeks to manage and prevent the spread of malware or malicious activity between computer systems within a network. Perimeter defense seeks to prevent the introduction of malware or stop malicious activities from entering a network. Network defenses commonly rely on a series of technologies known as intrusion detection systems (IDSs), intrusion prevention systems (IPS) or a hybrid IDPS. Most IDSs use one of three common detection methods to identify malicious traffic attempting to enter or transit within a network. First, signature-based detection compares traffic attempting to enter or already in a network to known or preconfigured attack patterns. This defense only works against known vulnerabilities (pre-existing malware) and therefore is less adaptable to rapid changes in the threat environment. The second type of IDS uses a statistical anomaly-based detect schema. Statistical anomaly-based detection uses snapshots of normal network behavior to create a "baseline." If a network exceeds this baseline, an anomaly-based detect schema identifies that there is anomalous activity that needs to be stopped. This type of defense is prone to false positives (identifications of problems where none exists) as traffic patterns change over time within and between networks. The third type of IDS is stateful-protocol analysis detection. This type of analysis focuses on predetermined profiles of normal activity. When non-normal activity occurs, it alerts human network defenders. Detecting malicious traffic is only the first step; a new class of products referred to as intrusion prevention systems attempts to stop an intrusion in progress. An IPS that detects a malicious remote connection to its network will halt the transfer of network traffic between the malicious connection and its network. IPS systems commonly work in tandem with IDS systems to ensure the defenses of a network.

Network and host-based security systems have substantially improved technical cyber defenses. Yet they remain vulnerable to advances such as polymorphic malware, which attempts to identify the defensive measures of a network or computer system and overcome them by changing its form. Human users pose another type of vulnerability that is difficult to mitigate – for example, when they inadvertently or knowingly introduce malicious software into a network. Technical defense is in many ways a game of whack-a-mole, in which defenders are constantly trying to plug holes all the while new holes keep appearing. The future of technical defense is likely going to include the use of AI to assist in the surveillance, monitoring and maintenance of computer systems and networks. One project developed by DARPA and named Mayhem has shown substantial progress against the world's top hackers at two recent hackers' events.[6]

Organizations across all levels are also developing agreements and institutions to facilitate the exchange of threat indicators. In the United States, a series of high-level public–private organizations called ISACs have formed around various critical industries. Organizations such as E-ISAC (electricity sector), FS-ISAC (financial services), Auto-ISAC (automotive), Aviation-ISAC, DIB-ISAC (defense industrial base) and more than a dozen other formal organizations share threat indicators between corporate and governmental partners in an attempt to get ahead of threats. These organizations are fee-based and the level of requisite defensive capabilities necessary to utilize the information they share remains above most small to medium firms. In the United States, a second, lower tier was proposed to address the challenges facing small to medium-sized entities. These groups, known as Information Sharing and Analysis Organizations (ISAOs), focus on information sharing. Both ISAOs and ISACs are designed to streamline the sharing of information horizontally within sectors, and vertically between sectors and the government. For example, these organizations can help with sharing indicators of compromise quickly, to minimize the time from indicator discovery to remediation. While some sectors' ISACs and ISAOs have become very robust and enable better defense, others remain relatively weak. In sum, cyber defense cooperation varies from one sector to another. The ISAC and ISAO model is being explored around the world. In 2017, the European Agency for Network and Information Security released a study on cooperative models for ISACs and collated best practices for implementation within Europe. The same year, the financial services ISAC (FS-ISAC) started building partnerships in Asia and began the process of developing centers headquartered in Singapore. Defense sharing and coordination are also growing within military alliances. In October 2018, NATO announced the establishment of its Cyberspace Operations Centre (CYOC) to better centralize cyberspace situational awareness and planning, and to coordinate operational concerns.[7]

Despite increases in information sharing across all levels, there remain strong incentives for many firms to be less than forthright regarding their breaches. Legal and reputation issues related to their products or services often constrain or slow organizations from sharing timely information that might prevent breaches within other organizations. While the trend is toward sharing, too much sharing might reveal weaknesses or cause clients to seek new firms. Incentivizing firms to share often requires negotiating policies that reduce the risks – including the legal liability – involved in sharing information about a compromise.

Beyond sharing threat information within organized networks, Internet and digital services providers have been pushed to address a variety of security challenges more directly. In 2012, US ISPs voluntarily began to work on addressing issues such as botnets, domain name fraud and Internet route hijacking. Many ISPs and telecommunications providers are currently seeking to address security challenges associated with data that reside both within their service areas and amongst their clients. However, there is no uniform international organizing principle and the ability of ISPs, Internet Exchange Points (IXPs) and content delivery firms to provide improved security has been met by legal challenges that have limited their success in liberal democracies and facilitated repression and censorship in more authoritarian states. The securitization of network traffic by the providers of the Internet remains a substantial challenge.

Combined, the technical and policy solutions examined in this section foster what IR scholars call deterrence by denial. Each of the steps undertaken above to build the defenses of computer systems and the networks they are a part of, as well as their users, increases the relative costs associated with attack. Denying vectors of attack across the three layers of cyberspace minimizes risks and requires potential adversaries to incur increased costs when attacking. Yet, despite all the available technology and policy, defense in cyberspace is and will probably remain for the foreseeable future inherently vulnerable. Each step undertaken to increase defense reduces risks, but no one solution – nor all in combination – eliminates risk. The inherent weaknesses of cyber defense via technical and policy solutions at the organizational level have pushed states and other sub-national jurisdictions to seek new means to deter malicious actors from engaging in cyberattacks. The next section focuses on the macro-policy options available to states and jurisdictions in their continuing efforts to create effective cyber defenses.

Defense through deterrence by punishment

Since defense in cyberspace is intrinsically imperfect, governments need to use various mechanisms to deter cyber threat actors. At its most basic, deterrence seeks to dissuade a potential adversary by signaling that the costs and/or risks of a given course of action they might take outweigh the benefits.[8] The most commonly examined form of deterrence emphasizes punishment. Deterrence by punishment operates at the international, national and sub-national levels. Deterrence that occurs at, or below, the national level most commonly falls into criminological frameworks that emphasize the individual level of analysis. Research in this area might seek to answer questions such as how to deter a hacker from attacking a local company for profit. Deterrence at the international level most commonly occurs through interstate interactions, but also includes state-to-non-state interactions, such as states interacting with transnational terrorist organizations.

In all cases, deterrence requires specific, credible signals backed up by sufficient resolve to exact punishment.[9] Deterrence requires specificity. Specificity at the state level is the identification of which acts perpetrated by another state constitute a violation that would cross a pre-identified "red line" or core interest of a state. Specificity within states is codified as acts that violate law. A violation by a state or non-state actor can both cross a red line and violate the national laws of the state it is attacking. Often a victim state will identify the types of violation and engage in deterrence through both domestic legal proceedings to punish the perpetrator and international actions for the same purpose. Credibility is the ability to exact punishment on a violator of a legal or political red line. Establishing credible punishments for cyberattacks is extremely challenging. Generally, the credibility of the state is not in doubt within states. The notion of de facto sovereignty holds that a state has the power to enforce the law within its territorial boundaries. Most states consistently demonstrate their resolve to enforce the law, thanks to policing and judicial systems. By contrast, when states interact amongst themselves, it is often difficult to signal both credibility – the ability to respond – and resolve – the will to respond.

Whether in the physical world or in cyberspace, exacting punishment requires accurate and timely attribution. Attribution in cyberspace is a substantial challenge to effective cyber deterrence.[10] Whether attempting criminological deterrence or interstate deterrence, accurately identifying the perpetrator of a digital attack requires substantial digital forensic and contextual information.[11] Attribution must also occur in a timely manner. If a perpetrator of a digital crime is not identified within the statute of limitations, he or she cannot be charged with a crime. While in interstate deterrence there is no formal statute of limitations, responding in an untimely manner to an attack is likely to be misinterpreted as a new attack.

Signals are the mechanism by which a state alerts potential violators of red lines or laws. The repeated prosecution of those who violate the law generally provides robust and unambiguous signals at the state and sub-state levels. Very often, these signals are ignored because criminal actors believe they are "able to get away with a crime." A perpetrator's belief that he or she can get away with a crime is rooted in an evaluation of the likelihood of being caught relative to the costs of being caught. While some crimes are driven by impulses, most cybercrimes require careful planning and foresight. At the domestic level, the process of establishing deterrence through criminological approaches – in particular, the prosecution of individuals or groups who violate the law – is hampered not by specificity or credibility, but rather by a lack of resolve to provide sufficient capabilities for law enforcement to attribute cyberattacks to a perpetrator at a level sufficient for criminal prosecution. When the deterrence of criminal actors is imperfect, violations of the law are more likely to occur than if it caught the perpetrator of every crime. Even if all crimes were prosecuted, it is likely that individuals would still, for a variety of reasons, attempt criminal acts in and through cyberspace.

Despite substantial resources, specific legal frameworks and a credible source of power, states are unable to achieve perfect criminological deterrence. All of the legal specificity present within a state and the credibility found within a criminological framework for the prosecution of crime are largely absent at the international level. The consensus among scholars and practitioners is that deterrence in cyberspace is plagued by a number of issues.[12] Cyberspace presents at least three core challenges to deterrence. First, victims of cyberattacks are often unaware that an attack has occurred. The average discovery time for data breaches in 2017 was 191 days.[13] Distinguishing between random or expected malfunctions in networks and systems and deliberately induced malfunctions is difficult and requires substantial resources, both human and financial. Moreover, after initial detection, data breaches in 2017 averaged 66 days between identification and containment.[14]

Second, beyond knowing that a cyberattack is occurring and preventing the damage from spreading, attributing the attack to a specific actor is often imprecise or dependent on substantial forensic analysis and contextual geopolitical factors that allow reasonable attribution to a given actor. In the case of Russian hacks of the DNC in 2015–16, the perpetrators' techniques, tactics and procedures provided both the forensic and geopolitical context necessary for reasonable attribution. Jon Lindsay points out that "attribution requires great technical expertise, analytical skill, and organizational coordination."[15] He goes on to write that, despite the attribution problem being hard to solve, it is more difficult in less vital instances of attack than it is in comparably important instances in which the amount of available information drawn from both forensic and non-forensic (geopolitical) means increases. More simply, the more geopolitically significant an attack, the more information about that attack is likely to be available, consequently making attribution easier. For deterrence to be credible, attribution is important.[16] The absence of accurate and substantiated attribution can lead to unnecessary escalation and retaliation against a third party that did not perpetrate a cyberattack. A response predicated on faulty attribution, or based on attribution with insufficient evidence, could even be in violation of international law.[17]

Third, international law requires that retaliation (the punishment side of deterrence) be proportionate. The calibration of a proportionate response to a cyberattack is difficult. Several factors must be taken into account, such as time, perceptions of proportionality, and existing technical capacity to respond. The average time it takes to recognize that an attack is under way or has taken place is almost 200 days. Moreover, the time to contain such an attack is approximately 60 days. Lengthy delays in actuating deterrence weaken the credibility associated with threats of punishment. If a state waited six months to respond to a conventional kinetic or nuclear attack, the credibility of a threatened punishment would be almost entirely lost. Following 9/11, it only took the United States a few weeks to have the first Central Intelligence Agency (CIA) operators and Special Forces responding to the Taliban and Al-Qaeda in the remote reaches of Afghanistan. Time is important for deterrence at any level, from punishing a criminal within a "statute of limitations" to punishing states for violating a red line. Calibrating the timing of the (counter-)attack and the subsequent perception of this attack by an adversary is difficult. If retaliation through cyberspace occurs but the state being punished does not recognize it has been attacked for more than 200 days, it is uncertain whether the punishment is in response to a violation of a stated red line, or is itself a new attack.

The proportionality of a retaliatory response is further challenged by the complexities of cyberspace itself. A successful cyberattack against a power station might warrant a successful return cyberattack against the attacking nation's electric grid. But, unlike in the physical world where bombs, missiles and the planes that carry them are reliable and work across a wide range of relevant cases, in cyberspace developing a retaliatory attack against an adversary takes time to plan, engineers to scope the consequences of various effects, and lawyers to assess whether the retaliation meets international legal standards. Such a process also assumes there is a proportionate target to attack. This might not always be the case. For instance, the United States presents a target-rich environment for would-be state hackers. But a state such as the Democratic People's Republic of Korea (DPRK – North Korea) has relatively few connections to cyberspace, and even fewer that constitute proportionate targets for a retaliatory cyberattack. Since readily available proportionate retaliatory cyberattacks are not a certainty, states are forced to consider options that extend beyond cyberspace. These cross-domain options – for instance, retaliating to a cyberattack through economic sanctions – cause decision-makers to worry about potential conflict escalation and have been used sparingly.

Although many nations state their intention to retaliate to cyber-attacks, the evidence that states actually do retaliate is far from conclusive.[18] There are few definitive cases in which there was a clear retaliatory response to a cyberattack. This situation can be explained by the fact that no single attack rises to the level of an "armed attack" or "a use of force" necessary under international law for a state to retaliate. Instead, the vast majority of cyberattacks occur just below the threshold of "armed attack" or "use of force." Cyber adversaries can essentially bleed their targets dry of information without doing any physical harm.[19] Storybox 7.1 explores the claim that Chinese cyber theft and espionage operations have caused the greatest transfer of wealth in human history.

Storybox 7.1 The greatest transfer of wealth in human history

In 2005, *Time* magazine ran an article about Shawn Carpenter, an employee at Sandia National Laboratories who had discovered a security breach within the Sandia computers.[20] Carpenter alerted US Army Counterintelligence, who later turned the investigation over to the FBI. What Carpenter encountered at Sandia was the beginning of one of the most pervasive intelligence penetrations of the US DoD and national laboratories up to that point – an operation codenamed "Titan Rain." But Titan Rain was only the beginning and was followed by more than 38 substantial breaches involving hundreds of government agencies and departments in dozens of countries around the world, as well as hundreds more private companies and human rights activists, including the Dalai Lama, over the next ten years.[21]

The story of Titan Rain and the subsequent mass theft, espionage and surveillance programs undertaken by the Chinese began when PLA colonels Liang Qiao and Wang Xiansui published their book on *Unrestricted Warfare*.[22] In their volume, the colonels emphasized a new series of military strategies to undermine the strategic and tactical position of an adversary without triggering a military conflict. Within the next five years, China began a rapid trajectory of informatization across the whole of its society, and developed a strategy focused on China's need to develop its technological prowess. Titan Rain and the broader Chinese cyber theft and espionage campaign are now among the most visible aspects of this strategy.

Throughout the more than 38 uniquely named operations, Chinese-affiliated actors stole terabytes-worth of data. Yet no single attack constituted an armed attack or a use of force. China's sustained theft and espionage are considered by many to be the single largest transfer of wealth (via intellectual property theft) in human history.[23]

In 2013, cybersecurity firm Mandiant released a detailed report on one Chinese actor: Unit 61398.[24] Less than a year later, the US Department of Justice indicted five members of this unit on 31 charges. Little more than a year after the indictment, rumors began circulating through official corridors in Washington, DC, that the United States was developing severe sanctions in response to repeated Chinese hacking.[25] The sanctions were being timed with an upcoming 2015 summit between Chinese President Xi Jinping and US President Barack Obama. Upon receiving word of the impending sanctions, China dispatched a high-level delegation to forestall their implementation.[26] Negotiations appeared to work out when both leaders reiterated a strong commitment to cybersecurity during a joint press conference at the close of the summit. The following year, cybersecurity firm FireEye (which bought Mandiant) released a follow-up report that indicated that Chinese economic espionage had significantly declined following the 2015 summit.[27]

This example illustrates the use of multiple levels of deterrence, ranging from a criminological approach to a formal and credible signal of impending retaliation in the form of sanctions. The initial indicators of success in response to this approach appear to have been a decline in economic espionage, but the long-term results of this deterrent approach remain uncertain. However, the process of deterring China from engaging in economic espionage in cyberspace took more than ten years, and in the end resulted not from retaliatory response in cyberspace, but through a cross-domain threat of sanctions and the use of indictments.

Organizing defense

The sections above have focused on organizational-level defense ranging from supply chains and software development life cycles to cybersecurity frameworks and macro-level state cyber deterrence strategies. In tandem with all of these efforts, states have begun to establish military and civilian organizations specifically devoted to cyber defense. Nadiya Kostyuk finds that the organization of cyber commands constitutes a signal to other states of an organizational capacity for cyber defense and offense.[28]

Over the last decade, multiple states have established and developed cyber defensive organizations. Strategic documents now frequently touch upon the role of cyber commands. While the section heading mentions organizing for defense, the reality is that most commands are dual-hatted and often straddle the divide between purely reactive and proactive forms of defense. More defense-oriented organizations focus on deterrence by denial to protect national infrastructures. They typically engage in defensive network operations to identify and eliminate threats as they arise. Specifically, Cyber Protection Teams provide insights into the critical networks and infrastructures of their state and play a key role in their defense.

The current US strategy for its cyber command leans more heavily on the proactive than the reactive side of cyber defense. "Persistent Engagement – Defend Forward," which we examined in chapter 5, is rooted in the idea that it is better to defend your own network from inside your adversaries' network or in a third-party state, rather than in your own networks. The United States has developed and resourced this strategy amidst legal and international uncertainty. The present belief is that this approach is having a meaningful impact on national cybersecurity, yet even its authors would admit they would prefer most states not to be persistently engaged or defending from third-party or adversarial networks. The result would be a complex mess of actors each acting in one another's networks, thereby further complicating the cybersecurity landscape.

More recently, sub-national commands have sprung up in large municipalities. The most prominent and well known of these is the New York Cyber Command run out of the New York Office of Technology and Innovation. The principal goal of these municipal-level cyber commands is to provide cybersecurity support to local government agencies in large jurisdictions. The resourcing of cybersecurity in large municipalities is still not the norm and does not extend to all, or even many, major municipalities. Below the major municipality level, most small and medium-sized cities simply develop a patchwork quilt of security procedures and standards constrained by local decision-makers' awareness and resources.

Although cyber commands at all levels play an increasingly important role in facilitating cybersecurity, there remains a wide stratification both across and within nations. Establishing and resourcing cyber commands sufficiently is no easy task. Even when they are fully resourced, it is unlikely they will prevent all attacks. Where no formal cybersecurity mechanisms exist or there are rotating local officials, cybersecurity is likely to get lost in the mix of changing politics and budget cycles. The result is that attacks are extremely common and can at times severely impede the functionality of government. The institutionalization of cyber commands establishes a bureaucratic weight that elevates cyber-security concerns of different levels of government, making the issue harder to ignore and thereby increasing security in aggregate over the long term.

Conclusion: the painful reality

The painful reality for defense and deterrence in cyberspace is that there remains, for the foreseeable future, no foolproof means of protecting computers, networks or their users in cyberspace. Since the challenges facing cyber defenders are so great, cyberspace is often referred to as an offense-dominant domain.[29] A preponderance of data currently indi-cates that defense in cyberspace is difficult, but primarily when facing espionage and theft. Some scholars contend that the balance between offense and defense is of little consequence, and that investment in cyber capabilities – whether offensive or defensive – matters most to achieve goals. Rebecca Slayton, for example, argues that the development costs of the exploits used to damage Iran's nuclear facilities at Natan exceeded the defensive costs undertaken by Iran to protect their networks and facilities, and the costs of repair to those facilities once damaged.[30] These direct cost–benefit analyses are helpful for conceptualizing raw inputs, but fail to consider the psychological impact that cyberattacks have. In the case of Iran, the Stuxnet worm caused significant distress and con-cern for engineers and within the military. In the absence of information on the source of their system failures, it was assumed they were experi-encing technical difficulties due to poorly sourced goods or engineering.

There are very few examples of cyberattacks that have achieved violent effects resulting in the physical destruction of property. Cases such as the Stuxnet attack on Iran's nuclear facilities at Natanz, the Iranian hacking of a spillway dam,[31] cyberattacks on a German steel mill in 2014,[32] and several others are relatively rare but stand out in the public conscious-ness. When attacks occur that rise to the level of an armed attack or use of force, they often make the problem of deterrence substantially easier. The more pervasive forms of theft and espionage require states to consistently develop and implement both technical and policy mecha-nisms to address increasingly sophisticated threats that do not readily fit within international legal frameworks related to acceptable retaliation.

The costs of organizing for cyber defense are expected to grow. In 2004, the global cybersecurity market was worth $3.5 billion; by 2017, that number exceeded $120 billion,[33] and by 2023 the market was estimated at $249.88 billion.[34]

Countries and companies are in a technical and financial race that seems unsustainable and appears to be making little dent in the overall trends of crime and espionage. Hardly a day goes by without a news story discussing yet another breach of a company or government agency somewhere in the world. To address the unsustainable nature of defense in cyberspace, states are trying to deter adversaries from engaging in further cyberattacks through multilateral institutions and bilateral signals. Yet, with a few exceptions, deterrence in cyberspace has largely failed to dissuade adversaries from attacking networks and the computers within them.

Discussion questions

1. Why are deterrence and defense so difficult in cyberspace?

2. What makes attribution so important to deterrence?

3. What should states prioritize – defense or deterrence?

Exercise

Select a country and draw a map of the key organizations responsible for cyber defense at the national level. Include a brief description of their core responsibilities and current strategy.

Additional resources

The *Cyber Defense Review*, at https://cyberdefensereview.army.mil.

Brantly, A. (ed.), *The Cyber Deterrence Problem* (Lanham, MD: Rowman & Littlefield, 2020).

Martin C. Libicki, *Cyberdeterrence and Cyberwar* (Santa Monica, CA: RAND, 2009), www.rand.org/content/dam/rand/pubs/monographs/2009/ RAND_ MG877.pdf.

National Institute of Standards Computer Security Resource Center, https:// csrc.nist.gov/publications/sp800.

8   Non-state threats: from cybercrime to terrorism

Reader's guide

- Quantitatively, non-state actors are the largest threat to cybersecurity.

- Cyber criminality is the most prominent non-state threat. The growing range of online criminal behavior includes forms of (cyber)trespassing, deception/fraud/extortion, theft and violence.

- Hacktivism targets the confidentiality, integrity and availability of data to further social and political ends. The term encompasses a broad range of actors, means and ends.

- "Cyberterrorism" refers to the use of cyberspace to commit terrorism. Achieving the type of political violence generally associated with terrorism in and through cyberspace is difficult. To date, organizations such as the Islamic State have demonstrated limited cyber offensive capabilities to spread and amplify their message.

- State actors increasingly rely on non-state actors to conduct unacknowledged operations in and through cyberspace. This trend has fostered a debate on the drivers and implications of so-called cyber proxies.

Although states inspire the greatest fear in cyberspace, they are not the most prolific malfeasant actor category or the most pervasive threat to the average netizen. Three categories of non-state actor generate the majority of havoc that occurs in cyberspace. Criminals, hacktivists and terrorists in combination far exceed states in volume and variety of daily attacks and thefts that occur in and through cyberspace. Criminal actors constitute the largest and most substantial threat to cybersecurity, trailed at a distance by hacktivists and terrorists.

The low barriers to entry and the wide reach and impact of cyberspace enable these non-state actors to pose security threats. For criminals, hacktivists and terrorists, the continued expansion of cyberspace and its associated technologies provides ample fertile ground for the development of capabilities within an environment that poses little risk to their physical safety. When asked why he robbed banks, the famous bank robber Willy Sutton responded: "because that's where the money is."[1] If criminals, hacktivists or terrorists were asked the same about their use of cyberspace, they would no doubt provide a similar response. For criminals, cyberspace is where the majority of the wealth and information of the world resides and transits each day. For hacktivists, it is the new public square, with moderate amounts of anonymity, allowing them to form robust groups able to work together with low costs for communications and organization. Lastly, for terrorists, cyberspace is where many potential recruits can be reached, and a medium through which they can elevate their power relative to states at a low cost and potentially high return on investment. The first three sections of this chapter examine each of these categories of actor and emphasize their motivations and the threats they pose. A fourth section focuses on so-called cyber proxies, and discusses the complex links between state and non-state threats in cyberspace.

Cyberspace is ripe for exploitation by non-state actors in most, but not all, states. In states where cyberspace is open and accessible, non-state actors have substantial room to maneuver, both legally and illegally. By contrast, in states where cyberspace is not friendly to non-state actors, such actors are often mobilized as proxies to enhance the cyber power of a state. The threats posed by non-state actors in and through cyberspace are substantial and, while unlikely to result in catastrophic attacks rising to the scale and complexity of a state-sponsored act of cyber war, the volume of non-state attacks can substantially overwhelm and challenge a state's capacity to respond to specific incidents. Addressing non-state threats in cyberspace requires resources. We examine these broad categories of non-state actors independently below to highlight their unique utilization of cyberspace and the challenges they present to states, from criminological to national security threats.

Criminals

Cybercrime is by far the most prolific and arguably impactful threat in cyberspace. The proliferation of malware, combined with its relative ease of use and online anonymity, enable a panoply of criminal endeavors. The FBI Internet Crime Complaint Center, in its 2022 report on

Internet crime, documented $10.3 billion in losses, based on approximately 800,944 reports over the course of one year. IBM estimates that the average cost of a data breach in 2023 was $4.45 million, up 15.3 percent over 2020.[2] Internet security firm McAfee estimates that total global cybercrime cost companies, individuals and governments $1 trillion in 2020, an increase of 50 percent from 2018.[3] This equates to a global GDP loss of approximately 1.1 percent for that year. Some estimates place the global impact of cybercrime much higher. Its impact varies widely by country, with North America, Europe and Central Asia, and East Asia and the Pacific, suffering the greatest financial losses.

Most conversations on cybercrime emphasize the financial losses incurred by victims. Cybercrime, however, encompasses multiple classes and categories of behavior. Early definitions of cybercrime focused on four categories of crime originating in, or occurring through, cyberspace or computers. These included cybertrespassing, deception and theft, cyber pornography and, finally, cyber violence.[4] For the purposes of this section, we examine cybertrespassing, deception/fraud/extortion, theft, violence, illicit commerce and a variety of sexual crimes. Cybercrimes involve criminal acts conducted on or with a computer, or within cyberspace. As this section illustrates, the expansion of cyberspace parallels a rise in criminal behavior online.

Cybertrespassing is the intentional unauthorized access to, or alteration, deletion, damage or destruction, or disruption of a computer, network, program or data. Trespassing in cyberspace is one of the most common criminal offenses and occurs across a variety of criminal contexts. One of the most famous examples of cybertrespassing was briefly examined in previous chapters: when Mathew Broderick's character in the movie *WarGames* hacks into his school's computers to change grades, hacks into software vendors to steal games, and breaks into NORAD's computer systems. While *WarGames* was a work of fiction, there are regular attempts globally by students to hack into and alter grades, steal tests, or a variety of other acts that constitute cybertrespassing. For instance, in April 2018, hackers attempted to hack a Fairfax County, Virginia, high school to alter grades from Fs to As.[5] The perpetrators were caught and charged by local police.

Cyber deception/fraud/extortion is the deliberate obfuscation and manipulation of intent, characteristics (physical, logical or human persona) and behaviors in cyberspace for the purposes of gaining access to or altering the intended functioning of a computer, network, program or user. Deception is the primary means by which criminals manipulate human users. Deception in cyberspace is often referred to as social engineering and can enable cybertrespassing or other criminal activities. The most famous form of cyber deception is that of the Nigerian Prince email scam, which attempted to prey upon unsuspecting recipients who might willingly transfer money to an unverified third party. Cyber deception resulting in fraud or extortion can take the form of email system compromises, the theft of personal data for use in identify theft, denials of service to reorient users to other services or networks, malware or scareware that falsely present users with warnings of system compromise, phishing and spoofing – the use of fake documents, emails or text messages to enable access to computers or networks.

An increasingly prolific form of cyber extortion is the use of malware that, when installed on a target, encrypts all files on that system. Known as ransomware, these attacks require a system's owner to pay a fee in bitcoin or another cryptocurrency to unlock their files. Ransomware attacks have been targeted at a wide array of institutions, businesses and individuals. Targets unwilling to pay a ransom run the risk of total data loss. Such attacks are increasing in number and diverse in their targets. One widely publicized attack occurred in 2016 when a hacker encrypted portions of the San Francisco Municipal Transportation Agency, including its ticket-purchasing terminals, and requested a $70,000 ransom. The transportation agency never considered paying the ransom and instead reinstalled the software on impacted systems. The payment of a ransom is not a guarantee that files will be decrypted as some implementations of ransomware are poorly written and fail to decrypt data even when the ransom is paid, as was the case of WannaCry in 2017. A lone grey hat hacker – Marcus Hutchens, also known online as MalwareTech – discovered that the WannaCry ransomware was calling back to an unregistered domain name. Once he registered the domain name, it created a kill switch that resulted in all infected systems calling back to that domain and subsequently resulted in their decryption.

Ransomware has become a scourge in cyberspace. The 2017 NotPetya attack on Ukraine leveraged an exploit in accounting software to distribute ransomware throughout Ukraine and global businesses resulting in billions of dollars of damages and shutting down global shipping for multiple firms. Another major ransomware, conducted by the ransomware gang DarkSide, resulted in the temporary shutdown of the Colonial Pipeline, a major oil pipeline that runs across much of the south-eastern United States, causing fuel shortages and increasing gasoline costs. Both the above attacks took place in a grey zone in which criminal groups likely act as proxy for a state actor – Russia in this case. Ransomware has grown to be one of the most damaging types of attacks globally and is perpetrated by a range of actors, from criminals that sell ransomware as a service – such as Hive, DarkSide, Revil, Dharma and LockBit – to more established criminal groups such as Conti and Lorenz. Targets of ransomware have been extremely widespread globally, including universities, hospitals, schools, casinos, transportation providers and many more. As with most cyberattacks, ransomware nearly always begins with deception or fraud, often in the form of social engineering.

Deception for fraud and extortion is the most common method criminal actors use to violate computers and networks. Metadata spoofing, the alteration of sender information, and the replication of common visual identifiers within emails, text messages or other communications media are common tactics. Figure 8.1 is an example of a spoofed email using both metadata (the sender poses as Amazon) and visual replication (the Amazon logos) to deceive the recipient. Typosquatting is another common form of deception used by criminals to replicate the look of a known website and involves registering a similar domain name accessed through the accidental misspelling of an intended website (e.g. typing foogle.com instead of google.com).[6] Criminals often use broad deception techniques that work well against large numbers of individuals. This

Figure 8.1 Phishing email example

Source: Softpedia[7]

approach seeks to maximize return on investment for the criminal. In certain instances, criminals leverage specific techniques or information to "spear phish" or "whale" a single (individual) target who might prove to be a lucrative mark. However, more time and effort are required for tailored deception for fraud and extortion, with limited increases in the probability for success.

Cyber theft is the theft of data or resources from a computer or network. The most commonly considered form of cyber theft is that of data theft for use in fraud. Theft can be achieved through a variety of means but is frequently instigated via the human persona layer. One of the largest incidents of cyber theft occurred in 2013 when hackers breached the point-of-sale systems of Target Corporation, the second-largest department store retailing in the United States, via the heating, ventilation and air conditioning units installed in stores. The hack resulted in the theft of 40 million debit and credit card numbers and 70 million records of personal information.[8] The theft of credit card information and personal data is a common occurrence. However, the Target hack led to a temporary multi-billion dollar decrease in Target's market capitalization, hundreds of millions of dollars in lost sales during the 2013 holiday season, $200 million in credit and debit card reissuance costs for banks, and an $18.5 million settlement with 47 states. The incident itself was not isolated and was followed several months later by an equally large data breach of American home improvement supplies company Home Depot in 2014.[9]

The Target and Home Depot hacks are part of a larger trend in criminal activities online. These activities seek the centralized accumulation of data in repositories. Attacks against corporate databases, email servers and point-of-sale systems often emphasize the theft of personally identifiable information (PII) that results in financial damage well beyond the initial corporate victim of an attack. The loss of PII, which is subsequently sold online in dark markets, leads to identity theft and results in substantial harm to individuals least able to address such challenges.

Data theft by cyber criminals is rampant, and the intersection of theft and organized criminal activities is growing and rapidly becoming a multi-billion-dollar industry.[10] A relatively new form of cyber theft seeks to exploit the victim's computational power. The theft of resources for the creation of botnets, collections of enslaved computers, has been around for quite some time and was used in the 2007 DDoS attacks against Estonia and the 2008 attacks against the Republic of Georgia.[11] The purchase of enslaved machines in botnets is a readily available service on the dark web. Figure 8.2 is an image of the logo of the Tech service

Figure 8.2 Logo of the Tech of the Islamic State

of the Islamic State, who provided information-technical solutions to avoid intelligence and law enforcement agencies. There are documented cases of members of the Islamic State purchasing DDoS capabilities via the dark web. The use of DDoS as a criminal tool to degrade or hold to ransom the websites of businesses, and the terrorist usage of the same tool to achieve political effects, highlight both the linkages between criminal and terror networks and the diffusion of tools and tactics across actor categories.

The utilization of botnets to create increasingly powerful DDoS attacks has begun to shift toward the creation of wealth through the theft of computational resources beyond extortion and political effects. Botnets stealing the computational resources of unsuspecting victims are available for sale in various time and scale increments.[12] While the theft of computer resources for botnets is not new, the rise of cryptocurrencies – virtual currencies representing monetary values equivalent to fiat currencies such as the US dollar – such as Bitcoin and Ethereum has resulted in the theft of computer resources for the purposes of mining for potential profits.[13] The theft of computer resources for cryptocurrency mining, a practice known as cryptojacking, steals the computer cycle resources, slowing down the functional operation of computers and increasing the energy consumption of those computers substantially. As the computational resources associated with mining cryptocurrencies have increased, the prevalence of cryptojacking has declined. This illustrates a technological feature of cybercriminality: criminals tend to look for the best return on investment. When that return on investment becomes too costly or the rewards for a particular type of exploitation decline due to technological change, criminals tend to shift their efforts to other targets of opportunity.

Corresponding to the rise in the value of cryptocurrencies was a dramatic increase in the number of attempts to steal the digital wallets that store the information (private keys) associated with the accumulated digital currency. Storybox 8.1 details one of the largest cryptocurrency heists in history.

Storybox 8.1 Cryptojacking for the state: Lazarus

In March 2022 the Ronin Network – a blockchain platform powering the popular mobile game Axie Infinity – had more than $600 million in cryptocurrency stolen from its wallet. Axie Infinity is an online video game based on non-fungible tokens (NFTs) that uses Ethereum-based cryptocurrencies to create, sell and manipulate axolotl-inspired digital pets referred to as Axies. The popularity of the game led to its rapid growth after 2018 and resulted in the company changing security settings in its back-end servers to accommodate a large influx of new users. The alterations to its security settings created a backdoor into the company's servers which allowed hackers to infiltrate and steal the private keys from the company's wallets.[14]

Cybersecurity firm Chainanalysis was tasked with investigating the hack and seeking out ways to recover as much of the stolen funds as possible.[15] Chainanalysis investigator Erin Plante led a team who discovered that the money had been stolen and then put into a service called Tornado Cash, an open source, non-custodial fully decentralized cryptocurrency "tumbler," a service designed to obscure the origin and destination of cryptocurrency funds rapidly and effectively across multiple wallets.[16]

Over the course of her team's investigation, Plante discovered that the perpetrator of the hack was the notorious North Korean hacker group the Lazarus Group, also known as the Guardians of Peace (from the 2014 hack and leak of confidential data from the film studio Sony Pictures Entertainment) and the WHOIS Group. Representatives of the FBI indicated that the Lazarus Group had stolen the money and laundered it with the intent of supporting the North Korean state in their pursuit of Weapons of Mass Destruction. Although the hack was discovered, and many of the subsequent destination wallets were identified, most of the $600 million was not recovered. As of this writing, only about $30 million was publicly acknowledged as recovered.[17] This hack highlights a potent criminal/state nexus examined later in this chapter in a section on cyber proxies.

Cyber theft for criminal ends is distinguishable from espionage in its profit-seeking motive. The breadth and depth of examples of cyber theft are far too numerous to list here. However, it is safe to say that, in line with the statistics presented in the introduction to this chapter, the problem of cyber theft is growing substantially year on year. Cybercrime is also diversifying in ways that reflect technological change. Cybercriminals tend to seek out the most profitable areas to the exclusion of others. While selling data from data breaches online can earn them money through credit card fraud, identity fraud and other nefarious means, the present large-scale criminal enterprise in cyberspace is ransomware.

Cyber violence is the utilization of cyberspace to achieve physical or psychological effects against target users or their systems. Unlike in the Bruce Willis action film *Live Free or Die Hard* (2007), it is unlikely that hackers are going to cause remote computers to explode and kill their users anytime soon. This is not to say that hackers have not achieved physical violence against computers or their associated systems in recent years. One of the earliest incidents of physical criminal violence achieved through hacking occurred a decade ago, when a 14-year-old modified a TV remote and used it to maneuver and derail trams in the city of Łódź, Poland, injuring 12 people.[18] Hacks that induce physical violence have been rare, but hackers have demonstrated the possibility for criminals to achieve physical violence.

The more pernicious and common forms of criminal violence in cyberspace have been cyberbullying and cyberstalking. Cyberbullying is "the willful and repeated harm inflicted through the use of computers, cell phones, and other electronic devices."[19] Cyberbullying is a more modern take on conventional bullying that has resulted in suicides and murders, and has been indicated as a contributing factor in mass shootings.[20] Some studies indicate that up to 28 percent of all students experience cyberbullying during their secondary school education.[21] While often overlooked in discussions on cybercrime, cyberbullying is a criminal offense that has resulted in numerous criminal convictions.

Closely related to cyberbullying, cyberstalking is the "repeated use of the Internet, e-mail, or related digital electronic communication devices to annoy, alarm, or threaten a specific individual or group of individuals."[22] All 50 states in the United States and most nations have enacted laws pertaining to stalking. Cyberstalking extends criminal acts of stalking into cyberspace and creates a pervasive and damaging set of conditions that harms victims.[23] In 2013, three members of the Matusiewicz family were sentenced to life in prison for cyberstalking resulting in death, when the family members engaged in physical and online surveillance and abuse of their victims, the ex-wife of one of the defendants and one of her children, in the US state of Delaware.[24] Criminal cyberstalking can be both technical and nontechnical – however, the common linking factor is the use of computers and associated technologies to threaten and harass victims. Criminal violence in cyberspace is complex and often extends violent acts found in traditional criminal activities to the new domain. Although cyberstalking and cyberbullying are often beyond the scope of broad cybercriminal analyses, they are unfortunately very common and result in substantial harm to victims.

Illicit marketplaces are commerce sites commonly hosted in dark web services, such as I2P and Tor, which provide customers with access to drugs, guns, credit and debit cards, hacking tools, pornography or a range of other illegal wares. The most famous illicit market, also referred to as a dark market, was Silk Road. Silk Road was a one-stop shop for a variety of drugs and illegal goods, run by an American, Ross William Ulbricht, also known as the "Dread Pirate Roberts." On February 4, 2014, the FBI indicted Ulbricht for narcotics trafficking conspiracy.[25] Dread Pirate Roberts ran what was, at the time, one of the largest dark markets, with thousands of users engaged in illicit sales using cryptocurrencies.[26] Dark markets in 2022 accounted for more than $470 million in yearly drug sales, and leverage transnational shipping and postal services as couriers.[27] Despite repeated takedowns by government authorities around the world, these markets continue to redeploy and sell illicit items. Figure 8.3 is an image from a weapons site that has since been taken down, but which purported to sell everything from landmines to rockets. The use of hidden services within Tor to host dark markets is extremely controversial as the technical construction and operation of Tor is partially funded by the United States government and is the result of a naval research laboratory's project. The challenge of halting dark markets is ongoing and will probably expand as cryptocurrencies become more common and encryption technologies make anonymous commerce increasingly feasible.

Sexual crimes via cyberspace include the transmission of images of child pornography, rape, mutilation, bestiality, enslavement and a variety of other associated crimes facilitated by cyberspace. Among all forms of crime, US law enforcement considers child pornography to be the most serious and damaging form of criminal behavior in cyberspace.[28] The FBI estimated that its analysts reviewed more than 26 million images and videos of abuse in 2015 alone.[29] The National Center for Missing and Exploited Children (NCMEC) reported locating more

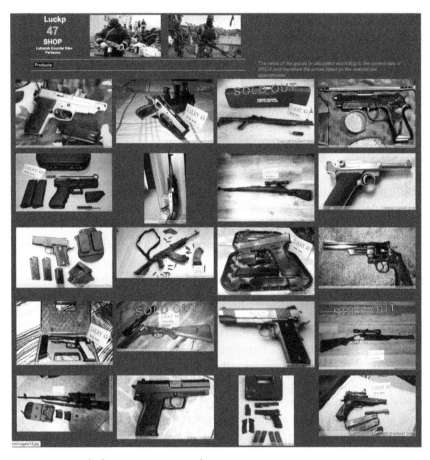

Figure 8.3 A dark net weapons market
Source: Accessed by the authors

than 10,500 victims of child pornography, with more than 4.4 million reports submitted.[30] One FBI investigation found that a single website showing child pornography hosted within Tor had 200,000 registered users.[31] NCMEC reported that it had identified an additional 4,260 new child pornography victims in 2021 alone and received more than 29.3 million reports of child pornography across 143 countries.[32] One man, Matthew Falder, leveraged cyberspace to blackmail 46 victims into sending increasingly explicit sexual images.[33] Three of his victims attempted to commit suicide.[34] The use of cyberspace for the facilitation and transmission of images and video for the blackmail of victims for the purposes of sexual crime, is unfortunately among the most common criminal activities within cyberspace. Very often, the investigation and subsequent prosecution of sex crimes facilitated in and through cyberspace require transnational cooperation among law-enforcement and intelligence agencies.

Although the impacts of economic cybercrime are often at the forefront of national and international discussions, the multitude of other criminal acts perpetrated in and through cyberspace is substantial and challenges all levels of jurisdictions from local communities to transnational bodies. Closely related, and often within the scope of cybercrime, is hacktivism. However, because the intentions of these individuals often – although not always – differ from "the purely criminal" intent, they are analyzed separately below.

Hacktivists

The term "hacktivist" combines "computer hacker" and "activist."[35] Hacktivism, while commonly associated with the collective known as Anonymous, has roots dating back to the early days of the Internet. Early hacktivists engaged in "digital sit-ins" by visiting sites or engaging in acts to consume the computer resources of an entity, to signal moral, ethical or political disfavor with the activities of an organization or entity.[36] Hacktivism commonly revolves around a variety of techniques meant to disrupt, or degrade, the operational status of servers or computers, through the use of DoS or DDoS attacks, social engineering, cross-site scripting (XSS),[37] injections of Structured Query Language (SQL – a language used to manage data)[38] or other minimally to moderately technical attacks. Although originally a means to engage in activism online for political, moral or ethical signaling, hacktivism expanded substantially when, in 2008, "anons" (anonymous users) of the popular site 4Chan formed an organic effort in response to a leaked video of actor Tom Cruise promoting the Church of Scientology.[39] Anons began coordinating efforts to attack the organization via various Internet fora and chatrooms. Prior to the 2008 attacks on the Church of Scientology, many anons hacked or engineered targets for the lulz (a pluralization of the term "LOL": "Laugh Out Loud").[40] Much of the early lulz-inspired hacking targeted individuals engaged in child pornography, businesses or organizations that could be easily spoofed for "fun," and gave hackers a sense of power over their victims as well as amusement. Most of these hacks are criminal in nature, but distinguished from the profit-seeking, violent and sexually exploitative acts discussed in the previous section.

Individuals with a wide range of skills populate the ranks of hacktivist communities. The distribution of skills skews toward those with limited technical hacking abilities, but this does not limit their participation in the operations – or #Ops – that their community plans. Tools such as the Low Orbit Ion Cannon (LOIC) – a DoS application – enable any user to engage in coordinated operations established by Anonymous. However, the impact of LOIC is relatively small compared to that of botnets managed by some of the collective's more talented hackers.

Anonymous is famous for its creed:

> *We are Anonymous.*
> *We are Legion.*
> *We do not forgive.*
> *We do not forget.*
> *Expect us.*

Anonymous is made up of members from nearly every country in the world. The collective functions as a decentralized and loosely coordinated group that plans and executes operations against various targets. Sometimes these operations are motivated politically, and sometimes they are for lulz. One of their most famous operations, Operation Avenge Assange, included attacking banking and credit card systems in response to the blocking of donations to file-sharing site Wikileaks, following the release of Chelsea Manning's documents. Operation Payback was a response to Bollywood companies attacking the popular peering site The Pirate Bay. Anonymous participants planned to attack Aiplex Software, the firm hired to DDoS The Pirate Bay, only to find it had already been DDoSed by an unknown hacktivist, and instead turned their attention to the Motion Picture Association of America, the International Federation of the Phonographic Industry, the Recording Industry Association of America and the British Phonographic Industry.[41] In 2015, Anonymous famously declared "war" on the Islamic State in the aptly named "OPISIS."[42] #OPISIS arose following the attacks on Charlie Hebdo in Paris and sought to identify and take down ISIS-affiliated Twitter accounts and websites around the world. Experts have found the impact of #OPISIS on the operational capacity of the Islamic State was negligible.[43]

Although the most famous grouping of hacktivists is Anonymous, they are probably not the most impactful. "Patriotic" hackers generally fall under the same rubric of hacktivism. Members of Anonymous have been instrumental in signaling displeasure to states following a variety of diplomatic incidents. Alex Klimburg writes that states can motivate, and often work in tandem with, non-state hackers to signal intentions to other states.[44] There have been numerous incidents of "patriotic hackers" coming to the "aid" of states in times of perceived crisis. In 2001, following the mid-air collision of a US surveillance plane and a Chinese fighter aircraft, Chinese hackers defaced a number of prominent websites in the United States. In 2007 and 2008, Russian "patriotic hackers" closely timed DDoS, XSS, SQL injections and a variety of other attacks against both Estonia and the Republic of Georgia, when international relations between these states and Russia hit new lows.[45]

Criminal cyber activities – such as financial crimes, and violent, harassing and sexual acts online – are often motivated for a variety of nefarious reasons. Similarly, the motivations of hacktivists are equally diverse, and complex. Simply hacking for lulz would not constitute hacktivism, and instead is more akin to low-level criminal deviance. Hacktivism spans a gambit of motivations, from libertarian ideals of freedom of information and anarchic tendencies, on one side, to highly motivated patriotic or nationalistic tendencies on the other side of the spectrum. Despite the alignment of the state and hacktivists' motivations on the patriotic side of the spectrum in some instances, the position of hacktivists is not static. Today's patriotic hacker can be tomorrow's anarchist or libertarian, following changes in laws or government policies. Slightly outside of the spectrum of hacktivism, which ranges from libertarian–anarchistic to patriotic–nationalistic ideas, is yet another category, best described as nihilistic, which focuses on the absence of belief.

Hacktivism and hacktivists have found a prominent home within popular culture, yet the overarching difficulty in engaging in highly complex cyber capability development at the individual level, or even through decentralized collectives, remains one of the largest impediments to making this category of hackers a substantial threat. Over the last two decades, many organizations have learned to deal with the techniques employed by hacktivists, such as XSS, SQL injection and even DDoS, thus impairing their impact. Hacktivists often reuse tools and resources and attack 1-day or 1-day+ exploits – meaning that they leverage exploits that have previously been discovered and might have been patched. The resources available to hacktivists are substantial within deep and dark websites. By pooling their efforts, hacktivists are increasingly able to access capabilities and resources that exceed those of any one individual. Yet their ability to coordinate and undertake large-scale operations remains limited by a number of costs – for instance, those associated with surveillance and reconnaissance. While the threat hacktivists present to states is limited, they are still able to cause some damage and can embarrass or even harm individuals, corporations and governments through doxing (the search for and publishing of private or identifying information about an individual on the Internet for malicious intent) or social engineering, among a variety of other potential exploits.

The diversity of actors and motivations driving cybercrime has spawned a robust literature on cyber criminology. Scholarship examines the range of motivational factors behind cybercrime, from financial, to sociological, to psychological. Although early analysis of virus writers found some common threads in the psychology of hackers and their divergent behaviors in online and offline environments,[46] most of the literature demonstrates that there is no single model to explain what drives hackers. Rather, there are a number of social constructions associated with hackers, some of which lead to more deviant behaviors than others.[47] What is known is that the overwhelming majority of cyber criminals are male, and often quite young. Although there are some older cyber criminals, much of the literature identifies a process of "aging out," with exceptions being made for more organized groups, such as ransomware groups. A cursory examination of the cybercrime literature reveals that the motivations for crime in online spaces are much more complicated than the quote from Willie Sutton at the beginning of this chapter would imply. There are, no doubt, profit motives, but there is also an inherent creativity – and therefore probably also narcissistic motives – to many of the acts of cybercrime being perpetrated. Where cybercrime leads to more explicit monetary reward, criminal behaviors in cyberspace are more likely to align with their analog counterparts. By contrast, however, where monetary gain is not involved, the literature provides a broad range of explanations, from youthful malfeasance to vindictive and predatory behaviors. In particularly well-documented cases, it is possible to witness the same hacker moving across different types of criminal and non-criminal or hacktivist behaviors. In other cases, more concrete motivations are obvious throughout. What links all theories of cybercrime is the use of connected technologies. Just as these technologies enable new forms of communication, commerce and so much more, they also enable new avenues for criminal behavior.

Inverting the issue, Holt and colleagues make the case that one pernicious issue associated with cybercrime is the lack of conventional law-enforcement attention paid to the subject.[48] Their data illustrate that law enforcement agencies generally do not consider criminal offenses occurring in and through cyberspace as analogous to crimes committed in the physical world.[49] Through training and education, it is important to increasingly elevate the issue of cybercrime within traditional policing circles. Until such time as the issue is taken seriously, the scale and scope of crime are likely to grow not solely because of technical capabilities, but also because of a lack of law enforcement.

Cyberterrorists

Since 9/11, an overwhelming amount of resources and research has been devoted to cyberterrorism. There have been many prognostications of forthcoming doom due to the terrorist use of cyberspace. Despite the multitude of articles written on the subject, both in the academic and the popular press, and the large number of successful cyberattacks conducted by "cyberterrorists," relatively few have resulted in meaningful consequences. Most terrorist-perpetrated cyberattacks have come in the form of XSS, SQL injection or the release of documents already publicly available. While the impact of terrorist cyberattacks has centered mainly on website defacement and document dumps of quasi-private information, terrorist use of cyberspace has changed the way in which terrorists organize, recruit and plan operations in the physical world. Early debates put a great deal of emphasis on understanding and preventing potential terrorist attacks in and through cyberspace. In the last few years, experts have increasingly emphasized the use of cyberspace for the organization and planning of terrorist incidents.

Cyberterrorists differ from both cyber criminals and hacktivists primarily in their motives. Differentiating between the motives of some cyberterrorists and some hacktivists requires walking a very thin line. At its most basic, cyberterrorism is the use of cyberspace to commit terrorism.[50] This definition begs the question of what constitutes terrorism. Terrorism, according to Bruce Hoffman, "is violence – or, equally important, the threat of violence – used and directed in pursuit of, or in service of, a political aim."[51] This definition, though it is debatable, reveals the greatest impediment to terrorism in cyberspace: the ability to commit or credibly threaten violence. Few violent cyber incidents have occurred in the young history of cyber conflict, other than accidental hacking and the use of a reprogrammed remote control in Poland by a teenager to crash streetcars. These incidents do not fit with common definitions of terrorism because they were apolitical. Achieving political violence through cyberspace is extremely difficult and requires a complex set of skills that can often only be provided by multiple individuals working together within a stable environment. Creating politically violent effects in cyberspace often requires advanced persistent presence within a remote system, which necessitates intelligence, surveillance and reconnaissance, and often C2 capabilities. The costs associated with developing a violent cyberattack are comparatively low for state actors, relative to other weapon systems, yet they are high for non-state actors such as terrorists, absent third-party funding. Storybox 8.2 discusses some of the hackers and hacks of the Islamic State in Iraq and Syria (ISIS).

Storybox 8.2 The ISIS hackers

Throughout late 2014 and into 2015, a group of ISIS-affiliated hackers known as teaMp0ison claimed credit for a variety of hacks, including the hacking of the Twitter and YouTube accounts of US Central Command (CENTCOM) on the same day that US President Barack Obama gave a speech on cybersecurity.[52] Hackers posted a variety of Tweets with missives against the United States and the coalition battling ISIS. One post said "In the name of Allah, the Most Gracious, the Most Merciful, the CyberCaliphate continues its CyberJihad," while another said: "American soldiers, we are coming, watch your back."[53] While briefly in control of CENTCOM's accounts, the hackers also posted what they claimed were classified documents stolen from CENTCOM and other US military and intelligence agencies. These claims were subsequently debunked.[54]

Analysis from the University of Toronto's Citizen Lab found evidence that ISIS-affiliated groups also probably engaged in targeting of human rights activists and others in Syria through social engineering and spyware.[55] Analyses from multiple sources indicate that the level of hacking skill within the various hacking teams in ISIS was relatively low. The cyber jihadis used a variety of readily available social engineering techniques and malware.

The most prominent ISIS hacker on teaMp0ison was a British Pakistani man named Junaid Hussain. Hussain had a previous criminal record, including an arrest for hacking into the email account of former British Prime Minister Tony Blair in 2012.[56] Hussain, other hackers from teaMp0ison, and other groups including Lizard Squad attempted to form what they referred to as the "Cyber Caliphate."[57] The Cyber Caliphate engaged in low- to moderate-level hacking and extensive social engineering. In addition to their hacking prowess, members including Hussain became well-known ISIS propagandists.

Junaid Hussain is thought to have been added to the Disposition Matrix, a US government "kill list" for high-level targets, primarily because of his propaganda efforts and ability to inspire "lone-wolf" terrorism, rather than his hacking skills. Hussain was killed in a drone strike on August 24, 2015, according to US government sources.[58] He is the only known hacker to have been deliberately targeted by a drone strike.

Although cyberterrorists have attracted much attention, their skill levels tend to be low to moderate. Those few terrorists who do possess substantial hacking skills have so far been unable to regroup and achieve a level of coordination comparable to large criminal enterprises, hacker collectives such as Anonymous, or states. Yet, despite a lack of numbers, members of Al-Qaeda and ISIS, among other terrorist groups, have made substantial headway into cyberspace in a variety of contexts. Most notably, hacker groups such as the Cyber Caliphate and others are responsible for a variety of website defacements and doxing.[59]

Cyberterrorists to date have almost exclusively gone after low-level targets, generally websites with known vulnerabilities. However, with state assistance from sponsoring regimes such as Iran, cyberterrorists might be able to substantially increase their capabilities. Although cyberterrorists are not presently a major threat to states, their attacks do impose costs and challenge a variety of smaller actors. Cyberterrorist doxing efforts have proven particularly disturbing and have led to the release of personal information on public officials around the world – most notably on members of the US military. Often the release of documents is accompanied by calls within terrorist propaganda channels to target the individuals named in the documents. To date, there are no known instances in which individuals named within such documents were subsequently killed by terrorists.

Terrorists most commonly use cyberspace to organize and coordinate their activities, communicate propaganda and recruit new members.[60] In November 2008, terrorists from Lashkar-e-Taiba (LeT) killed more than 172 people in an attack on hotels and streets in Mumbai, India. Subsequent investigations found that the terrorists had leveraged mobile communications, online groups and Google Earth mapping to plan and organize the resources for the attack. Since then, dozens of physical attacks have similarly relied on cyberspace to plan and coordinate terror in the physical world. One of the most notable attacks occurred in 2015 when ISIS-inspired attacks on Paris led to the deaths of 137.

The reach and messaging of terrorist organizations are both extended and amplified within cyberspace. Services such as Twitter (now "X") and Facebook provide a readily available and accessible platform for group organization and mobilization.[61] While the use of these platforms by terrorists is widespread, it is not without challenges. Intelligence and law-enforcement agencies have long sought to use the open distribution of information on these platforms to identify, interdict or capture terrorists in advance of, or following, attacks. Their efforts have forced terrorists to adopt new tactics to avoid being caught, using encryption and software or protocols that enable or facilitate anonymity.[62] Terrorists have also shown a moderate level of interest in the utilization of cryptocurrencies such as bitcoin, to evade restrictions on money laundering and financial transfers for criminal or illicit purposes.[63]

Starting in 2015, the US Army Cyber Command began directly targeting ISIS and Al-Qaeda networks in what has become known as Joint Task Force (JTF) Ares. This effort has sought to identify and neutralize the online presence of various terrorist organizations.[64] Some US policy-makers have criticized this initiative, feeling that JTF Ares did not accomplish enough.[65] US military efforts to engage and counter online terrorist organization and coordination have been frustrated by the speed with which terrorists have been able to quickly and effectively reconstitute their online networks. Attempts to remove terrorists from cyberspace have been frequently referred to as a "whack-a-mole" concept, after the famous carnival game where a player attempts to bonk one mole on the head, only to have others quickly rise to take its place in nearby locations. For the foreseeable future, the challenge of combatting terrorists online is likely to remain. New reports indicate an increased effort by transnational terrorist organizations to leverage the dark web to recruit and organize out of sight of intelligence and law-enforcement agencies.[66] Given the trend toward more online coordination, it is likely that future terrorists will organize and generate effects that challenge states, leading to attacks or exploits that are comparable to those orchestrated by larger hacker collectives and criminal organizations.

Cyber proxies

Although this chapter has focused principally on cyber criminals, hacktivists and terrorists as discrete unitary actors, there are many instances where state and criminal, private, or hacktivist actors work in a synergistic relationship. Both Russia and China are known for fostering very close relationships between state and non-state and, frequently, criminal actors. Although the linkage between state and non-state actors has been well known and documented over the last 30 years, recent literature has begun to pull apart the logic of this linkage and identify some of the mechanisms by which it functions.

In one of the first academic studies of cyber proxies, Tim Maurer examined the relationship between the state and the legitimate use of force and began the process of identifying a growing trend of state actors, including China, Russia and North Korea, using domestic hackers as an extension of the state.[67] The expression "cyber proxies" refers to a range of actors not directly affiliated with a state who are coerced or induced by this state to engage in cyber operations that can be beneficial to both the hacker(s) and the state. Proxy actors offer a buffer, a partially – or even wholly – plausibly deniable means of action with no direct or apparent ties to the state. Maurer identifies three categories of proxies with a range of different skillsets: individuals, small informal networked groups of people, and more formal, hierarchical groups.[68] Actors within these groups range from individual hacktivists and cybercriminals all the way up to private companies and organized crime groups. Further research seeks to explain why proxy actors engage in cyber operations on behalf of states actors. Justin Canfil identifies three main rationales: ideological zeal, nationalism and money.[69] Another explanatory factor focuses on the role of state coercive actions.[70]

In his seminal research on semi-state actors in cybersecurity, Florian Egloff identifies that states have historically used proxy actors to undermine adversaries in areas where state jurisdiction is difficult to enforce.[71] Historically, the English used privateers to harass adversary merchant vessels on the high seas.[72] In recent years, several well-documented cases have shown that individuals or groups who engaged in criminal activity were effectively co-opted to produce or facilitate Russian state activities. When law enforcement in the target state detected and sought these proxy actors, they would seek the protection of their home state.[73]

Although cyber proxies seemingly offer a solution for attacking states to blur the attribution of cyber operations to them, there are dilemmas present in working with such actors. By definition, proxy actors fall outside the formal control of the state. They can turn against their state sponsor or act without the full knowledge or consent of state authorities, fostering political agendas that exceed a given mandate.[74] Regardless of how proxies are used, what tools they are given and what their targets are, their use opens up a gray area in international law that seeks to circumvent the norms and rules of state interaction. As some states expand their reliance on proxy actors, there is a risk that the deniability they seek for their actions becomes increasingly implausible. Adversaries will simply see the actions of proxies as the directed actions of the state on behalf of which they are acting. This could lead to limited forms of escalations or proxy fights between states which negatively impact cyberspace stability. Disaggregating proxy behavior and state behavior in cyberspace is difficult and is likely to become even more so as the use of proxies increases. These questions are likely to attract more scholarly and political attention over the next decade.

Conclusion: governing malicious non-state actors

Although the biggest threats to national security in cyberspace originate at the state level, non-state actors pose substantial challenges across a variety of interest areas central to the functioning of stable societies. Malicious non-state actors cost individuals, businesses and states vast sums of money on an annual basis. The use of the Internet for criminal or terrorist activities harms the reputations, and degrades the digital and physical safety, of the average netizen. Curtailing malicious activities in cyberspace is time-consuming and costly.

To date, state efforts to do so have been unsuccessful, even in repressive countries such as China and Russia. China, through its use of the Great Firewall and domestic surveillance mechanisms, has one of the most censored and controlled domestic cyberspaces in the world. Yet, despite all these controls, China remains home to a substantial number of bots, cyber criminals and hacktivists who actively seek to avoid censorship and surveillance.[75] Since the 1980s, Russia has used a variety of means to control its growing domestic cyberspace. Most notably, Russia has employed intercept devices that monitor all traffic on domestic networks and can engage in deep-packet inspection of that traffic.[76] Russia, too, remains one of the most prolific points of origin for cybercrime.

The use of control, censorship and surveillance in domestic cyberspaces tends to affect the civil liberties of citizens, in direct contravention of many of the goals originally promoted by early users and developers of the Internet. And while these controls often limit domestic cyber criminals targeting domestic actors – for instance, Russian cyber criminals are less likely to hack other Russians or the Russian government, and Chinese cyber criminals are less likely to hack other Chinese – these measures are unlikely to apply beyond the state's borders. Hacktivists from repressive countries are also more likely to target their ire outside of their domestic cyberspaces.

The proliferation of cybercrime is likely to continue and intensify as more and more users and their computers come online. Cyberspace is a target-rich environment. The saying goes that there are two types of people or companies in cyberspace: those who have been hacked and know it, and those who have been hacked and do not know it. Statistically, the probability of being hacked in cyberspace in a given year is greater than 100 percent. These hacks are almost always the result of criminals attempting to steal information or data to generate a profit.

At the international level, states banded together as early as November 23, 2001 to sign the Budapest Convention on Cybercrime, which seeks to harmonize laws relating to cybercrime and facilitate multilateral legal assistance to investigate and prosecute cyber criminals. There are now 70 parties to the Convention. In addition, there are 23 signatories and countries that have been invited to accede. Although the Budapest Convention has a broad base of adoption, it does not cover a number of important countries, including Russia and China.

Since the signing of the Budapest Convention, the volume of cybercrime has increased substantially and shows no signs of abatement. There is rarely a week that passes in which there is not a news story detailing a large cyber breach of a major company, hospital or organization. What these articles often overlook is the heavy toll that the cybercrime can take on individuals, in the form of identity theft or stolen financial resources. Non-state actors who actively seek to violate the laws of states – whether for profit, lulz or terrorist objectives – challenge law-enforcement and intelligence agencies at all levels. At the lowest levels of criminal jurisdiction, most police departments simply do not have qualified staff to assess or investigate cybercrime. In higher jurisdictions, the volume of cases is overwhelming. In the near term, the challenges faced by states in addressing non-state cyber threat actors are likely to grow.

Discussion questions

1. Who are non-state actors in cyberspace and why do they create so many problems for states?

2. Why is cyberterrorism so difficult to accomplish?

3. What is the impact of cybercrime on individuals within different societies?

Exercise

Write a two-page assessment of a non-state threat actor that is active in cyberspace for a senior policy-maker. The assessment should include the following sections:

– A **summary** using bullet points
– A brief **background** section on the threat actor
– **Intentions**: What does the group want to achieve?
– **Capabilities**: What capabilities does the group have to back up these intentions?
– **Activities**: What is the group (already) doing?
– **Obstacles** to the threat posed by the group
– **Expected impact** of the threat and **prospects** (expected developments)

Additional resources

Florian Egloff, *Semi-state Actors in Cybersecurity* (Oxford University Press, 2022).

Marc Goodman, *Future Crimes: Everything Is Connected, Everyone Is Vulnerable and What We Can Do about It* (New York: Doubleday, 2015).

Parmy Olson, *We Are Anonymous: Inside the Hacker World of LulzSec, Anonymous, and the Global Cyber Insurgency* (New York: Back Bay Books, 2013).

Gabriel Weimann, *Terrorism in Cyberspace: The Next Generation* (New York: Columbia University Press, 2015).

9   Cybersecurity and democracy

Reader's guide

- Cyberspace is what we make of it. It is both a "liberation technology" that empowers humans in their pursuit for freedom, and a means to surveil people and curtail their freedom.

- There is an imbalance in cyberspace between the power of governments and companies on the one hand, and civil society on the other hand. Several organizations seek to redress this imbalance by offering advice to civil-society activists and journalists.

- The debate on encryption crystalizes the tension between citizens who want to encode their data, and government agencies who want to maintain access to some encrypted data for security purposes. The one side underlines encryption's role in privacy, civil liberties and cybersecurity; the other contends it protects criminals.

- Technological advances in cyberspace can reinforce discrimination. Asymmetries of access to cyberspace and its resources are a key form of discrimination. Automated systems are not free from bias: algorithms can also contribute to unjustified treatment based on ethnicity, sexual orientation and other identity markers.

- The tensions between security imperatives and liberal democratic norms in cyberspace provide fertile ground to pursue ethical debates about the moral principles that govern various actors' behavior.

Cyberspace has provided a platform for the expansion of democracy. At national and local levels, e-government offers new or increasingly well-established forms of accessibility to public services. The Internet is sometimes described as a "liberation technology," fostering democratization throughout the world. However, as our daily lives increasingly rely on the Internet and its connectivity, governments have also used cyberspace to expand their surveillance efforts, fostering important debates and concern about human rights and civil liberties in the digital era. While social media played a key role in the Arab Spring (2010–12) and the EuroMaidan movement in Ukraine (2013–14),[1] their effect cannot be separated from broader political and societal implications. Authoritarian governments, fearing the power of social media, have not hesitated in restricting or banning access to certain parts of their domestic Internets, using broad surveillance powers to curtail free speech.[2] Cyberspace is a powerful medium for mobilizing citizens and organizing democracy, yet it can also be used by states to control and manipulate their societies and limit human freedom.

This chapter first presents the core tension between democracy and security in cyberspace. The second section examines claims that the Internet is a "liberation technology" and related criticisms. Third, we show how states have leveraged cyber capabilities to target civil-society activists and critiques. One important measure to protect our digital data – whether at rest on a computer or in transit – is encryption. The fourth section explores the debate on encryption and the limits of digital privacy. Fifth, we move on to concern about cyber discrimination, another example of how technological advances – specifically the use of AI – bring about opportunities but also threaten human rights. The last section takes a step back to consider how insecurity in and through cyberspace raises broader ethical questions about moral reasoning, values and standards of behavior.

Democracy and security in cyberspace

Early Internet enthusiasts championed notions of freedom and independence. They envisioned that cyberspace would liberate humans due to its decentralized nature. The Internet did not need a constitution, or a political process, it was an emancipatory space controlled by users and established to share ideas and experiments: WWW users were free to express themselves and interact however they wanted. This openness, and the liberties provided by the Internet, were essential to its early success. However, as researchers Ronald Deibert and Rafal Rohozinski note, "just because a technology has been invented for one purpose does not mean that it will not find other uses unforeseen by its creators."[3]

Governments have always been and remain dominant actors in cyberspace, and have used the Internet to further both democracy and national security. From this perspective, cyberspace has simply provided new ground for pre-existing processes and tensions, between democracy and security, to express themselves. At the end of the twentieth century, governments embraced the Internet to develop new instruments of governance. The Internet offered a new means to provide citizens with information about public services, political processes and choices, a practice known as e-government. Increasingly, digital devices became tools to facilitate online citizens' participation in political processes – for example, through online voting.[4] Together, these new modes of action were expected to promote greater efficiency and effectiveness, and a more citizen-centric government.[5] However, as state actors expanded their digital footprint, the percentage of the population with access to computers remained relatively low, and the development of e-democracy stalled.[6]

At the dawn of the twenty-first century, a growing number of countries invested in national cybersecurity, re-affirming the pre-existing tension between security and democracy. This tension is particularly clear when focusing on the national level of analysis. National security can be defined as the possibility for inhabitants of a state to live in the absence of internal and external threat to the quality of their life and values. To protect a people's way of life, including the democratic system of government and liberal democratic values such as freedom of speech and privacy, intelligence and security agencies use special powers that threaten, and sometimes infringe upon, these values. In democracies, security agencies seek to defend an open society by secret means. Beyond strategic-level declarations, governments keep most of their cybersecurity practices secret, to protect the methods through which they wield cyber power. Throughout the world, cyber commands, SIGINT agencies and domestic law-enforcement agencies operate secretly to protect the comparative advantages they develop over their adversaries. Their reliance on secrecy limits governmental transparency and, by extension, democratic accountability. Without sufficient information on government cyber operations, citizens cannot assess the decisions public authorities make on their behalf. Instead, they have to rely on representatives – the head of government and select members of parliament – who have access to sensitive government information and make cyber policy decisions.

Cybersecurity policy decisions are particularly important because government security agencies benefit from surveillance powers that encroach upon individual privacy. Privacy, defined as the condition of being free from observation or disruption by other people, is an international human right guaranteed by the Universal Declaration of Human Rights of 1948 and the International Covenant on Civil and Political Rights of 1966. International law holds that individuals have the right to consent to or refuse the use of their personal data by secondary or third parties. Privacy is not an absolute right – government authorities can interfere with this right but they must justify encroachments. Government officials generally invoke national security to deploy special surveillance powers. In this context, surveillance, in and beyond cyberspace, is supposed to constitute a temporary restriction to the rights of a few suspect individuals, accepted in the pursuit of the greater societal interest of national security.

The extent to which governments conduct cyber surveillance in exceptional circumstances is a point of debate. Domestic security services collect information in cyberspace to identify and monitor suspected criminals, spies and terrorists. They sometimes monitor political dissenters and opposition groups – subversive elements – who have the potential to turn to violent action or (in autocratic countries) threaten the legitimacy of the regime. Government security services have struggled historically to differentiate legitimate political dissenters from subversive elements that truly threaten society.[7] What constitutes legitimate government surveillance is contentious and constantly evolving. Government overreach in this domain can stymie public debate and freedom of expression. Public expectations regarding surveillance can sometimes also have a "chilling effect" on society, in the sense that the simple awareness of the existence of surveillance can restrain social activism and free expression. At the extreme end of the spectrum, excessive government surveillance threatens democracy, instead of protecting it. There is substantial evidence that the same technologies once heralded as facilitating liberation are now constraining it. Research suggests that the trend is increasingly moving away from a human rights-based order in digital spaces.[8] The movement away from a rights-based order is in part facilitated by the increasing capabilities of states to collect large volumes of data on nearly every action of its citizens.

There are many ways privacy can be threatened online. Internet users all leave a digital footprint when they visit websites, send emails and submit information online. Some elements are left intentionally – a birth date or a picture shared on X (formerly Twitter), for instance. Other data are left unintentionally by visiting websites and clicking on links. Each computer has an IP address that is used to surf on the web, which reveals the location and type of device used to access specific parts of the Internet.[9] Data on Internet browsing habits can help governments, private companies and malicious actors identify individuals online. Storybox 9.1 discusses growing public concern about online privacy in the aftermath of the global surveillance disclosures of 2013.

Storybox 9.1 The global surveillance disclosures of 2013

In Spring 2013, international media revealed details of a global surveillance network set up by the NSA and partner agencies across the world. The revelation emanated from a cache of highly classified documents stolen by then NSA contractor Edward Snowden. Snowden leaked these documents to a group of journalists, who subsequently published them in newspapers such as the *Guardian*, the *Washington Post* and *Der Spiegel*. The Snowden leaks contained thousands of top-secret documents shedding light on the surveillance efforts of the "Five Eyes" network – composed of intelligence agencies in Australia, Canada, New Zealand, the United Kingdom and the United States – and partner countries (including Denmark, France, Germany, Israel, Italy, the Netherlands, Norway, Singapore, Spain and Switzerland).

The most widely discussed revelations focused on a series of programs with mysterious codenames, such as PRISM and Xkeyscore. Through the implementation of PRISM, the NSA uses selectors – an email address, for instance – to collect stored Internet communications from major companies, including Apple, Google and Skype. According to a PowerPoint presentation leaked by Edward Snowden, PRISM is the main source of raw intelligence used for NSA analytic reports.[10] Another program, Xkeyscore, allowed the NSA and a number of partner agencies in other countries to search and analyze global Internet data.

These revelations caused outrage around the world because they suggested that the US government and its partners were collecting Internet data in bulk. For many critics and concerned citizens around the globe, these revelations raised the specter of omnipresent government surveillance described in George Orwell's dystopian novel *Nineteen Eighty-Four*, or practiced by the East German Ministry for State Security, the Stasi.[11]

Critics question whether government agencies should be allowed to collect data on large populations of presumably innocent people. While modern intelligence agencies do collect tremendous amounts of data, they do not actively monitor and analyze all the individuals whose data have been collected. From the perspective of the US government, PRISM and Xkeyscore were originally authorized by Congress, and legal. Beyond legalities, the global surveillance disclosures raised public awareness and triggered a broad public debate on Internet surveillance.

The debate on Internet privacy expands well beyond the reach of government intelligence agencies. Both government and private-sector organizations are data hungry and seek to obtain personal information online to inform and orient their decisions.[12] The amount of data they gather is particularly worrying because no organization seems to be immune to data breaches that can leave sensitive personal information in the hands of criminals.[13] In response to growing concerns about online privacy, the EU passed the GDPR to harmonize data protection across Europe. The GDPR allows European users to have easier access to the data that website owners hold about them, and establishes a clear responsibility for organizations to obtain the consent of people they collect information about, among other measures.[14] One hope is that creating more accountability for organizations that handle people's personal information will force them to develop more comprehensive data protection policies and assessments.

A liberation technology

Optimists argue that cyber technologies can help foster social change that encourages liberal democratic values. Scholar Larry Diamond defines liberation technology as "any form of information and communication technology that can expand political, social, and economic freedom," from computers to mobile phones to the Internet and social media.[15] Social media platforms like YouTube and X (formerly Twitter) can be used to report news, express opinions and expose wrongdoing. From this perspective, online media provide powerful tools for transparency and monitoring government activities. The practice of cyberactivism, a form of political mobilization in and through cyberspace, relies on the Internet to organize political activities such as demonstrations and street protests.[16]

There is no question that, in some circumstances, the Internet does empower individuals and strengthen civil society. Larry Diamond details how China's blogosphere has provided room to open a domestic public sphere, in spite of strong government censorship.[17] In one case, online indignation forced the Chinese government to investigate the death of a rural migrant, Sun Zhigang, after he was incarcerated and beaten to death by local police in the city of Guangzhou. The government eventually decided to change its national regulation and closed the detention centers that were used to hold rural migrants in custody prior to repatriation.[18] In 2011, social media facilitated the Arab Spring, a series of demonstrations, protests and riots that spread from Tunisia to the rest of the Arab world. In a region where freedom of speech and freedom of press are limited, youth used the Internet to exchange political ideas, spread information and organize protests against repressive governments.[19] Storybox 9.2 examines the role digital media played in the EuroMaidan movement, which has affected Ukrainian politics since 2013.

Storybox 9.2 The EuroMaidan movement

In 2013, a wave of demonstrations and protests followed the Ukrainian government's decision to suspend the signature of an association agreement with the EU. The movement, which began on November 21, 2013 in Maidan Nezalezhnosti (Independence Square) was nicknamed "EuroMaidan," and supported through a number of social media accounts such as @euromaidan on Twitter (now X) and the євромайдан–euromaydan page on Facebook. With the help of digital media, fueled by growing public concern with government corruption and human rights violations, among other issues, the movement grew significantly. Protests eventually led to the 2014 Ukrainian revolution, ousting Ukrainian President Viktor Yanukovych and resulting in the overthrow of his government.

Activists, news media and political scientists have all pointed out the importance of social media in the EuroMaidan movement. Social media helped mobilize the population rapidly, sometimes leading to near-spontaneous actions. Digital tools helped protesters connect to one another – thanks, for example, to the use of hashtags.[20] Following Yanukovych's decision not to sign the EU agreement, activists promptly assembled online to criticize the administration. Social media helped activists communicate about the protest, and the broader situation in Ukraine, to domestic and international audiences. They also helped activists organize protests, sharing information about flyers and slogans, setting up a legal assistance service for victims of government repression, and field hospitals for protesters.[21]

The use of social media also provides a uniquely detailed source of data for researchers to study social movements and a number of other phenomena relevant to national and international politics. However, the digital world cannot provide a window into everything. Social media were an important part of the success of the EuroMaidan movement, but not the sole facilitator. Pre-existing social networks and other types of media – digital, in print, and television – interacted with social media to amplify the protest and bring about social and political change in Ukraine.[22] Scholars continue to debate the extent to which digital platforms can foster durable change and sustained civic engagement. In addition to technology, a number of other variables affect political change, including political culture, leadership and the level of organization within a movement.[23]

The US government famously embraced the potential of the Internet as a tool for democracy promotion in its 2011 International Strategy for Cyberspace. This strategy expressed US support for fundamental freedoms and privacy in cyberspace and offered to support civil-society actors in achieving these freedoms throughout the world.[24] Then-Secretary of State Hillary Clinton famously defended Internet freedom, noting that "governments should not prevent people from connecting to the Internet and websites or each other."[25] This notion builds on pre-existing civil and political rights and is often attached to online free expression and the right to access the Internet to connect to others.[26] In practice, the US government has supported the development of software, including Tor, that provides online protection by disguising the source and endpoint of online interactions. Tor allows individuals to surf the web without anyone knowing who and where they are. Egyptian dissidents relied on Tor to protect their identity during the Arab Spring.

However, cyberspace is not a one-dimensional domain dominated by its potential for liberation. Two-thirds of all Internet users live in countries where criticism of the government is subject to censorship.[27] China and Russia, among other nations, perceive Internet freedom as a way for Western culture and values to infiltrate their societies and foment dissent. The contrast could hardly be starker between these different perspectives on what constitutes a security risk or a right.[28] While the Internet may have been invented with the ideals of freedom of expression and access to information in mind, other purposes have emerged throughout its development. Pessimistic voices in the debate on cybersecurity and democracy highlight governments' capabilities to control and filter the Internet to identify and punish dissenters. Critics point out that governments can leverage their concerns about cyber warfare to securitize cyberspace and justify extraordinary surveillance measures to the population. The same social media used to organize popular protest and widen the public sphere in the Arab world and beyond can be used by governments to identify dissenters and put them in jail.

Reductions in Internet freedom can take many forms. Filtering technologies, such as the Great Firewall of China, limit citizens' access to specific sites and resources in cyberspace. Governments can monitor and track online activities, to support arrests and prosecutions based on behaviors or actions in cyberspace.[29] The Chinese government has tried to eliminate anonymous communications and networking by requiring the registration of real names to blog or comment, and monitoring cyber cafés. However, there is simply too much information online for governments to monitor everything.

A multiplicity of national approaches to what is allowed on the Internet continues to dictate its use. Even in the most advanced liberal democracies, complete freedom of expression on the Internet does not exist. Among other limitations, liberal democracies have been keen to protect intellectual property, legislating on music rights and cracking down on illegal download platforms, such as Napster and The Pirate Bay. Citizens are also protected from online slander and hate speech in various countries. Other countries choose to more directly restrain access to Internet websites and services based on national values. In Pakistan, laws concerning blasphemy have been used to ban access to Facebook, which hosted cartoons of the Prophet Muhammad.[30]

In the last decade, the emergence of alternative news websites and fake news raised important questions on the impact of the Internet on public debate. The rise of disinformation and fake news long predate the Internet era,[31] but their impact in the Internet age is extensive and in many ways subverts reality for individuals seeking information in online spaces.[32] Larry Diamond emphasizes "the fine line between pluralism and cacophony, between advocacy and intolerance, and between the expansion of the public sphere and its hopeless fragmentation."[33] While the Internet can help establish a public debate and support civil society, it can also divide people and foment dissent.[34] Cyberspace, in turn, is what people make of it.

Whose cybersecurity?

While a significant part of the IR literature on cyberspace focuses on nation states, understanding the effect of cybersecurity on individuals is equally important. Aaron Brantly argues that the main losers in the current cyber arms race are not states but the activists who are struggling to keep up with the tremendous resources of state actors and corporations that invest in cybersecurity, cyber espionage and cyber operations.

As states develop more powerful cyber capabilities, they can use them not only against their adversaries, but also on civilian populations.[35] For instance, a company based in the United Kingdom developed a complex spyware named FinFisher. This software was sold and used by repressive regimes in Egypt, Bahrain and Uganda to spy on political opponents.[36] In other cases, innovations developed for cybercrime are re-used by governments to spy on foreign agents, or even on their own citizens.[37] Brantly shows that the development of new cyber capabilities is often followed by decreases in civil liberties, and argues that major democracies should invest more significantly in facilitating freedom of connection and expression online.[38]

Recently, the Pegasus spyware scandal provided further evidence of massive state surveillance campaigns against human and civil rights activists and journalists in dozens of countries around the world. Pegasus leverages a 'zero click' exploit, meaning the spyware requires no interaction or click to operate in a system. This capability was developed by Israeli firm NSO Group, which was authorized to sell its product to dozens of countries.[39] Though several specialized groups such as the Citizen Lab at the University of Toronto had identified the existence of this spyware several years ago, a list of 50,000 phone numbers of potential Pegasus targets was leaked to nonprofit organizations Forbidden Stories and Amnesty International in 2021. The 2 nonprofits worked with 17 media partners across the world to verify the information and tease out its political implications, generating ample media coverage.[40] The spyware has since been discovered on thousands of activists' and journalists' phones and even on the phones of French President Emanual Macron and Morocco's King Mohammed VI. We now know that Pegasus has been used to intimidate, track, arrest and murder perceived enemies of the state in both authoritarian states such as Saudi Arabia and more democratic states, including India[41] and Mexico.[42]

The recognition of the imbalance between the power of governments and companies and of civil society has fostered the emergence of public-interest groups supporting Internet freedom. Organizations such as the Citizen Lab – an interdisciplinary laboratory based at the University of Toronto – the Electronic Frontier Foundation (EFF) and others actively support less capable cyber actors. The weak position of civil-society actors is reinforced by what one author calls their careless practices. In one stunning example, advocacy group Reporters Without Borders unknowingly propagated a link to a malicious website posing as a Facebook petition to release the Tibetan activist Dhondup Wangchen.[43] To combat these kinds of mistakes, organizations such as the Citizen

Lab provide free support to human rights groups and teach them best practices in cybersecurity. Storybox 9.3 presents the findings of an investigation co-led by the Citizen Lab, and shows some of the difficulties confronted by public-interest groups in this context.

Storybox 9.3 GhostNet

In a seminal report entitled "Tracking GhostNet," an international team of researchers led by the Citizen Lab at the University of Toronto uncovered a vast electronic spying operation infecting 1,295 computers in 103 countries. Their investigation started when researchers at the University of Toronto were asked by the office of the Dalai Lama to examine its computers for signs of malware. Their initial analysis found that the computers had indeed been infected, and the team decided to pursue their investigation through technical scouting and laboratory analysis. The researchers set up a honey-pot computer that helped them identify malicious servers and observe the tactics, techniques and procedures used by the attacker(s) to infect computers and to access and retrieve data from them.[44]

Their analysis opened a window into a broad cyber operation that had infiltrated hundreds of computers throughout the world, stealing troves of potentially sensitive documents, mostly in Asian countries. The main tool used by the hackers behind GhostNet – an open-source and widely available trojan known as gh0st RAT – allowed attackers to gain complete control of a computer.[45] This malware was used to retrieve data from high-value targets located in ministries of foreign affairs, embassies, international organizations and NGOs.

Though the researchers could not directly attribute the computer network exploitation, they found that four control servers were based in China, and one in Southern California. However, they remained reluctant to pin responsibility on the Chinese government. Another state actor could have compromised proxy computers in China to achieve deniability. Non-state actors, working for profit or out of patriotism, could also have conducted the operation.[46]

Protecting information stored on digital devices and communicated through cyberspace has become easier in the last decade, not least thanks to the effort of organizations such as the Citizen Lab, the EFF and the Guardian Project.[47] These organizations recommend a number of free tools that are available online to support digital privacy. This includes software that provides disk encryption, email encryption, secure text messages and video services, secure browsing services and VPNs, to name a few. These tools are particularly important for activists living in undemocratic countries, where failing to secure online activities can become the difference between freedom and incarceration.[48] They can also be important in democracies, to help users protect their online activities from cyber criminals and other online threats. Most online freeware provides sufficient cyber defense against neighbors, colleagues and common cyber criminals. However, the capabilities of specialized companies and many governments are much more difficult to protect against. In those more extreme cases, effective cybersecurity might require users to adapt and limit the ways they use computers. While encryption tools enable highly secure browsing and communication, there is no perfect cybersecurity.

Encryption and cyber (in)security

The debate on encryption gained prominence in the 1990s, when the administration of President Bill Clinton proposed for federal law-enforcement agencies to hold a decryption key that would facilitate wiretaps. Opponents were disturbed that this would give undue power to government officials, and the government proposal was eventually withdrawn.[49] Advocates of strong public encryption – such as the EFF – point out that the "power of ciphers" protects citizens when they communicate, bank and shop online. For them, more cryptography is inherently beneficial. On the other side, critics – mostly government intelligence and security agencies – point out that encryption protects "foreign spies, terrorists and criminals when they pry, plot and steal."[50] For Daniel Moore and Thomas Rid, these antithetical positions are over-stated and flawed. The problem is less with encryption itself than how it is used. They argue that encryption should be used as often as possible, but not all the time, especially not as it relates to cryptographically ena-bled services.[51] They recommend encrypting personal communications and data to enable better privacy and freedom of speech. However, they condemn the use of encryption for online exchange platforms and mar-ketplaces, specifically on the dark web – a distinct cyberspace network supporting cryptographically hidden sites and accessible through specific software such as Tor. These services provide anonymous browsing and hosting of exchanges through a browser. While anonymous browsing should be welcomed, anonymous exchanges are more problematic.

Research shows that encryption helps develop marketplaces that mostly benefit criminals who want to sell or buy fake passports, drugs, weapons and other illegal goods and services. For Rid and Moore, the individuals creating these websites should have to give their names to service providers. Outside of these specific circumstances, user anonymity should be protected to support free speech.[52] The solution Rid and Moore provide is helpful, but it does not resolve the dilemma over encryption. Storybox 9.4 examines the case of the San Bernardino shooters in the United States and presents the dispute that ensued over the decryption of a mobile phone, between the FBI and Apple.

Storybox 9.4 The Apple–FBI debate over digital privacy

The rise of encryption limits government agencies' ability to access data on digital devices. Technology companies such as Apple have used encryption as a marketing tool. Developing encryption locks that are difficult, sometimes even impossible, to break is a selling point to attract customers who want to protect their digital data. Strong encryption has frustrated law-enforcement agencies, which have repeatedly asked companies such as Apple to provide them with a key to access encrypted data on their customers' digital devices and support their investigations. But IT companies have been reluctant to do so. They are concerned that any means of bypassing encryption would create a weakness that hackers and foreign spies might be able to exploit against their customers.

The dispute between Apple and the FBI concerns the extent to which a US court can compel manufacturers to assist government in unlocking mobile phones whose data is encrypted. In 2015 and 2016, Apple received and objected to a dozen court orders seeking to compel the company to use its capabilities to extract data from iPhones to assist criminal investigations. In the most well-known case, the FBI tried to force Apple to create new software that would enable it to unlock an iPhone used by Syed Rizwan Farook, one of the shooters involved in a terrorist attack in San Bernardino, California, that killed 14 and injured 22. FBI officials said that the data in Farook's phone might hold vital clues for their investigation. The company refused to cooperate on the grounds that it would violate its right to due process, claiming that forcing it to write new software would be a violation of free speech (writing code can be considered as a form of free speech in the United States). From Apple's perspective, helping law enforcement to bypass the phone password protection would create unwanted vulnerabilities in its products. Privacy advocates, Apple and other technology companies were also worried that cooperating with the government would create a precedent. If Apple complied with the US government, it might then be forced to cooperate again in the future, and not only with US agencies but perhaps also with China, Russia and other less democratic countries.[53]

Eventually the US government withdrew its request to Apple after it reached out to an Israeli cybersecurity company that was able to unlock the device.[54] Since then, Apple has developed stronger encryption on its newer devices, making it technically impossible to unlock passwords or extract data from the devices it produces. The Apple versus FBI story raises broader questions about trust in the digital era. Who should we trust our digital data with? The government? Technology companies? Or only ourselves?

Digital discrimination

As cyberspace becomes increasingly ubiquitous and complex, new technologies, governance regimes and conflicts continue to undermine human rights in online spaces. Human rights violations are often deliberate acts by state or non-state actors who seek to maintain regime stability, undermine opposition or even, at times, provide security as interpreted by the state elite. Amid all the external cybersecurity threats and challenges individuals face, technologies themselves are increasingly reinforcing forms of discrimination. Digital discrimination can manifest itself in multiple ways, including access asymmetries based on geography (rural versus urban divides), education and income.[55] One of the more prevalent forms of discrimination arises due to the algorithms upon which digital services depend. An algorithm is a set of commands or rules followed by computers to perform calculations. Artificial Intelligence (AI) and Machine Learning (ML) are two fields of studies in computer science that have transformed the use of algorithms and become particularly pervasive in cyberspace. While there is no single type of AI and ML, most of these algorithms depend upon vast quantities of training data and on decisions made by programmers that can and do lead to discriminatory outcomes. Algorithmic discrimination – when automated systems contribute to unjustified treatment based on race, ethnicity, class, sexual orientation, religion, age, education and other markers of identity – can undermine the basic rights and the cyberse-curity of individuals.[56] This form of discrimination is often subtle and can reinforce existing societal discrimination, making it difficult to dif-ferentiate. Its implications are widespread. Firms use algorithms to help in hiring decisions, municipalities to help in parole decisions, universi-ties to aid in admissions decisions, and healthcare providers to influence care decisions. No longer can individuals simply secure their devices using the latest anti-virus software or encrypt their files, they must also contend with an ecosystem of services in which algorithms influence and shape their life experiences in both online and offline spaces.

Digital discrimination can be inadvertently or deliberately built into systems. When adversaries at any level (state, non-state, private, indi-vidual, etc.) understand how a given AI or ML algorithm functions, they can manipulate it to achieve preferential benefits or negatively harm potential targets. Cybersecurity extends beyond simply keeping intrud-ers out and ensuring systems function as designed. The code underlying these systems and the services upon which cyberspace depends affect human security more broadly. While algorithms can increase efficiency and provide insights into phenomena that were once obscured, they can also lead to individuals being compared to animals, self-driving cars failing to see pedestrians, medical devices administering too much or too little medication, employers hiring homogeneous workforces. The networks and devices that comprise cyberspace are in part reflections of human nature and activities, both good and bad. It would be naïve to assume that the algorithms that govern cyberspace are free from bias and infallible to mistakes. Cyberspace, just like any other domain of human activity, raises broad questions about moral principles and values.

Ethics and cyber activities

Much of the discussion in this chapter has focused on areas where cyberspace and its associated technologies either empower or undermine human rights and democracy. The issues raised above and throughout the book pose profound ethical and moral challenges. They force users and operators, states, firms and non-state actors to make decisions that often have uncertain or risky outcomes. As a result, scholars have increas-ingly sought to develop an understanding of the ethics of cyber conflict and operations.[57] They are asking questions about the distinction of targets in cyberspace, privacy of users, appropriateness of surveillance and the sale of surveillance capabilities, the use and abuse of intellectual property, the offsetting of human decisions to algorithms, the centrality of data and its collection, and the legitimate use and users of force in cyberspace.[58] Just as in the physical world, establishing and applying a single ethical framework for all actions in and through cyberspace is not practical. Ethical appraisal of each situation and activity benefits from considering multiple lenses. Storybox 9.5 below examines the ethical issues of allowing non-state actors to engage in military cyber operations against an adversary state.

Storybox 9.5 Anonymous and Ukraine

On February 24, 2022, the Russian Federation began a full-scale, unprovoked invasion of its neighbor Ukraine. The invasion did not just take place on land, by sea and in the air, it also extended to cyberspace. Although Ukraine had spent the better part of the previous eight years developing its national cybersecurity infrastructures,[59] its cyber defenses were incomplete and its capacity to engage in cyberspace with its substantially more powerful neighbor remained constrained.[60] In the immediate aftermath of the invasion, with critical infrastructure and government websites and services under sustained cyber assault, Ukrainian officials put out a call to international hacker fora for help in resisting the Russian Federation.[61] This call made its way into global hacker communities and was picked up by the hacker collective Anonymous.

Within hours of the invasion of Ukraine, Anonymous initiated cyberattacks against multiple Russian entities, including the Central Bank of Russia, Russia's space agency Roscosmos, Russian oil giant Gazprom, and property management and telecommunications firms.[62] Anonymous hacked into databases, doxed (stole and dumped documents and account credentials of Russian firms), blocked Russian and Belarussian websites, hijacked media and streaming services, and more.[63] These activities were conducted at the request of the Ukrainian state but without official sanction or official direction and targeting. The result was a collective movement to degrade Russian capabilities in cyberspace.

The request by Ukraine for assistance and the subsequent provision of assistance by Anonymous and other hackers around the world fall into an ethical gray area. Using non-state actors to fulfill state military functions violates the laws of war. The practice is similar to seventeenth- and eighteenth-century privateering under letters of mark.[64]

The lack of direction and the indiscriminate targeting of public and private assets also violate the laws of war and if done in the physical world would have potentially constituted war crimes. Yet, the facts of this case are convoluted. A powerful state was attacking its far weaker neighbor. Ukraine in this instance faced an existential crisis in a fight for its survival. In this moment it sought to mobilize every potential resource to its aid to slow down and undermine the Russian Federation.

Anonymous responding to Ukraine's call for help could also have inadvertently embroiled other states into the conflict if the Russian Federation had chosen to hold those states accountable for the actions of their citizens. If the call for help to the global hacker community was unethical, did Ukraine's need to maintain its survival create an exception that justified this call? What if the Russian Federation had attacked a near-peer state such as China or the United States – whose survival might not be at stake. Would similar calls and use of non-state actors to indiscriminately attack targets in the Russian Federation then be illegal and unethical?

The ethics of actions in cyberspace are often compared to their physical world equivalents. Frequently these comparisons are adequate and applicable. Yet the nuances of cyberspace, not least the way in which it spans virtual and physical domain that extends out into nearly every part of the world, can make some issues more complex. At present, there remains inconsistency in behavior between physical and virtual spaces. In the early days of the Internet, there was a caption to a cartoon by Peter Steiner published in the *New Yorker* on July 5, 1993, that stated, "On the Internet nobody knows you're a dog." Perceived anonymity in online spaces enables both good and bad behavior. It is a critical attribute of human rights, but it is also an enabler of vitriol and malfeasance. As the domain evolves and events continue to transpire, the ethical parameters of individual, firms and states in cyberspace will become increasingly clear. Yet, because the technologies are constantly evolving, ethics in cyberspace will remain, at least in part, unsettled.

Conclusion

The advent of cyberspace has expanded traditional debates about security and democracy in the digital world. Early Internet users were very attached to the free flow of information and conceived of cyberspace as a haven of freedom. However, the expansion of cyberspace has also been marked by the development of new security tools and threats. These tools have been used by governments to monitor populations for good and bad reasons. But they have also been available beyond governments, to activists seeking to advance democracy and to criminals and terrorists seeking to protect their identities.

Long-existing tensions between liberal democratic values and security practices have not disappeared in cyberspace. States are still trying to regulate and control the digital world. They use new and evolving tools in ways that both enhance and limit individual freedoms in online spaces. They establish rules and laws that foster and undermine cybersecurity. Concurrently, malicious actors also try to exploit the domain for their own material or psychological gain. The interwoven nexus of actors, actions and technologies is resulting in challenges both to cybersecurity and to democracy and human rights more broadly. New tools in cyberspace do not guarantee freedom or control. Why and how cyberspace is used largely depend on political and societal factors that vary across the globe. The Internet does not create fundamentally new choices between security and democracy, but provides an evolving platform for reaffirming these choices and reflecting upon the core values that drive individuals and communities.[65] In this sense, the Internet is what people make of it. Cyberspace is a cause for both optimism and pessimism, and, as such, illustrates the complexity of modern societies.

Discussion questions

1. How far should governments be able to encroach on liberties to provide for cybersecurity?

2. Has cybersecurity become essential to democracy?

3. Was Apple right to resist the FBI demand to crack an iPhone linked to the San Bernardino attacks?

4. Was Ukraine's use of Anonymous in the early days of Russia's invasion ethical?

Exercise

Go on the Freedom House's website and visit the "Global Freedom Status" map. Click on the "Internet Freedom" option at the bottom left and select one country on which there is data. Use the country report to explain relevant scores and what they tell us about the state of Internet freedoms in this country.

Additional resources

Aaron Brantly, "Utopia Lost – Human Rights in a Digital World," *Applied Cybersecurity and Internet Governance* 1/1 (2022): 25–43.

Ronald J. Deibert, *Black Code: Surveillance, Privacy, and the Dark Side of the Internet* (Toronto: McClelland & Stewart, 2013). An eponymous documentary directed by Nicholas de Pencier was released in 2016.

Timothy Edgar, *Beyond Snowden: Privacy, Mass Surveillance, and the Struggle to Reform the NSA* (Washington, DC: Brookings Institution, 2017).

10   The futures of cybersecurity

Reader's guide

- There is a multitude of possible futures, some of them more desirable than others. Examining current trends provides a small window into some of the opportunities and challenges that characterize emerging technologies.

- The IoT is expanding and will continue to expand the boundaries of cyberspace into our daily lives, compounding vulnerabilities and underlining the need for further regulation.

- The growing role played by AI in contemporary society is forcing and will continue to force many (security) professionals to adapt their practices to focus increasingly on overseeing machines and their users.

- The boundaries between humans and machines will become increasingly blurred, providing new opportunities to augment our lives as well as raising further concern about privacy and liberties.

- Quantum computing is poised to make the most computationally intensive tasks solvable in far shorter periods of time. Such a capability will undermine most if not all current forms of encryption.

The future of cybersecurity will be complex. As humans invest more time and resources in cyberspace, the digital realm will become increasingly multifaceted, and so will cybersecurity. In the coming decades, cyberspace will continue to grow in influence at all levels of society. The number of Internet-enabled devices is expected to expand substantially from 20 billion in 2020 to more than 100 billion by 2050. These devices will pervade every aspect of modern life, from the rise of smart cities to new biotechnologies, and collect zettabytes-worth of data daily, requiring increasingly robust capabilities to process, interpret and secure big data. Quantum computing and other emerging technologies are poised to expand processing power at unfathomable rates, redefining human–machine interactions. The confluence of greater numbers of devices, increasing automation and faster computing offers both challenges and opportunities for the future of cybersecurity. Yet, despite all the technological advances over the horizon, the inherently human – and therefore complex and imperfect – nature of cybersecurity will remain.

The best experts in any field frequently get it wrong when they write about the future. Futurists prefer to discuss an array of alternative futures to reflect the infinite number of possible permutations originating in the present. Using scenarios to plot possible futures can help strategic planning and identify research priorities, but they should not be treated as predictions. In the best cases, they are informed hypotheses whose implications can orient cybersecurity planning and practices.[1] For example, Jason Healey, the former Director of the Cyber Statecraft Initiative at the Atlantic Council in Washington, DC, imagines five possible futures of cyber conflict and cooperation based on three key factors: offense–defense balance, the intensity and kinds of cyber conflict, and the intensity and kinds of cyber cooperation. His "most likely" scenario is one that imagines cyberspace as a "conflict domain" where cyber terror and cyber war coexist with normal use of the Internet for communication and commerce. Another plausible scenario plots a balkanized Internet divided by national interests and intranets. Healey's preferred future is a "paradise cyberspace" that is secure, and where espionage, warfare and crime are all extremely difficult.[2]

Thinking about a multitude of possible futures for cybersecurity keeps the door open for different understandings of cyberspace to coexist. This concluding chapter focuses on possible developments and highlights some of the puzzles confronting scholars and practitioners as they ponder over the shape that a desirable cyber future might take. A common method for thinking about futures is to extrapolate from current trends to anticipate changes. The sections below highlight four interconnected trends that are frequently discussed in the contemporary debate on cybersecurity: the IoT; the rise of AI; deepening of human–machine interactions; and quantum computing. These trends offer a small window into the future that allows us to examine some – but not all – of the key developments in the field, related threats and opportunities, and their policy implications. Given the growing complexity of cyberspace as a socio-technical domain, greater engagement from the humanities and social sciences will improve our understanding of cybersecurity. To tackle emerging challenges, researchers need to study how humans and societies interact in and through the digital realm.

Toward an ever more interconnected world: the Internet of Things

The IoT has and will continue to significantly expand the physical and digital frontiers of cyberspace in the coming decades. The concept of IoT is best understood as an ecosystem of connected sensors attached to everyday devices and appliances, from vehicles to door locks, thermostats, fridges, security cameras and so on.[3] Together, these sensors "collect and transmit data (sensing)," feed it to "systems that interpret and make use of the aggregated information (processing), and actuators that, on the basis of this information, take action without direct human intervention (actuation)."[4] IoT Analytics, a research firm that tracks the number of activated IoT devices, found that by the end of the fourth quarter of 2022 14.3 billion IoT devices were online and they estimated that the number would rise to 16.7 billion by the end of 2023.[5]

The growing physical presence of connected devices will significantly increase the flow of data in cyberspace, and will require the development of new standards to maintain interoperability between billions of connected digital tools.

With applications in every sector of society, from agriculture to finance and health, the IoT will significantly expand the scope and scale of cybersecurity needs. Each new Internet-enabled device provides an entry point into cyberspace, as well as new opportunities to shape human lives in and through cyberspace in both positive and negative ways. IoT devices are a major point of weakness in the cybersecurity landscape. Many devices lack basic security features and rely upon default passwords, giving attackers easy access to them.

Experts warn that the emergence of the IoT will boost cyberattack capabilities. The growing ecosystem of devices already provides fertile ground for hackers to develop large botnets. The convergence of billions of devices across multiple sectors is likely to increase the potential scale of these disruptions. A single attack will be able to affect more devices and users and is likely to result in amplified socio-economic effects.[6] The IoT will also open new vectors for holding individual data or access ransom. For example, hackers might one day lock users out of their personal vehicle, home or appliances until a ransom is paid.

The more we interact with the Internet in our everyday life, the larger the data footprint we leave behind. Interconnected devices increasingly transfer large amounts of personal data in cyberspace, generating deeper concerns about privacy, and raising the political stakes of cybersecurity. The IoT will increase surveillance capacities to an unprecedented level, allowing resourceful cyber actors to collect new types of data in greater quantities. In 2018, media revealed how popular fitness trackers allowed companies to monitor the movement of national security professionals working in military bases around the world.[7] An interconnected system of billions of sensors provides a tremendous source of information, not only for governments to conduct domestic and foreign surveillance, but also for data-hungry companies and non-state threat actors.[8]

While none of the risks highlighted in this section is fundamentally new, their scale and scope are likely to significantly affect the way users approach cybersecurity. When cyberspace is everywhere, traditional boundaries between the home and workplace, public and private sphere, and related security practices will become harder to distinguish.[9] As IoT dominates our daily lives, cybersecurity will become just security.[10] Users of IoT devices often do not know or recognize that they are using devices connected to the Internet. The pervasiveness of IoT is increasingly fading to the background as users interact with Alexa, Google, Siri or other AI assistants in the world around us. Our lights, gaming devices, garage doors, refrigerators and more are connected and, as we become more accustomed to them being connected, we lose visibility into the novelty and the potential vulnerabilities that these devices bring with them. For the better part of a decade, the FBI and other organizations have recommended explicitly segmenting home networks between IoT devices and more comprehensive computing devices such as home computers and smart phones, but rarely are these recommendations implemented. Instead, we add devices to networks and hope for the best. Yet the manufacturers of these devices build in product life cycles that frequently do not align with our personal and professional lives. A person who installs smart light-switches in their home does not anticipate that the security for these devices – if maintained at all by the original vendor – will likely only last three to five years. Just as computer operating systems lose support after several years, so too do IoT devices. Yet who is going to change their refrigerator when it no longer receives security patches from its vendor? The reality of the IoT does not align with the way in which individuals live their lives. As a result, the IoT not only introduces initial systemic vulnerabilities, but also creates compounding vulnerabilities over time.

At present, there is little to no regulation associated with the IoT. Standards bodies seek to foster buy-in on security, but not all vendors participate in certain standards and those that do must often charge higher prices for their products. As products age, who or what will guarantee the confidentiality, integrity and availability of our data in this connected future?[11] Key security actors, in governments and beyond, increasingly need to develop new concepts and technologies to protect and process the massive amounts of data generated by the IoT. More importantly, they need to understand the systemic vulnerabilities that these evolving markets and devices are creating.[12]

Artificial Intelligence

The expansion of the IoT and advances in data types and uses have dramatically increased over the last five years. As of 2023, worldwide daily data production was estimated to be approximately 1,000 petabytes or the equivalent of 223,101,000 high-resolution movies of 4.7 Gigabytes each.[13] This data comes in all shapes and sizes. It is generated by everything from users uploading YouTube and TikTok videos to sensors monitoring seismic activity, weather patterns and so on. The ability to process large volumes of data remains one of the defining challenges of big data. The velocity at which data are produced or changed, and the variety of data types, contribute to the complexity of big data. Scholars and practitioners generally define big data as "the information assets characterized by such a high volume, velocity and variety [as] to require specific technology and analytical methods for its transformation into value."[14]

Individuals and organizations increasingly use assistive technologies to extract information and meaning out of the ever increasing volume, velocity and variety of data.[15] At the forefront of this data revolution are substantial advances in AI, a branch of computer science focusing on "programming machines to perform tasks that replicate or augment aspects of human cognition."[16] By 2018, 87 percent of US cybersecurity professionals and 60 percent of those in Japan reported their organizations already used AI as part of their cybersecurity strategy.[17] By 2023, this number was closer to 100 percent for all organizations globally. It should be noted that the complexity of the AI used by different organizations varies substantially. AIs are software programs using algorithms that can learn and adapt to new inputs without assistance from human programmers. AIs perform tasks faster and more accurately than most, if not all, equivalent human users attempting to keep up with a deluge of data such as malware samples.[18] In the years ahead, AI models will help identify, anticipate and respond more swiftly to cyber threats, including malware, malicious IPs and websites.

When the first volume of this book came out, the idea of AI writing code was still in the realm of science fiction. Advances over the intervening years have seen massive leaps forward in the development of LLMs that can write code for nearly any application, conduct data analysis, solve complex questions, hold near human-quality conversations, translate texts or audio in near real-time and much more. Figure 10.1 shows a demonstration of code written by ChatGPT 4 (an LLM) to solve a common problem faced by type 1 diabetics in dosing the correct amount of insulin before eating a meal. In this figure, the LLM provides instructions on implementing code within Apple's iOS programming language Swift, and offers a sample code basis from which to develop a program.

Many students and readers will be familiar with ChatGPT as they are increasingly using it to write or edit papers and assist with other work assignments. Similarly, many professors are also faced with the challenge

```
import UIKit

class ViewController: UIViewController {

    // UI Outlets
    @IBOutlet weak var carbohydrateTextField: UITextField!
    @IBOutlet weak var ratioTextField: UITextField!
    @IBOutlet weak var resultLabel: UILabel!

    override func viewDidLoad () {
        super.viewDidLoad()
    }

    // Function to calculate insulin dose
    func calculateInsulinDose(carbs: Double, ratio: Double) ->
Double {
        return carbs / ratio
    }

    // Action for the calculate button
    @IBAction func onCalculateButtonTapped (_ sender: Any) {
        guard let carbsString = carbohydrateTextField.text,
              let ratioString = ratioTextField.text,
              let carbs = Double(carbsString),
              let ratio = Double(ratioString) else {
            resultLabel.text = "Invalid input"
            return
        }

        let insulinDose = calculateInsulinDose(carbs: carbs, ratio:
ratio)
        resultLabel.text = "Insulin dose: \(insulinDose) units"
    }
}
```

Figure 10.1 ChatGPT 4 output snippet of an application to determine insulin dosing for type 1 diabetics

of creating assignments that cannot be solved with ChatGPT, a task that has become increasingly difficult. ChatGPT is only one type of advanced AI in a field that is becoming crowded with advances that are changing the way in which people work. Generative AI is undermining the job security of content creators in many fields and shifting the way humans interact with different types of technology. ChatGPT is able to scan nearly the entire corpus of publicly accessible material on the Internet to generate its responses. Analysis of this vast trove of data far exceeds human capabilities. Microsoft's Bing search and Edge browser now both come with embedded LLM functionality.

LLMs are only the tip of a deeper iceberg of change that is taking place. Generative adversarial networks (GANs) are a class of machine learning frameworks able to create images of people who do not exist, swap the faces of people in real time on live video broadcasts, create new works of art, write symphonies, and much more. Much of what was once considered to be limited to human creativity has steadily shifted toward AI as well. Many mobile phones now allow users to create digital twins of their operators with simulated voices and responses. Digital twins are being used for healthcare and marketing analytics to predict human behaviors.[19] Cars with embedded AI can track and model the actions of their drivers, other drivers on the road, and road conditions to change driving behavior and enhance safety or offload the responsibilities of human drivers in certain circumstances. As AI becomes increasingly prominent in our lives, it will raise a growing range of security concerns.

At the intersection of increasingly large volumes of data and advances in AI, cybersecurity involves controlling data and algorithms. The convergence of big data, cloud computing and the IoT generates vast amounts of personal data. These data, combined with AIs, provide novel insights into human behavior that often extend well beyond the standard user's experience. Predictive analytics, behavioral modeling and more are changing our world. These developments raise public concern about the availability of personal data in cyberspace. Experts point out that a deterioration of privacy might be mirrored by an increasing level of societal acceptance of infringement on privacy.[20] Powerful AIs allow those that wield them to better target their interactions with individual users. Similarly, hackers exploit big data and AI to better identify potential targets and develop more sophisticated attacks, such as using LLMs and GANs to generate targeted social engineering campaigns. The growing role played by AI will force security professionals to adapt their practices to focus increasingly on overseeing machines and their users. AI does not work perfectly and the potential for error remains, not least because embedded code-based and data-based biases limit the fidelity of AI outputs. In one notable case, a crime prediction tool, which combined criminal data to tell officers where to focus their prevention efforts, was found to significantly amplify racially biased policing.[21] While AI offers many promises, humans remain essential to developing, using, making sense of and securing cyberspace.

Human–machine interactions

A third trend suggests that the boundaries between humans and machines will become increasingly blurred. Contemporary research on the brain–machine interface already allows humans to interact with computers by thought. Companies such as Neuralink and academic research labs at multiple institutions have begun seeking ways to build brain–computer interfaces – also known as brain–machine interfaces – that can reduce seizures, control prosthetics or assist in communication through AI voices, in computer text, or cursor movements on screens. Multiple fields of research now use the term "cyborgs" to identify individuals who bridge human–machine interactions. The merging of biological data and digital devices presents tremendous opportunities to improve standards of living. Recent experiences have seen tetraplegic patients directly control robotic prosthetic limbs from electrodes placed in their brain.[22] In 2016, the first artificial pancreas system was approved, and subsequent efforts in both expert and lay communities have continued to develop and implement AI to increasingly regulate bodily functions in real time.[23] These changes have fostered research investigating issues pertaining to body area networks in which devices arrayed on different parts of the body work together to create hybrid systems of communication and control.[24] Further research in this area examines whether the bridging of humans and machines creates national security risks that might undermine the capabilities of militaries to fight and win wars.[25]

As these advances continue to progress, new concerns are arising over bio-surveillance and the impact of new technologies on personal privacy. A scenario developed by the Center for Long-Term Cybersecurity at the University of Berkeley hypothesizes an "Internet of Emotion" in which computer devices – directly able to track our hormone levels, heart rate, facial expressions and voice – will be able to read our emotions and touch "the most sensitive aspects of human psychology." In this future, the report concludes, "managing and protecting an emotional public image and outward mindset appearance become basic social mainte-nance."[26] In the worst case, this is a future in which Internet users' privacy will increasingly fall prey to psychological manipulations and blackmail.

The possibility of a future in which AI directly augments human intel-ligence has encouraged researchers to examine the need for appropriate human-centered safeguards and ethical considerations in the develop-ment of AI technologies.[27] In recent years, a number of prominent TV shows – from *Black Mirror* to *Westworld* – have used fiction to explore the ethical implications of a future dominated by new forms of AI. As AI becomes more prominent, the role of humans will evolve increasingly toward oversight and management of computer systems. Automation requires guardians to ensure the continuity of the values, ethics and policies that define human societies. Prominent thinkers are currently debating whether humans should always have the ultimate say in this context, or whether machines might be able to act as their own masters.[28]

Both humans and machines will continue to generate cybersecurity vulnerabilities. Humans will continue to forget to install the latest secu-rity patch, fall for phishing attacks, and leave phones or other devices improperly secured. Computers will continue to have bugs, coded biases, hardware system flaws or flawed data inputs. As technologies change and humans and machines adapt and evolve, cybersecurity will remain necessary. Yet there is one invention on the horizon that portends a monumental shift in our understanding of ourselves and our universe; the next section focuses on this advance and explores its implications.

Quantum computing

Quantum computing is a branch of computer science poised to revolutionize the processing of data. It is likely to offer the first major revolution in fundamental computer architectures and logic since their invention prior to World War II. Quantum computers will allow for more complicated computational structures beyond binary 1s and 0s. Rather than a binary choice, a quantum computer faced with solving a maze does not need to try each turn independently to get from start to finish. Because it uses theories from quantum mechanics (a branch of physics) such as superposition (the ability of a particle to be in multiple states or positions simultaneously), it can explore all potential turns within a maze concurrently to find the solution of the maze far more rapidly than a conventional computer. Quantum computing is making substantial advances. In December 2023 IBM announced the first ever 1,000-qubit quantum processor.[29] Prior to this, the most recent advance by IBM, Google's 70-qubit system, could solve problems in seconds that the world's fastest conventional supercomputer could only solve in 47 years.[30] It is difficult to fathom the profound change that this sort of capability presents to the world. The speed with which quantum computing can solve even the most complicated problems could undermine most if not all current forms of encryption and offer potentially revolutionary advances in computational power, making the most computationally intensive tasks solvable in far shorter periods of time. Advances such as quantum computing and AI are expected to open new areas of research for fields as diverse as medicine and physics. In medicine, quantum computers could identify billions of new protein configurations or potential drug combinations that could cure human diseases. There is a great deal of hope associated with the potential of quantum computing. Scientists around the world are pondering what difficult questions they might answer if they had such a powerful computer. Yet at the same time, governments worry that the creation of such a tool will give the nation that possesses this technology an insurmountable lead that will dramatically change the global balance of power.

While quantum computers are making great strides, their ability to consistently solve problems and achieve stable states required for computation is still a work in progress. Most quantum computers must be kept extremely cold (near absolute zero), making their widespread use and adoption in the near future unrealistic. Major private firms and states are investing heavily into quantum computing, and the trajectory of advances over the previous 10 years has moved the science from theory to prototypes. Recent advances are substantially increasing the computational power of these devices, to a point where they are likely to become increasingly usable. Yet, less than a decade ago, most AI discussed in the previous section was in its nascent stages of development. In the intervening time, the technology has advanced to a place once thought impossible. It is likely that in another decade or so, quantum computing will also push the boundaries of science, engineering, computing and cybersecurity.

Conclusion: adapting to the evolving cybersecurity environment

Understanding current trends and alternative futures provides a foundation for considering the need for new cybersecurity policies and regulations. As computer systems and their interactions with humans become more diverse and complex, experts worry about the extent to which governments, businesses and broader society will be able to maintain security and privacy online.[31] Many of the cybersecurity trends discussed in this conclusion suggest a future in which privacy will decrease. If this is the case, policies and regulations will need to adapt to maintain acceptable levels of privacy. Commentators worry that the fast pace of technological change is outstripping laws and policies.[32] For instance, researchers have expressed concern that current cybersecurity policies do not adequately address human vulnerabilities, such as insider threats, and the risk posed by individuals bringing their own devices to work and taking those same devices back home.[33]

In a highly complex and decentralized environment, multiple divides – between countries, industries and organizations – will require more coordinated efforts to develop coherent cybersecurity regulations and practices. Cybersecurity scholar Benoit Dupont warns that "the escalation and acceleration of data flows may lead to a dilution of security responsibilities if adequate regulatory obligations are not developed and implemented."[34] The concept of multistakeholderism, introduced in chapter 3, might not be enough to overcome these divisions. New concepts and theories will be necessary to better understand and explain the governance of cybersecurity, and to help decision-makers develop and implement common regulations.

The growing complexity of cyberspace and cybersecurity threats will widen the gap between those that can achieve some degree of security and those that cannot. An ISOC report on "Paths to Our Digital Future" identifies a growing divide, not between those who have and do not have access to the Internet, but between those who have the skills and capabilities to protect their data and those who do not.[35] In a highly complex and divided environment, powerful states, companies and collectives will continue to dominate, while individual users struggle to understand the implications of their online activities. Cybersecurity is a booming sector that will require not only new technologies but also a steady influx of human talent.[36] The dearth of cybersecurity skills is already a major problem for many organizations. The tremendous growth of cybersecurity occupations poses pressing challenges in the fields of talent acquisition and education. The search for cyber talent will continue to create opportunities for non-state actors and companies, but also for groups of hackers, to sell their services to the highest bidders. Education and training will remain essential to foster tomorrow's cyber-security workforce.

A seminal report by the Internet Society on the future of the Internet notes that "new thinking, new approaches and new models are needed across the board, from Internet policy to addressing digital divides, from security approaches to economic regulations."[37] This book has provided a starting point for understanding some of the defining concepts and issues confronting contemporary cybersecurity. While cybersecurity has long been considered a topic for engineers and computer scientists, the last two decades have witnessed growing engagement from scholars and students in the social sciences and humanities. These disciplines are uniquely placed to make sense of the rapid changes and multiple dimensions of cybersecurity. From the individual to the organizational, national and international, the social sciences have a unique capacity to contribute to the analysis of cybersecurity.

Throughout the book, we have shown how the study of human and social relationships – specifically, of politics and international relations – provides insights into cybersecurity. Despite the pessimism and tech-nological determinism that mark some of the debate on the futures of cyberspace, the human and political nature of cyberspace also provides ground for optimism. Whatever the future of cybersecurity will be, understanding its core challenges and the role humans continue to play in shaping this domain is essential.

Additional resources

Tech4Humanity Lab, Case studies, at https://tech4humanitylab.org/case-stu dies.

World Economic Forum, Cybersecurity Futures 2030. New Foundations, White Paper, December 2023.

Notes

Introduction

1 Norbert Wiener, *Cybernetics: Or, Control and Communication in the Animal and the Machine* (New York: MIT Press, 1961).

2 John Arquilla and David Ronfeldt, "Cyberwar Is Coming!" *Comparative Strategy* 12/2 (1993): 141–65.

3 US Joint Chiefs of Staff, Joint Publication 3-12 (R), "Cyberspace Operations," Washington, DC, 2013, https://irp.fas.org/doddir/dod/jp3_12r.pdf.

4 Chris Demchak and Peter Dombrowski, "Cyber Westphalia: Asserting State Prerogatives in Cyberspace," *Georgetown Journal of International Affairs* (2013): 29–38.

5 William Gibson, *Neuromancer* (New York: Ace Books, 1984).

6 Craig Timberg, "The Real Story of How the Internet Became So Vulnerable," *Washington Post*, May 30, 2015, www.washingtonpost.com/sf/business/2015/05/30/net-of-insecurity-part-1.

7 AV-Test Institute, "Malware," www.av-test.org/en/statistics/malware.

8 Symantec, "Norton Cyber Security Insights Report Global Results 2017," www.nortonlifelock.com/us/en/newsroom/press-kits/ncsir-2017.

9 James Andrew Lewis, Hanna L. Malekos Smith and Eugenia Lostri, "The Hidden Cost of Cybercrime," CSIS/McAfee, 2020, 3, www.csis.org/analysis/hidden-costs-cybercrime.

10 Jonathan Vanian, "Here's How Much Businesses Worldwide Will Spend on Cybersecurity by 2020," *Fortune*, October 12, 2016, fortune.com/2016/10/12/cybersecurity-global-spending.

11 Alina Sylyukh, "A Year after San Bernardino and Apple–FBI, Where Are We on Encryption?" National Public Radio, December 3, 2016, www.npr.org/sections/alltechconsidered/2016/12/03/504130977/ayear-after-san-bernardino-and-apple-fbi-where-are-we-on-encryption.

12 Aaron F. Brantly, "Innovation and Adaptation in Jihadist Digital Security," *Survival* 59/1 (2017): 79–102.

13 David E. Sanger and William J. Broad, "Pentagon Suggests Countering Devastating Cyberattacks with Nuclear Arms," *New York Times*, January 16, 2018, www.nytimes.com/2018/01/16/us/politics/pentagonnuclear-review-cyberattack-trump.html.

1 The expanding scope of cybersecurity

1 Paul E. Ceruzzi, *Computing: A Concise History* (Cambridge, MA: MIT Press, 2012), 27; Graeme Philipson, "A Short History of Software," in *Management, Labour Process and Software Development: Reality Bites*, ed. Rowena Barrett (New York: Routledge, 2005), 14–15.
2 Ceruzzi, *Computing*, 6–7.
3 Loyd Searle, "The Bombsight War: Nordern vs. Sperry," *IEEE Spectrum* (1989): 60–4.
4 Ceruzzi, *Computing*, 33–7, 41.
5 Ibid., 46–7.
6 Philipson, "A Short History of Software," 15–17.
7 Beverley Steitz, "A Brief Computer History," 2006, http://people.bu.edu /baws/brief%20computer%20history.html.
8 Philipson, "A Short History of Software," 18.
9 Ceruzzi, *Computing*, 58–63.
10 Brad A. Myers, "A Brief History of Human–Computer Interaction Technology," *ACM Interactions* (1998): 47–8.
11 Martin Campbell-Kelly et al., *Computer: A History of the Information Machine* (New York: HarperCollins, 2017), 186–8.
12 Camille Ryan and Jamie M. Lewis, *Computer and Internet Use in the United States: 2015* (Washington, DC: US Census Bureau, 2017), 3.
13 Pew Research Center, "Global Computer Ownership," March 18, 2015, www.pewglobal.org/2015/03/19/internet-seen-as-positive-influence-on-educa tion-but-negative-influence-on-morality-in-emerging-anddeveloping-nations/technology-report-15.
14 Derek S. Reveron, "An Introduction to National Security and Cyberspace," in *Cyberspace and National Security: Threats, Opportunities, and Power in a Virtual World*, ed. Derek S. Reveron (Washington, DC: Georgetown University Press, 2012), 7.
15 David C. Mowery and Timothy Simcoe, "Is the Internet a US Invention? An Economic and Technological History of Computer Networking," *Research Policy* 31 (2002): 1369–70.
16 Reveron, "An Introduction to National Security and Cyberspace," 7; Michael Warner, "Intelligence in Cyber – and Cyber in Intelligence," in *Understanding Cyber Conflict*, ed. George Perkovich and Ariel E. Levite (Washington, DC: Georgetown University Press, 2018), 24.
17 Peter W. Singer and Allan Friedman, *Cybersecurity and Cyberwar: What Everyone Needs to Know* (Oxford University Press, 2014), 16.
18 Mowery and Simcoe, "Is the Internet a US Invention?" 1373.
19 Ibid., 1373.
20 Barry M. Leiner et al., "The Past and Future History of the Internet," *Communications of the ACM* 40/2 (1997): 104.

21 Mowery and Simcoe, "Is the Internet a US Invention?" 1372.
22 Ceruzzi, *Computing*, 123; Thomas Rid, *Rise of the Machines: A Cybernetic History* (London: Scribe, 2016), 181–94.
23 Gibson, *Neuromancer*, 69.
24 Mowery and Simcoe, "Is the Internet a US Invention?" 1375.
25 A supercomputer has a high level of performance compared to general-purpose computers in use at the time.
26 Mowery and Simcoe, "Is the Internet a US Invention?" 1371; Ceruzzi, *Computing*, 131.
27 Mowery and Simcoe, "Is the Internet a US Invention?" 1376–7.
28 Singer and Friedman, *Cybersecurity and Cyberwar*, 20.
29 Mowery and Simcoe, "Is the Internet a US Invention?" 1378; Edward Skoudis, "Evolutionary Trends in Cyberspace," in *Cyberpower and National Security*, ed. Franklin D. Kramer, Stuart H. Starr and Larry K. Wentz (Washington, DC: National Defense University, 2009), 149.
30 "A Brief History of Wi-Fi," *The Economist*, June 10, 2004, 26; Ceruzzi, *Computing*, 139–40.
31 Darcy DiNucci, "Fragmented Future," *Print* 53/4 (1999): 32.
32 Milton L. Mueller, *Networks and States: The Global Politics of Internet Governance* (Cambridge, MA: MIT Press, 2010), 1; Mary McEvoy Manjikian, "From Global Village to Virtual Battlespace: The Colonizing of the Internet and the Extension of Realpolitik," *International Studies Quarterly* 54/2 (2010): 381–401.
33 Skoudis, "Evolutionary Trends in Cyberspace," 156–7.
34 White House, National Security Decision Directive 145, "National Policy on Telecommunications and Automated Information Systems Security," September 17, 1984, 1.
35 Clifford Stoll, *The Cuckoo's Egg: Tracking a Spy through the Maze of Computer Espionage* (New York: Doubleday, 1989); Wayne Madsen, "Intelligence Agency Threats to Computer Security," *International Journal of Intelligence and CounterIntelligence* 6/4 (1993), 413–88; Clifford Stoll, "Stalking the Wily Hacker," *Communications of the ACM* 31/5 (1988): 484–97.
36 John Arquilla and David F. Ronfeldt, *Cyberwar Is Coming!* (Santa Monica, CA: RAND, 1992); Eric Harnett, "Welcome to Hyperwar," *Bulletin of the Atomic Scientists* 48/7 (1992): 14–21.
37 Michael Warner, "Cybersecurity: A Pre-history," *Intelligence and National Security* 27/5 (2012): 781–99.
38 Fred Kaplan, *Dark Territory: The Secret History of Cyber War* (New York: Simon & Schuster, 2017), 57–79.
39 Vin McLellan, "Case of the Purloined Password," *New York Times*, July 26, 1981, F4.

40 British Broadcasting Corporation, "Bill Gates's Desert Island Playlist," January 31, 2016, www.bbc.co.uk/news/magazine-35442969.

41 For a short timeline of cybercrimes, see Symantec, "Cybercrime Time-Line," www.symantec.com/region/sg/homecomputing/library/cybercrime.html.

42 Andrew Murray, *Information Technology Law: The Law and Society* (Oxford University Press, 2016), 357–8.

43 Jessica Johnston, *Technological Turf Wars: A Case Study of the Computer Antivirus Industry* (Philadelphia: Temple University Press, 2009).

44 This test was first revealed by CNN, which has also made a video of the test available on its website. See Jeanne Meserve, "Mouse Click Could Plunge City into Darkness, Experts Say," *CNN*, September 27, 2007, http://edition.cnn.com/2007/US/09/27/power.at.risk/index.html.

45 White House, "The National Strategy to Secure Cyberspace," February 2003, ix, https://georgewbush-whitehouse.archives.gov/pcipb.

46 For an overview of cybersecurity organizations and strategies in a number of developed countries, see: NATO Cooperative Cyber Defence Centre of Excellence, "National Cyber Security Organisation," https://ccdcoe.org/national-cyber-security-organisation.html.

47 Lev Grossman, "Attack of the Love Bug," *Time*, May 15, 2000, 37.

48 "Turk, Moroccan Nabbed in Huge Worm Case," *CNN*, August 26, 2005, http://money.cnn.com/2005/08/26/technology/worm_arrest; Skoudis, "Evolutionary Trends in Cyberspace," 167.

49 Mandiant Threat Intelligence Center, "APT1: Exposing One of China's Cyber Espionage Units," 2011, 20, www.fireeye.com/content/dam/fireeye-www/services/pdfs/mandiant-apt1-report.pdf.

50 "European Repository of Cyber Incidents (EuRepoC)," May 2023, https://eurepoc.eu/database.

2 What is cyberspace?

1 Kaplan, *Dark Territory*.

2 Tibi Puiu, "Your Smartphone Is Millions of Times More Powerful than All of NASA's Combined Computing in 1969," October 12, 2015, www.zme science.com/research/technology/smartphone-powercompared-to-apollo-432.

3 Rid, *Rise of the Machines*.

4 Gibson, *Neuromancer*.

5 Greg Conti and David Raymond, *On Cyber: Towards an Operational Art for Cyber Conflict* (n.p.: Kopidion Press, 2017).

6 Thomas C. Folsom, "Defining Cyberspace (Finding Real Virtue in the Place of Virtual Reality)," *Tulane Journal of Technology and Intellectual Property* 9/1 (2007): 75.

7 Kuehl cited in Franklin D. Kramer, "Cyberpower and National Security: Policy Recommendations for a Strategic Framework," in *Cyberpower and National Security*, ed. Kramer, Starr and Wentz, 4.

8 *Oxford Dictionaries*, s.v. "Electronic," https://en.oxforddictionaries.com/de finition/electronic.

9 *Oxford Dictionaries*, s.v. "Electromagnetic spectrum," https:// en.oxforddic tionaries.com/definition/electromagnetic_spectrum.

10 US Joint Chiefs of Staff, Joint Publication 3-12 (R), "Cyberspace Operations."

11 Brandon Valeriano and Ryan C. Maness, *Cyber War versus Cyber Realities: Cyber Conflict in the International System* (New York: Oxford University Press, 2015); Lucas Kello, *The Virtual Weapon and International Order* (New Haven, CT: Yale University Press, 2017); Alexander Klimburg, *The Darkening: The War for Cyberspace* (New York: Penguin Books, 2017).

12 Amy Nordrum, "Popular Internet of Things Forecast of 50 Billion Devices by 2020 Is Outdated," *IEEE Spectrum*, August 18, 2016, https://spectrum .ieee.org/tech-talk/telecom/internet/popular-internet-ofthings-forecast-of -50-billion-devices-by-2020-is-outdated.

13 Om Malik, "Gigaom | 100G, 200G, 400G: Internet's Core Is Getting Fatter to Meet Our Tech Planet's Bandwidth Demand," August 16, 2013, https://gigaom.com/2013/08/16/100g-200g-400g-internets-coreis-getting-fatter-to-meet-our-tech-planets-bandwidth-demand; Rounak Jain, "Cisco's New Router Can Go up to 25 Terabytes per Second – but It's Not the Fastest Speed that Money Can Buy," *Business Insider*, December 12, 2019, www.businessinsider.in/tech/news/ciscos-new-router-can-go-25-terabytes-per-second-but-its-not-the-fastest-speed-that-money-can-buy/articleshow/72487162.cms.

14 Ramakrishnan Durairajan et al., *InterTubes* (New York: ACM Press, 2015), 565–78.

15 Tom Parfitt, "Georgian Woman Cuts Off Web Access to Whole of Armenia," *Guardian*, April 6, 2011, www.theguardian.com/world/2011 /apr/06/georgian-woman-cuts-web-access.

16 Maddie Stone, "What Would Happen If a Massive Solar Storm Hit the Earth?" August 20, 2015, https://gizmodo.com/what-would-happen-if-a-massive-solar-storm-hit-the-eart-1724650105.

17 David Kravets, "It's Official: Sharks No Longer a Threat to Subsea Internet Cables," *ArsTechnica*, July 10, 2015, https://arstechnica.com/tech-policy /2015/07/its-official-sharks-no-longer-a-threat-to-subsea-internet-cables.

18 Louis Matsakis, "What Would Really Happen If Russia Attacked Undersea Internet Cables," *Wired*, January 15, 2018, www.wired.com/story/russia -undersea-internet-cables.

19 Asma Ali Zain, "Cable Damage Hits One Million Internet Users in UAE," *Khaleej Times*, February 4, 2008, www.khaleejtimes.com/nation/general /cable-damage-hits-one-million-internet-users-in-uae.

20 "Packet Switching History," www.livinginternet.com/i/iw_packet_inv .htm.

21 Lawrence G. Roberts, "The Evolution of Packet Switching," *Proceedings of the IEEE* 66/11 (1978): 1307–13.

22 Katie Hafner and Matthew Lyon, *Where Wizards Stay Up Late: The Origins of the Internet* (New York: Simon & Schuster, 1996).

23 Vinton G. Cerf and Robert E. Kahn, "A Protocol for Packet Network Intercommunication," *Data Communications of the IEEE Communications Society* 22/5 (1974): 1–13.

24 Matthew G. Naugle, *Network Protocols* (New York: McGraw-Hill Professional, 1999).

25 "Exploiting Heartbleed," *Infosec Institute*, April 18, 2014, http:// resources .infosecinstitute.com/exploiting-heartbleed.

26 Brian Krebs, "AshleyMadison Hack – Krebs on Security," September 23, 2015, https://krebsonsecurity.com/tag/ashleymadison-hack.

27 Adrian Bridgewater, "20% of Cyber-Attacks Attributed to Conficker Worm," *SCMagazine*, December 7, 2015, www.scmagazineuk.com/news /20-of-cyber-attacks-attributed-to-conficker-worm/article/535571.

28 Brett Hawkins, "Case Study: The Home Depot Data Breach," *SANS Institute InfoSec Reading Room*, January 2015, www.sans.org/reading-room /whitepapers/breaches/case-study-home-depot-databreach-36367; Xiaokui Shu et al., "Breaking the Target: An Analysis of Target Data Breach and Lessons Learned," arXiv (January 2017), 1–10, https://arxiv.org/pdf/1701 .04940.

29 Ron Ross, Michael McEvilley and Janey Carrier Oren, *Systems Security Engineering* (Gaithersburg, MD: National Institute of Standards and Technology, 2016).

30 Dan Mayer, "Ratio of Bugs Per Line of Code," November 10, 2012, www .mayerdan.com/ruby/2012/11/11/bugs-per-line-of-code-ratio.

31 Lance Ulanoff, "Ford Ready to Innovate, but Not at the Expense of Customer Needs," *Mashable*, May 21, 2015, https://mashable.com/20 16/05/31/mark-fields-ford-codecon; David Flynn, "New Mercedes-Benz E-Class Has More Lines of Computer Code than an Airbus A380," *Australian Business Traveller*, August 30, 2016, www.ausbt.com.au/new-me rcedes-benz-e-class-has-more-lines-of-computercode-than-an-airbus-a380.

32 Ben Collins and Joseph Cox, "Jenna Abrams, Russia's Clown Troll Princess, Duped the Mainstream Media and the World," *Daily Beast*, November 2, 2017, www.thedailybeast.com/jenna-abrams-russias-clown-troll-princess-duped-the-mainstream-media-and-the-world.

33 Ned Kock, "E-Collaboration and E-Commerce in Virtual Worlds," *International Journal of E-Collaboration* 4/3 (2008): 1–13.

34 Aaron F. Brantly, "The Cyber Losers," *Democracy and Security* 10/2 (2014): 132–55.

35 Paul Syverson, "A Peel of Onion," *Proceedings of the 27th Annual Computer Security Applications Conference* (2011): 123–37.

36 Aaron F. Brantly, *The Decision to Attack: Military and Intelligence Cyber Decision-Making* (Athens: University of Georgia Press, 2016).

37 A plausibly deniable operation that pretends to originate from a third party.

38 Marc Goodman, *Future Crimes: Everything Is Connected, Everyone Is Vulnerable and What We Can Do about It* (New York: Doubleday, 2015); Brantly, "Innovation and Adaptation in Jihadist Digital Security."

39 Steve Durbin, "Insiders Are Today's Biggest Security Threat," *Recode*, May 24, 2016, www.recode.net/2016/5/24/11756584/cyberattack-data-breach -insider-threat-steve-durbin.

40 Fran Howarth, "The Role of Human Error in Successful Security Attacks," *SecurityIntelligence*, September 2, 2014, https://securityintelligence.com /the-role-of-human-error-in-successful-security-attacks.

3 Governing cyberspace

1 Working Group on Internet Governance, "Report," June 2005, www.wgig .org/docs/WGIGREPORT.pdf.

2 Laura DeNardis, *Protocol Politics: The Globalization of Internet Governance* (Cambridge, MA: MIT Press, 2009).

3 Steven Levy, *Hackers: Heroes of the Computer Revolution* (Sebastopol, CA: O'Reilly Media, 2010), 7–10.

4 Janet Abbate, *Inventing the Internet* (Cambridge, MA: MIT Press, 2000); Hafner and Lyon, *Where Wizards Stay Up Late*.

5 Network Working Group, "Request for Comments: 2, [unknown title]," n.d., https://tools.ietf.org/html/rfc2, and "Request for Comments: 3, Documentation Conventions," April 1969, https://tools.ietf.org/html /rfc3.

6 Sandra Braman, "The Interpenetration of Technical and Legal Decision-Making for the Internet," *Information, Communication & Society* 13/3 (2010): 309–24.

7 Network Working Group, "Request for Comments: 322, Well Known Socket Numbers," March 26, 1972, https://tools.ietf.org/html/rfc322.

8 Network Working Group, "Request for Comments: 1083, IAB Official Protocol Standards," December 1998, https://tools.ietf.org/html/ rfc1083.

9 Jovan Kurbalija, *An Introduction to Internet Governance*, 7th edn. (Geneva: DiploFoundation, 2016).

10 US Government, "Improvement of Technical Management of Internet

Names and Addresses; Proposed Rule," in *Federal Register*, vol. LXIII (Washington, DC: Office of the Federal Register, 1998).

11 Laura DeNardis, *The Global War for Internet Governance* (New Haven, CT: Yale University Press, 2014).

12 Ryan Singel, "Pakistan's Accidental YouTube Re-routing Exposes Trust Flaw in Net," *Wired*, February 25, 2008, www.wired.com/2008/02/pakistans-accid.

13 Arielle Pardes, "What Is GDPR and Why Should You Care?" *Wired*, May 24, 2018, www.wired.com/story/how-gdpr-affects-you.

14 Bill Marczak and John Scott-Railton, "Keep Calm and (Don't) Enable Macros: A New Threat Actor Targets UAE Dissidents – the Citizen Lab," Citizen Lab, May 29, 2016, https://citizenlab.ca/2016/05/stealth-falcon.

15 Fergus Hanson, *Revolution @State: The Spread of Ediplomacy* (Sydney: Lowy Institute for International Affairs, 2012).

16 Sue Pleming, "U.S. State Department Speaks to Twitter over Iran," *Reuters*, June 16, 2009, www.reuters.com/article/idUSWBT011374.

17 Netmundial, "NetMundial Multistakeholder Statement," Sao Paulo, Brazil, April 24, 2014, http://netmundial.br/netmundial-multistakeholder-statement.

18 Jeremy Malcolm, "Internet Governance and the NETmundial Initiative: A Flawed Attempt at Turning Words into Action," Electronic Frontier Foundation, August 28, 2014, www.eff.org/deeplinks/2014/08/internet-governance-and-netmundial-initiative-flawed-attempt-turningwords-action.

19 Robert O. Keohane and Joseph S. Nye, *Power and Interdependence: World Politics in Transition* (Boston: Little, Brown, 1977).

20 Alexander Wendt, "Anarchy Is What States Make of It," *International Organization* 46/2 (1992): 391–425.

21 Mark Raymond and Laura DeNardis, "Multistakeholderism: Anatomy of an Inchoate Global Institution," *International Theory* 7/3 (2015): 572–616.

22 Adam Segal, "Holding the Multistakeholder Line at the ITU," *Council on Foreign Relations*, October 21, 2014, www.cfr.org/report/holding-multistakeholder-line-itu.

23 Milton Mueller, *Will the Internet Fragment? Sovereignty, Globalization and Cyberspace* (Malden, MA: Polity, 2017).

24 Bob Price, "Portugal Hints at What the American Internet Could Eventually Look Like without Net Neutrality," *Business Insider*, December 14, 2017, www.businessinsider.com/net-neutrality-portugal-how-american-internet-could-look-fcc-2017-11.

25 Melissa Locker, "John Oliver Is Calling on You to Save Net Neutrality, Again," *Time*, May 8, 2017, http://time.com/4770205/john-oliver-fcc-net-neutrality.

26 Video: Burger King, "Whopper Neutrality," January 24, 2018, www.youtu be.com/watch?v=ltzy5vRmN8Q.

27 Council of Europe, Convention on Cybercrime, Budapest, November 23, 2001, www.coe.int/en/web/conventions/full-list/-/conventions/rms/09000 01680081561.

28 Alex Grigsby, "The UN GGE on Cybersecurity: What Is the UN's Role?" Council on Foreign Relations, April 15, 2015, www.cfr.org/blog/un-gge -cybersecurity-what-uns-role.

29 Michael N. Schmitt, *Tallinn Manual on the International Law Applicable to Cyber Warfare: Prepared by the International Group of Experts at the Invitation of the NATO Cooperative Cyber Defence Centre of Excellence* (Cambridge University Press, 2013); Michael N. Schmitt and Liis Vihul, *Tallinn Manual 2.0 on the International Law Applicable to Cyber Operations* (Cambridge University Press, 2017).

30 Heather Harrison Dinniss, *Cyber Warfare and the Laws of War* (New York: Cambridge University Press, 2012).

31 Aaron F. Brantly, "The Most Governed Ungoverned Space: Legal and Policy Constraints on Military Operations in Cyberspace," *SAIS Review of International Affairs* 36/2 (2016): 29–39.

32 Catherine Lotrionte, "A Better Defense: Examining the United States' New Norms-Based Approach to Cyber Deterrence," *Georgetown Journal of International Affairs* (2016): 75–88.

33 Josephine Wolff, *Cyberinsurance Policy: Rethinking Risk in an Age of Ransomware, Computer Fraud, Data Breaches, and Cyberattacks* (Cambridge, MA: MIT Press, 2022), 111–49.

34 Department of the Treasury, "Potential Federal Insurance Response to Catastrophic Cyber Incidents," *Federal Register* 87/188, September 29, 2022, 59161-3.

35 Barack Obama, "Cyber-Insurance Metrics and Impact on Cyber-Security," Washington, DC: The White House, https://obamawhitehouse.archives .gov/files/documents/cyber/ISA%20-%20Cyber-Insurance%20Metrics %20and%20Impact%20on%20Cyber-Security.pdf.

36 Joseph R. Biden, "National Cybersecurity Strategy 2023," Washington, DC: The White House, March 2023, www.whitehouse.gov/wp-content /uploads/2023/03/National-Cybersecurity-Strategy-2023.pdf.

37 Federal Trade Commission, "Cyber Insurance," www.ftc.gov/business-guidance/small-businesses/cybersecurity/cyber-insurance.

38 Angelica Marotta et al., "Cyber-Insurance Survey," *Computer Science Review* 24 (2017): 35–61.

39 Nir Kshetri, "The Economics of Cyber-Insurance," *IEEE IT Professional* 20/6 (2019): 9–14.

40 Sasha Romanosky et al., "Content Analysis of Cyber Insurance Policies:

How Do Carriers Price Cyber Risk?" *Journal of Cybersecurity* 5/1 (2019): 1–19; Ranjan Pal et al., "Will Cyber-Insurance Improve Network Security? A Market Analysis," *IEEE INFOCOM 2014 – IEEE Conference on Computer Communications* (2014): 235–43.

41 European Union Agency for Cybersecurity, "Cyber Insurance: Fitting the Needs of Operators of Essential Services?" February 23, 2023, www.enisa.europa.eu/news/cyber-insurance-fitting-the-needs-of-operators-of-essential-services.

4 Cyber capabilities and insecurity

1 US Joint Chiefs of Staff, Joint Publication 3-12 (R), "Cyberspace Operations."

2 Stanley Sandler, *World War II in the Pacific: An Encyclopedia* (New York: Routledge, 2015).

3 Michael Dobbs, *One Minute to Midnight: Kennedy, Khrushchev, and Castro on the Brink of Nuclear War* (New York: Vintage Books, 2009).

4 Homer, *The Iliad & the Odyssey* (New York: Barnes & Noble Books, 2008).

5 Peiter Mudge Zatko, "If You Don't Like the Game, Hack the Playbook," presentation at DARPA Cyber Colloquium, November 7, 2011, Arlington, VA.

6 US House of Representatives, Committee on Oversight and Government Reform, Subcommittee on Information Technology, "Wassenaar: Cybersecurity and Export Control," 114th Congress, 2nd sess., January 12, 2016, https://oversight.house.gov/hearing/wassenaar-cybersecurity-and-export-control.

7 Jacob Benjamin and Michael Haney, "Nonproliferation of Cyber Weapons," *2020 International Conference on Computational Science and Computational Intelligence* (2020): 105–8; Thomas Reinhold and Christian Reuter, "Toward a Cyber Weapons Assessment Model – Assessment of the Technical Features of Malicious Software," *IEEE Transactions on Technology and Society* 3/3 (2022): 226–39.

8 Aaron F. Brantly, "Public Health and Epidemiological Approaches to National Cybersecurity: A Baseline Comparison," in *US National Cybersecurity: International Politics, Concepts and Organization*, ed. Damien Van Puyvelde and Aaron F. Brantly (New York: Routledge, 2017), 91–109.

9 Kevin Mitnick and William L. Simon, *Ghost in the Wires: My Adventures as the World's Most Wanted Hacker* (New York: Little, Brown and Company, 2011).

10 Choong Nyoung Kim, Kyung Hoon Yang and Jaekyung Kim, "Human Decision-Making Behavior and Modeling Effects," *Decision Support Systems* 45/3 (2008): 517–27; Isabella Corradini, Enrico Nardelli and

Tareq Ahram, *Advances in Human Factors in Cybersecurity, AHFE Virtual Conference on Human Factors in Cybersecurity* (Cham: Springer, 2020).

11 IBM Global Technology Services, "IBM Security Services 2014 Cyber Security Intelligence Index," https://media.scmagazine.com/documents/82/ibm_cyber_security_intelligenc_20450.pdf.

12 Author conversation with Vice Admiral Nancy A. Norton, March 2018.

13 Mayer, "Ratio of Bugs Per Line of Code."

14 Dick O'Brien, "ISTR Ransomware 2017," *Internet Security Threat Report,* July 2017, www.symantec.com/content/dam/symantec/docs/security-center/white-papers/istr-ransomware-2017-en.pdf.

15 Ibid.

16 National Audit Office, "Investigation: WannaCry Cyber Attack and the NHS," October 27, 2017, www.nao.org.uk/report/investigation-wannacry-cyber-attack-and-the-nhs.

17 Alejandro Calleja and Juan Caballero, *A Look into 30 Years of Malware Development from a Software Metrics Perspective* (Cham: Springer, 2016), 325–45.

18 Brett Stone-Gross et al., "The Underground Economy of Fake Antivirus Software," in *Economics of Information Security and Privacy III*, ed. Bruce Schneier (New York: Springer, 2013), 55–78.

19 Brian Krebs, "Shadowy Russian Firm Seen as Conduit for Cybercrime," *Washington Post*, October 13, 2007, A15.

20 Rhys Blakely, Jonathan Richards and Tony Halpin, "Cybergang Raises Fear of New Crime Wave," *The Times*, November 10, 2007, 13.

21 David Bizeul, "Russian Business Network Study," 2007, www.bizeul.org/files/RBN_study.pdf.

22 John Markoff, "Before the Gunfire, Cyberattacks," *New York Times*, August 13, 2008, A1.

23 Bizeul, "Russian Business Network Study."

24 Shadow Server Foundation, "AS40989 RBN as Rbusiness Network," www.shadowserver.org/wp-content/uploads/2019/04/RBN-AS40989.pdf.

25 John Leyden, "Bulletproof Hosts Stay Online by Operating out of Disputed Backwaters," *Register*, October 5, 2017, www.theregister.co.uk/2017/10/05/bulletproof_hosting.

26 David E. Sanger, David Barboza and Nicole Perlroth, "China's Army Is Seen as Tied to Hacking against U.S.," *New York Times*, February 19, 2013, A1.

27 Mandiant Threat Intelligence Center, "APT1."

28 Ibid.

29 Ibid., 8.

30 Ibid., 3.

31 Ibid., 2.

32 Giora Engel, "Deconstructing the Cyber Kill Chain," DarkReading, November 18, 2014, www.darkreading.com/attacks-breaches/deconstruc ting-the-cyber-kill-chain/a/d-id/1317542; Lockheed Martin, "The Cyber Kill Chain," www.lockheedmartin.com/en-us/capabilities/cyber/cyber-kill -chain.html.

33 Sydney J. Freedberg Jr., "Cyber Command Lawyer Praises Stuxnet, Disses Chinese Cyber Stance," *Breaking Defense*, March 12, 2012, https://bre akingdefense.com/2012/03/cyber-commandlawyer-praises-stuxnet-disses -chinese-cyber-stanc.

34 Kim Zetter, *Countdown to Zero Day: Stuxnet and the Launch of the World's First Digital Weapon* (New York: Broadway Books, 2014).

35 Jason Healey, *A Fierce Domain: Conflict in Cyberspace, 1986 to 2012* (Arlington, VA: Cyber Conflict Studies Association, 2013).

36 Aaron F. Brantly, Nerea M. Cal and Devlin P. Winkelstein, *Defending the Borderland: Ukrainian Military Experiences with IO, Cyber, and EW* (West Point, NY: US Army Cyber Institute, 2017), www.dtic.mil/dtic/tr/fulltext /u2/1046052.pdf.

37 US Department of Justice, "Fugitive Computer Hacker Arrested in North Carolina," February 15, 1995, www.justice.gov/opa/pr/Pre_96/ February95/89.txt.html.

38 Chris Williams, "Today the Web Was Broken by Countless Hacked Devices – Your 60-Second Summary," *Register*, October 21, 2016, www.th eregister.co.uk/2016/10/21/dyn_dns_ddos_explained.

39 Mandiant Threat Intelligence Center, "APT1."

40 Stoll, *The Cuckoo's Egg*.

41 Herbert Lin, "Operational Considerations in Cyber Attack and Cyber Exploitation," in *Cyberspace and National Security*, ed. Reveron, 37–56.

42 David E. Sanger, *The Perfect Weapon: War, Sabotage, and Fear in the Cyber Age* (New York: Crown Publishers, 2018).

43 Aaron F. Brantly, "The Violence of Hacking: State Violence and Cyberspace," *Cyber Defense Review* 2/1 (2017): 1–19.

44 Richard A. Clarke and Robert K. Knake, *Cyber War: The Next Threat to National Security and What to Do about It* (New York: Ecco, 2010).

45 Kello, *The Virtual Weapon and International Order*; Thomas Rid, "Cyber War Will Not Take Place," *Journal of Strategic Studies* 35/1 (2012): 5–32; Erik Gartzke and Jon R. Lindsay, "Weaving Tangled Webs: Offense, Defense, and Deception in Cyberspace," *Security Studies* 24/2 (2015): 316–48.

46 Richard Forno and Anupam Joshi, "How U.S. 'Cyber Bombs' against Terrorists Really Work," *Scientific American*, May 13, 2016, www.scientific american.com/article/how-u-s-cyber-bombs-againstterroristsreally-work.

5 Cybersecurity and strategy

1 Damien Van Puyvelde and Aaron F. Brantly (eds.), *US National Cybersecurity: International Politics, Concepts and Organization* (Abingdon: Routledge, 2017), 2–3.

2 See Brandon Valeriano, Benjamin Jensen and Ryan C. Maness, *Cyber Strategy: The Evolving Character of Power and Coercion* (Oxford University Press, 2018).

3 For a classic definition, see Arnold Wolfers, "National Security as an Ambiguous Symbol," *Political Science Quarterly* 67/4 (1952): 483–4.

4 Alan G. Stolberg, "Crafting National Interests in the 21st Century," in *U.S. Army War College Guide to National Security Issues*, vol. II: *National Security Policy and Strategy*, ed. J. Boone Bartholomees Jr. (Carlisle, PA: Strategic Studies Institute, 2012), 13–14.

5 Joseph S. Nye, "Get Smart: Combining Hard and Soft Power," *Foreign Affairs* 88/4 (2009): 160–3.

6 John Sheldon, "The Rise of Cyberpower," in *Strategy in the Contemporary World*, ed. John Baylis, James J. Wirtz and Colin S. Gray (Oxford University Press, 2013), 306.

7 Daniel T. Kuehl, "From Cyberspace to Cyberpower: Defining the Problem," in *Cyberpower and National Security*, ed. Kramer, Starr and Wentz, 39.

8 Tina Highfill and Christopher Surfield, "New and Revised Statistics of the U.S. Digital Economy 2005–2021," Bureau of Economic Analysis, U.S. Department of Commerce, November 2022, www.bea.gov/system /files/2022-11/new-and-revised-statistics-of-the-us-digital-economy-2005 -2021.pdf; Yi Wu, "Understanding China's Digital Economy: Policies, Opportunities, and Challenges," *China Briefing*, August 11, 2022, www.ch ina-briefing.com/news/understanding-chinas-digital-economy-policies-op portunities-and-challenges/#:~:text=Statistics%20also%20show%20that %20the,expansion%20of%20digital%20infrastructure%20construction.

9 Joseph S. Nye, "Hard, Soft, and Smart Power," in *The Oxford Handbook of Modern Diplomacy*, ed. Andrew F. Cooper, Jorge Heine and Ramesh Thakur (Oxford University Press, 2013), 559–74.

10 Kramer, Starr and Wentz (eds.), *Cyberpower and National Security*, xvi.

11 Kuehl, "From Cyberspace to Cyberpower: Defining the Problem," 41–2.

12 W. Alexander Vacca, "Military Culture and Cyber Security," *Survival* 53/6 (2011): 159.

13 James J. Wirtz, "Cyber War and Strategic Culture: The Russian Integration of Cyber Power into Grand Strategy," in *Cyber War in Perspective: Russian Aggression against Ukraine*, ed. Kenneth Geers (Tallinn: NATO Cooperative Cyber Defence Centre of Excellence, 2015), 30.

14 Alastair Iain Johnston, "Thinking about Strategic Culture," *International*

Security 19/4 (1995): 32–64; R. Uz Zaman, "Strategic Culture: A 'Cultural' Understanding of War," *Comparative Strategy* 28/1 (2009): 82–3.

15 European Union Agency for Cybersecurity, "A Governance Framework for National Cybersecurity Strategies," February 2023, www.enisa.europa .eu/publications/a-governance-framework-for-national-cybersecurity-stra tegies.

16 US Department of State, "A Declaration for the Future of the Internet," April 2022, www.state.gov/wp-content/uploads/2022/04/Declaration-for -the-Future-for-the-Internet.pdf.

17 Nigel Inkster, *China's Cyber Power* (Abingdon: Routledge, 2016).

18 Greg Austin, *Cyber Policy in China* (New York: Polity, 2014).

19 Jon R. Lindsay, "Introduction: China and Cybersecurity – Controversy and Context," in *China and Cybersecurity: Espionage, Strategy, and Politics in the Digital Domain*, ed. Jon R. Lindsay, Tai Ming Cheung and Derek S. Reveron (Oxford University Press, 2015), 1–2.

20 Kathrin Hikle, "How China Polices the Internet," *Financial Times*, July 25, 2009, 2.

21 Lindsay, "Introduction: China and Cybersecurity," 10–11.

22 Chris Demchak and Peter Dombrowski, "Rise of a Cybered Westphalian Age," *Strategic Studies Quarterly* 5/1 (2011): 45.

23 Gary King, Jennifer Pan and Margaret E. Roberts, "How Censorship in China Allows Government Criticism but Silences Collective Expression," *American Political Science Review* 107/2 (2013): 326–43.

24 Valeriano, Jensen and Maness, *Cyber Strategy*, 146.

25 Singer and Friedman, *Cybersecurity and Cyberwar*, 139.

26 Zhuge Jianwei et al., "Investigating the Chinese Online Underground Economy," in *China and Cybersecurity*, ed. Lindsay, Cheung and Reveron, 87–120.

27 Singer and Friedman, *Cybersecurity and Cyberwar*, 142; Valeriano, Jensen and Maness, *Cyber Strategy*, 144–5.

28 Jeffrey B. Jones, "Confronting China's Efforts to Steal Defense Information," The Belfer Center for Science and International Affairs, May 2020, www.belfercenter.org/sites/default/files/2020-05/ChinaStealing .pdf.

29 Timothy L. Thomas, "Nation-State Cyber Strategies: Examples from China and Russia," in *Cyberpower and National Security*, ed. Kramer, Starr and Wentz, 468–75.

30 David E. Sanger and Nicole Perlroth, "N.S.A. Breached Chinese Servers Seen as Security Threat," *New York Times*, March 22, 2014.

31 Lindsay, "Introduction: China and Cybersecurity," 17.

32 Valeriano, Jensen and Maness, *Cyber Strategy*, 146.

33 Lindsay, "Introduction: China and Cybersecurity," 7.

34 Ronald J. Deibert, *Black Code: Surveillance, Privacy, and the Dark Side of the Internet* (Toronto: McClelland & Stewart, 2013), 21–6.

35 Valeriano, Jensen and Maness, *Cyber Strategy*, 150.

36 Robert Sheldon and Joe McReynolds, "Civil–Military Integration and Cybersecurity: A Study of Chinese Information Warfare Militias," in *China and Cybersecurity*, ed. Lindsay, Cheung and Reveron, 190; Nigel Inkster, "The Chinese Intelligence Agencies: Evolution and Empowerment," in *China and Cybersecurity*, ed. Lindsay, Cheung and Reveron, 35–7.

37 Dmitry (Dima) Adamsky, "From Moscow with Coercion: Russian Deterrence Theory and Strategic Culture," *Journal of Strategic Studies* 41/1–2 (2018): 41–2.

38 Andrei Soldatov and Irina Borogan, *The Red Web: The Struggle between Russia's Digital Dictators and the New Online Revolutionaries* (New York: Public Affairs, 2015).

39 Thomas, "Nation-State Cyber Strategies: Examples from China and Russia," 483–4.

40 Tracy Staeder, "Why Russia Is Building Its Own Internet," *IEEE Spectrum*, January 17, 2018, https://spectrum.ieee.org/tech-talk/telecom/internet/could-russia-really-build-its-own-alternate-internet.

41 Sergey Medvedev, "Data Protection in the Russian Federation: Overview," *Thomson Reuters Practical Law*, December 1, 2017, https://uk.practicallaw.thomsonreuters.com/2-502-2227.

42 Nicholas Gvodsev, "The Bear Goes Digital: Russia and Its Cyber Capabilities," in *Cyberspace and National Security*, ed. Reveron, 175.

43 "Russia Internet: Law Introducing New Controls Comes into Force," *BBC News*, November 1, 2019, www.bbc.com/news/world-europe-50259597.

44 Shannon Bond and Bobby Allyn, "Russia Is Restricting Social Media. Here's What We Know," NPR, March 21, 2022, www.npr.org/2022/03/07/1085025672/russia-social-media-ban.

45 K. J. Yossman, "Russia Passes Censorship Law Threatening Imprisonment, Forced Labor over 'Fake News,'" *Variety*, March 4, 2022, https://variety.com/2022/politics/news/russia-censorship-law-fake-news-1235196208.

46 Adam Satariano, "How Russia Took Over Ukraine's Internet in Occupied Territories," *New York Times*, August 9, 2022, www.nytimes.com/interactive/2022/08/09/technology/ukraine-internet-russia-censorship.html.

47 Thomas, "Nation-State Cyber Strategies: Examples from China and Russia," 476; Gvodsev, "The Bear Goes Digital," 175.

48 Timothy L. Thomas, "Russian Reflexive Control–Theory and the Military," *Journal of Slavic Military Studies* 17/2 (2004): 237.

49 Wirtz, "Cyber War and Strategic Culture," 35.

50 Valeriano, Jensen and Maness, *Cyber Strategy*, 110.

51 Office of the Director of National Intelligence, "Background to 'Assessing

Russian Activities and Intentions in Recent US Elections': The Analytic Process and Cyber Incident Attribution," January 6, 2017, www.dni.gov/files/documents/ICA_2017_01.pdf.

52 Ibid., 5.

53 Matthew Rosenberg, Charlie Savage and Michael Wines, "Russia at Work on U.S. Midterms, Spy Chiefs Warn," *New York Times*, February 14, 2018, A1.

54 Valeriano, Jensen and Maness, *Cyber Strategy*, 131.

55 Jean-Baptiste Jeangène Vilmer, "Successfully Countering Russian Electoral Interference: 15 Lessons Learned from the Macron Leaks," *CSIS Brief*, 2018, 2–4.

56 Ibid.

57 Gvodsev, "The Bear Goes Digital," 179.

58 Julie Anderson, "The Chekist Takeover of the Russian State," *International Journal of Intelligence and CounterIntelligence* 19/2 (2006): 247–50.

59 Sergei Modsetov cited in Gvodsev, "The Bear Goes Digital," 176.

60 Jack Jarmon and Pano Yannakogeorgos, *The Cyber Threat and Globalization: The Impact on U.S. National and International Security* (New York: Rowman and Littlefield, 2018), 133–7.

61 Gvodsev, "The Bear Goes Digital," 180–1.

62 White House, Presidential Decision Directive/NSC-63, "Critical Infrastructure Protection," May 22, 1998, https://fas.org/irp/offdocs/pdd/pdd-63.htm.

63 See, for example, White House, "National Strategy to Secure Cyberspace," 2003; "National Defense Strategy of the United States of America," March 2005, 16; Chairman of the Joint Chiefs of Staff, "National Military Strategy for Cyberspace Operations," December 2006, www.hsdl.org/?view&did=3 5693; "National Defense Strategy of the United States of America," June 2008, 1; "National Defense Strategy of the United States of America," 2011; "National Security Strategy of the United States of America," December 2017, 12–13; "National Defense Strategy of the United States of America: Sharpening the American Military's Competitive Edge," 2018, 6.

64 US Department of Defense, "The DoD Cyber Strategy," April 2015, 15, 27, http:// archive.defense.gov/home/features/2015/0415_cyber-strategy /final_2015_ dod_cyber_strategy_for_web.pdf.

65 Richard J. Harknett, "United States Cyber Command's New Vision: Why It Matters," Lawfare, March 23, 2018, www.lawfareblog.com/unitedstates -cyber-commands-new-vision-what-it-entails-and-why-it-matters.

66 Scott Jasper, "U.S. Cyber Threat Intelligence Sharing Frameworks," *International Journal of Intelligence and CounterIntelligence* 30/1 (2016): 53–65.

67 Damien Van Puyvelde, "From Information to Cybersecurity: Bridging the Public–Private Divide," in *US National Cybersecurity*, ed. Van Puyvelde and Brantly, 177–94.

68 White House, "Presidential Policy Directive 41 – United States Cyber Incident Coordination," July 26, 2016.

69 Michael P. Fischerkeller, Emily O. Goldman and Richard J. Harknett, *Cyber Persistence Theory: Redefining National Security in Cyberspace* (Oxford University Press, 2022).

70 Valeriano, Jensen and Maness, *Cyber Strategy*, 195.

71 Ibid., 179.

72 US Cyber Command, "Achieve and Maintain Cyberspace Superiority: Command Vision for US Cyber Command," 2018, www.hsdl.org/?view& did=812923.

73 UK Government, "National Cyber Security Strategy 2016 to 2021", www.gov.uk/government/publications/ national-cyber-security-strategy-2016-to-2021; Ministère de la Défense, "Pacte Défense Cyber," February 7, 2014; Saïd Haddad, "Le Cyberespace ou la construction d'un 'champ de confrontation à part entière,'" in *La Cyberdéfense. Politique de l'espace numérique*, ed. Amaël Cattaruzza, Didier Danet and Stéphane Taillat (Paris: Armand Collin, 2018), 44–51.

74 See, for example: White House, Remarks by President Obama and President Park of the Republic of Korea in Joint Press Conference, October 16, 2015, https://obamawhitehouse.archives.gov/the-pressoffice/2015/10 /16/remarks-president-obama-and-president-parkrepublic-korea-joint -press.

75 NATO Cooperative Cyber Defence Centre of Excellence, "Cyber Security Strategy Documents," October 18, 2018, https://ccdcoe.org/ cyber-security-strategy-documents.html and "Incyder: International Cyber Developments Review," https://ccdcoe.org/incyder.html.

76 US Department of Commerce, Bureau of Industry and Security, "Commerce Implements New Export Controls on Advanced Computing and Semiconductor Manufacturing Items to the People's Republic of China (PRC)," October 7, 2022, www.bis.doc.gov/index.php/documents /about-bis/newsroom/press-releases/3158-2022-10-07-bis-press-release-ad vanced-computing-and-semiconductor-manufacturing-controls-final/file.

77 Ana Swanson, "U.S. Issues Final Rules to Keep Chip Funds out of China," *New York Times*, September 22, 2023, www.nytimes.com/2023/09/22/us /politics/us-final-rules-chip-makers-china.html.

78 Swanson, Ana, "The CHIPS Act Is About More than Chips: Here's What's in It," *New York Times*, February 28, 2023, www.nytimes.com/2023/02 /28/business/economy/chips-act-childcare.html.

79 Council of the Executive Office of the President of the United States,

Select Committee on Artificial Intelligence of the National Science and Technology Council, "National Artificial Intelligence Research and Development Strategic Plan 2023 Update," May 2023, www.whitehouse .gov/wp-content/uploads/2023/05/National-Artificial-Intelligence-Resear ch-and-Development-Strategic-Plan-2023-Update.pdf.

80 Chris Miller, *Chip War: The Fight for the World's Most Critical Technology* (New York: Simon & Schuster, 2022).

81 "US Threat Gives ASML New Headache on China Exports," Reuters, June 30, 2023, www.reuters.com/breakingviews/us-threat-gives-asml-new-hea dache-china-exports-2023-06-30.

82 Demchak and Dombrowski, "Rise of a Cybered Westphalian Age," 35.

83 Brian Mazanec, "The Outlook for Constraining International Norms for Offensive Cyber Operations," in *US National Cybersecurity*, ed. Van Puyvelde and Brantly, 40–54.

84 Jon R. Lindsay and Derek S. Reveron, "Conclusion: The Rise of China and the Future of Cybersecurity," in *China and Cybersecurity*, ed. Lindsay, Cheung and Reveron, 346–7; Jarmon and Yannakogeorgos, *The Cyber Threat and Globalization*, 98.

85 John Rollins, "U.S.–China Cyber Agreement," CRS Insight, October 16, 2016, https://fas.org/sgp/crs/row/IN10376.pdf. For an analysis, see Gary Brown and Christopher D. Yung, "Evaluating the US–China Cybersecurity Agreement, Part 1: The US Approach to Cyberspace," *Diplomat*, January 19, 2017, https://thediplomat.com/2017/01/evaluating-the-us-china-cyb ersecurity-agreement-part-1-the-usapproach-to-cyberspace.

6 From cyber war to cyber conflict

1 Michael N. Schmitt, "Classification of Cyber Conflict," *Journal of Conflict & Security Law* 17/2 (2012): 245.

2 Harold Hongju Koh, "International Law in Cyberspace," keynote address at the US Cyber Command Inter-agency Legal Conference, Ft. Meade, MD, September 18, 2002.

3 Singer and Friedman, *Cybersecurity and Cyberwar*, 120.

4 See, for example, Mike McConnell, "To Win the Cyber-war, Look to the Cold War," *Washington Post*, February 28, 2010.

5 Colin Gray, *Another Bloody Century: Future Warfare* (London: Orion Books, 2006), 37.

6 Carl von Clausewitz, *On War*, ed. Michael Howard and Peter Part (Princeton University Press, 2008), 6.

7 Gray, *Another Bloody Century*, 105.

8 Arquilla and Ronfeldt, "Cyber War Is Coming!" 144.

9 Ibid., 147.

10 See, for example, Donald Rumsfeld, "Transforming the Military," *Foreign*

Affairs 81/3 (2002): 20–32; John Ferris, "A New American Way of War? C4ISR, Intelligence and Information Operations in Operation 'Iraqi Freedom': A Provisional Assessment," *Intelligence and National Security* 81/3 (2003): 155–74; Eliot Cohen, "Changes and Transformation in Military Affairs," *Journal of Strategic Studies* 27/3 (2004): 395–407.

11 See, for example, David Betz, "The Mystique of 'Cyberwar' and the Strategic Latency of Networked Social Movements," *Strategic Insights* 10 (2011): 61–77; Martin C. Libicki, "Why Cyber War Will Not and Should Not Have Its Grand Strategist," *Strategic Studies Quarterly* 8/1 (2014): 30.

12 Damien McGuinness, "How a Cyber Attack Transformed Estonia," BBC, April 27, 2017, www.bbc.co.uk/news/39655415.

13 John Arquilla, "Cyberwar Is Already upon Us: But Can It Be Controlled?" *Foreign Policy* 192 (2012): 84.

14 David A. Fulghum and Robert Wall, "Israel Shows Electronic Prowess," *Aviation Week & Space Technology*, November 25, 2007.

15 Gary McGraw, "Cyber War Is Inevitable (unless We Build Security In)," *Journal of Strategic Studies* 36/1 (2013): 112.

16 Clarke and Knake, *Cyber War*, 64–8.

17 US House of Representatives, Committee on Science, Space, and Technology, Subcommittee on Technology and Competitiveness, Hearing: Computer Security, "Statement of Winn Schwartau," 102nd Congress, 1st sess., June 27, 1991, 10; Neil Munro, "The Pentagon's New Nightmare: An Electronic Pearl Harbor," *Washington Post*, July 16, 1995, C3.

18 US Department of Defense, Remarks by Secretary Panetta on Cybersecurity to the Business Executives for National Security, New York City, October 11, 2012, http://archive.defense.gov/transcripts/transcript.aspx?transcripti d=5136.

19 See, for example, Gordon Corera, "If 2017 Could Be Described as 'Cyber-geddon,' What Will 2018 Bring?" BBC, 30 December 2017, www.bbc .co.uk/news/technology-42338716; video: Kevin Mandia, "FireEye CEO Says Midterm Elections Are Vulnerable to a Russian Hack," Bloomberg, February 20, 2018, www.bloomberg.com/news/videos/2018-02-20/firee ye-ceo-says-midterm-elections-vulnerable-torussia-hack-video. For a media critique, see Ryan Singel, "Richard Clarke's *Cyber War*: File under Fiction," *Wired*, April 22, 2010, www.wired.com/2010/04/cyberwar-richard-clarke.

20 Rid, "Cyber War Will Not Take Place"; Rid, *Cyber War Will Not Take Place* (London: Hurst, 2013).

21 Rid, *Cyber War Will Not Take Place*, xv.

22 Ibid., 10.

23 Ibid., 15–27.

24 Kim Zetter, "How Digital Detectives Deciphered Stuxnet, the Most Menacing Malware in History," *Wired*, July 11, 2011.

25 Ralph Langner, "To Kill a Centrifuge: A Technical Analysis of What Stuxnet's Creators Tried to Achieve," November 2013, www.langner.com /wp-content/uploads/2017/03/to-kill-a-centrifuge.pdf.

26 Ellen Nakashima and Joby Warrick, "Stuxnet Was Work of U.S. and Israel Experts, Officials Say," *Washington Post*, June 2, 2012.

27 Ron Rosenbaum, "Richard Clarke on Who Was behind the Stuxnet Attack," *Smithsonian Magazine*, April 2012, www.smithsonian mag.com/history/richard-clarke-on-who-was-behind-the-stuxnet-attack- 160630516.

28 Kapersky, "Shamoon the Wiper – Copycats at Work," *Securelist*, August 16, 2012, https://securelist.com/shamoon-the-wiper-copycats-at-work/57 854.

29 Chris Bronk and Eneken Tikk-Ringas, "The Cyber Attack on Saudi Aramco," *Survival* 55/2 (2013): 81–96.

30 Fahmida Y. Rashid, "Inside the Aftermath of the Saudi Aramco Breach," *DarkReading*, August 8, 2015, www.darkreading.com/attacks-breaches/in side-the-aftermath-of-the-saudi-aramco-breach.

31 Ibid.

32 McGraw, "Cyber War Is Inevitable (unless We Build Security In)," 109– 19; Timothy J. Junio, "How Probable Is Cyber War? Bringing IR Theory Back into the Cyber Conflict Debate," *Journal of Strategic Studies* 36/1 (2013): 125–6.

33 John Stone, "Cyber War Will Take Place!" *Journal of Strategic Studies* 36/1 (2013): 103.

34 Valeriano and Maness, *Cyber War versus Cyber Realities*, 29.

35 Betz, "The Mystique of 'Cyberwar,'" 65.

36 Myriam Dunn Cavelty, *Cyber-Security and Threat Politics: US Efforts to Secure the Information Age* (London: Routledge, 2008), 1–7.

37 Sheldon, "The Rise of Cyberpower," 306.

38 Valeriano and Maness, *Cyber War versus Cyber Realities*, 5. See also Chris C. Demchak, *Wars of Disruption and Resilience: Cybered Conflict, Power, and National Security* (Athens: University of Georgia Press, 2011).

39 Brandon Valeriano and Ryan Manness, "The Fog of CyberWar," *Foreign Affairs*, November 21, 2012, www.foreignaffairs.com/articles/2012-11-21 /fog-cyberwar.

40 Valeriano and Maness, *Cyber War versus Cyber Realities*, 16; Jon R. Lindsay, "Stuxnet and the Limits of Cyber Warfare," *Security Studies* 22/3 (2013): 401–4.

41 Curt Merlo, "How an Entire Nation Became Russia's Test Lab for Cyberwar," *Wired*, June 20, 2017, www.wired.com/story/russianhackers-at tack-ukraine.

42 Ibid.

43 Brandon Valeriano and Ryan Maness, "The Coming Cyberpeace," *Foreign Affairs*, May 13, 2015, www.foreignaffairs.com/articles/2015-05-13/coming-cyberpeace.
44 Erik Gartzke, "The Myth of Cyberwar: Bringing War in Cyberspace Back Down to Earth," *International Security* 38/2 (2013): 42–3.
45 Ibid., 57.
46 Martin C. Libicki, *Cyberdeterrence and Cyberwar* (Santa Monica, CA: RAND, 2009), 25; Rid, "Cyber War Will Not Take Place," 16.
47 Gartzke, "The Myth of Cyberwar," 46–7.
48 For a similar argument, see Betz, "The Mystique of 'Cyberwar,'" 63–4.
49 Gartzke, "The Myth of Cyberwar," 49; Lindsay, "Stuxnet and the Limits of Cyber Warfare," 404.
50 Ronald J. Deibert, Rafal Rohozinski and Masashi Crete-Nishihata, "Cyclones in Cyberspace: Information Shaping and Denial in the 2008 Russia–Georgia War," *Security Dialogue* 43/1 (2012): 18.
51 Lindsay, "Stuxnet and the Limits of Cyber Warfare," 371.
52 Lionel Beehner et al., *A Contemporary Battlefield Assessment* (West Point, NY: Modern War Institute, 2018).
53 Arquilla, "Cyberwar Is Already upon Us," 84–5.
54 Sarah P. White, *Understanding Cyberwarfare: Lessons from the Russia–Georgia War* (West Point, NY: Modern War Institute, 2018), 6–8.
55 Peter Dombrowski and Chris C. Demchak, "Cyber War, Cybered Conflict, and the Maritime Domain," *Naval War College Review* 67/2 (2014): 73.
56 US Army War College, "Strategic Cyberspace Operations Guide," June 1, 2016, 15, archive.org/details/USAWCStrategicCyberOpsGuide; US Joint Chiefs of Staff, Joint Publication 3-0, "Joint Operations," Washington, DC, January 17, 2017, GL-8, http://irp.fas.org/doddir/dod/jp3_0.pdf.
57 James E. Cartwright, "Memorandum: Joint Terminology for Cyberspace Operations," November 2010, 3–6, https://nsarchive.gwu.edu/document/21369-document-10; United States Army War College, "Strategic Cyberspace Operations Guide," 17.
58 Valeriano and Maness, *Cyber War versus Cyber Realities*, 32.
59 Brantly, Cal and Winkelstein, *Defending the Borderland*, 40.
60 Juan Andres Guerrero-Saade, "AcidRain: A Modem Wiper Rains Down on Europe," *Sentinel One*, March 31, 2022, www.sentinelone.com/labs/acidrain-a-modem-wiper-rains-down-on-europe; Kim Zetter, "Viasat Hack 'Did Not' Have Huge Impact on Ukrainian Military Communications, Official Says," *Zero Day*, September 26, 2022, www.zetter-zeroday.com/p/viasat-hack-did-not-have-huge-impact?utm_source=%2Fsearch%2Fviasat&utm_medium=reader2.
61 Guerrero-Saade, "AcidRain."
62 "KA-SAT Network Cyber Attack Overview," VIASAT, March 30, 2022,

https://news.viasat.com/blog/corporate/ka-sat-network-cyber-attack-over
view.

63 Guerrero-Saade, "AcidRain."

64 Zetter, "Viasat Hack."

65 Nadiya Kostyuk and Aaron F. Brantly, "War in the Borderland through Cyberspace: Limits of Defending Ukraine through Interstate Cooperation," *Contemporary Security Policy* 43/3 (2022): 498–515.

66 Ibid.

67 Ibid.

68 United States Army Training and Doctrine Command, "Multi-domain Battle: Evolution of Combined Arms for the 21st Century, 2025–2040," December 2017, i, www.tradoc.army.mil/wp-content/uploads/2020/10/MDB_Evolutionfor21st.pdf.

69 Herbert Lin, *Cyber Threats and Nuclear Weapons* (Redwood City, CA: Stanford University Press, 2021).

70 Andrew Futter, *Hacking the Bomb: Cyber Threats and Nuclear Weapons.* (Washington, DC: Georgetown University Press, 2018).

71 Michael J. Mazarr, Bryan Frederick and Yvonne K. Crane, *Understanding A New Era of Strategic Competition* (Santa Monica, CA: RAND Corporation, 2022).

72 Fischerkeller, Goldman and Harknett, *Cyber Persistence Theory.*

73 Ibid.

74 Ibid., 61.

75 Ibid.

76 Gregory J. Rattray, *Strategic Warfare in Cyberspace* (Cambridge, MA: MIT Press, 2001).

77 Erica D. Borghard and Shawn W. Lonergan, "Cyber Operations as Imperfect Tools of Escalation," *Strategic Studies Quarterly* 13/3 (2019) 122–45; Jacquelyn Schneider, "What War Games Tell Us about the Use of Cyber Weapons in a Crisis," Council on Foreign Relations, 2018, https://cfr.org/blog/what-war-games-tell-us-about-use-cyber-weapons-crisis.

7 Organizing deterrence and defense in cyberspace

1 Ben Buchanan, "Cyber Deterrence Isn't MAD; It's Mosaic," *Georgetown Journal of International Affairs* 4 (2018): 130–40.

2 Clausewitz, *On War*, 119.

3 Office of the President of the United States, "National Strategy for Global Supply Chain Security," Washington, DC, 2012, https://obamawhite house.archives.gov/sites/default/files/docs/national_strategy_for_global _supply_chain_security_implementation_update_public_version_final2 -26-131.pdf.

4 Andy Greenberg, "A Critical Intel Flaw Breaks Basic Security for Most

Computers," *Wired*, January 3, 2018, www.wired.com/story/critical-intel-flaw-breaks-basic-security-for-most-computers.

5 George Mutune, "23 Top Cybersecurity Frameworks," CyberExperts, 2023, https://cyberexperts.com/cybersecurity-frameworks/#:~:text=23%20Top%20Cybersecurity%20Frameworks%201%201.%20ISO%20IEC,COBIT8%20...%208%208.%20COSO9%20...%20More%20items.

6 Chris Bing, "Mayhem, the Tech behind the DARPA Grand Challenge Winner, Now Used by the Pentagon – CyberScoop," *Cyberscoop*, August 11, 2017, www.cyberscoop.com/mayhem-darpa-cyber-grand-challenge-dod-voltron.

7 "Cyber Defense," NATO, September 14, 2023, www.nato.int/cps/en/natohq/topics_78170.htm.

8 Alexander L. George and Richard Smoke, *Deterrence in American Foreign Policy: Theory and Practice* (New York: Columbia University Press, 1974), 11.

9 Aaron F. Brantly, "The Cyber Deterrence Problem," in *Proceedings of the 10th International Conference on Cyber Conflict, NATO Cyber Defense Center of Excellence* (Tallinn: IEEE, 2018), 31–54.

10 Thomas Rid and Ben Buchanan, "Attributing Cyber Attacks," *Journal of Strategic Studies* 38/1–2 (2015): 4–37.

11 Jon R. Lindsay, "Tipping the Scales: The Attribution Problem and the Feasibility of Deterrence Against Cyberattack," *Journal of Cybersecurity* 1/1 (2015): 53–67.

12 Will Goodman, "Cyber Deterrence: Tougher in Theory than in Practice?" *Strategic Studies Quarterly* 4/3 (2010): 102–35; Valeriano and Maness, *Cyber War versus Cyber Realities*.

13 Ponemon Institute, "2017 Cost of Data Breach Study," research report, June 2017, https://documents.ncsl.org/wwwncsl/Task-Forces/Cybersecurity-Privacy/IBM_Ponemon2017CostofDataBreachStudy.pdf.

14 Ibid.

15 Lindsay, "Tipping the Scales," 58.

16 Martin C. Libicki, *Cyberspace in Peace and War* (Annapolis: Naval Institute Press, 2016).

17 Schmitt and Vihul, *Tallinn Manual 2.0*.

18 Valeriano and Maness, *Cyber War versus Cyber Realities*.

19 Josh Rogin, "NSA Chief: Cybercrime Constitutes the 'Greatest Transfer of Wealth in History,'" *Foreign Policy*, July 9, 2012, https://foreignpolicy.com/2012/07/09/nsa-chief-cybercrime-constitutes-thegreatest-transfer-of-wealth-in-history.

20 Nathan Thornburgh, "The Invasion of the Chinese Cyberspies (and the Man Who Tried to Stop Them)," *Time*, September 5, 2005.

21 Jon R. Lindsay and Tai Ming Cheung, "From Exploitation to Innovation:

Acquisition, Absorption, and Application," in *China and Cybersecurity*, ed. Lindsay, Cheung and Reveron, 51–86.

22 Inkster, *China's Cyber Power*.
23 Rogin, "NSA Chief."
24 Mandiant Threat Intelligence Center, "APT1."
25 Ellen Nakashima, "U.S. Developing Sanctions against China over Cyberthefts," *Washington Post*, August 30, 2015, www.washington post.com/world/national-security/administration-developing-sanctions-against-china-over-cyberespionage/2015/08/30/9b2910aa-480b-11e5-8ab4-c73967a143d3_story.html.
26 Sanger, *The Perfect Weapon*.
27 FireEye, "Redline Drawn: China Recalculates Its Use of Cyber Espionage," June 20, 2016, www.fireeye.com/blog/threat-research/2016/06/ red-line-drawn-china-espionage.html.
28 Nadiya Kostyuk, "Allies and Diffusion of State Military Capacity," *Journal of Peace Research* 61/1 (2024): 44–58.
29 Gartzke and Lindsay, "Weaving Tangled Webs."
30 Rebecca Slayton, "What Is the Cyber Offense–Defense Balance? Conceptions, Causes, and Assessment," *International Security* 41/3 (2017): 72–109.
31 Joseph Berger, "A Dam, Small and Unsung, Is Caught Up in an Iranian Hacking Case," *New York Times*, March 25, 2016, www.nytimes.com /2016/03/26/nyregion/rye-brook-dam-caught-incomputer-hacking-case .html.
32 Kim Zetter, "A Cyberattack Has Caused Confirmed Physical Damage for the Second Time Ever," *Wired*, January 8, 2015, www.wired.com/2015/01 /german-steel-mill-hack-destruction.
33 Steve Morgan, "2018 Cybersecurity Market Report," Cybersecurity Ventures, February 17, 2018, https://cybersecurityventures.com/ cybersecurity-market-report.
34 "Size of Cybersecurity Market Worldwide from 2021 to 2030," Statista, August 30, 2023, www.statista.com/statistics/1256346/worldwide-cyber -security-market-revenues/#:~:text=According%20to%20Next%20Move %20Strategy%20Consulting%2C%20the%20global,is%20forecast%20to %20exceed%20657%20billion%20U.S.%20dollars.

8 Non-state threats: from cybercrime to terrorism

1 Federal Bureau of Investigation, "Willie Sutton," www.fbi.gov/history/fa mous-cases/willie-sutton.
2 "Cost of a Data Breach Report 2023," *IBM Security*, 2023, www.ibm.com /downloads/cas/E3G5JMBP.
3 Zhanna Malekos Smith and Eugenia Lostri, "The Hidden Costs of

Cybercrime," McAfee, 2022, https://companies.mybroadband.co.za/axiz/fi les/2021/02/eBook-Axiz-McAfee-hidden-costs-of-cybercrime.pdf.

4 Thomas J. Holt, George W. Burruss and Adam M. Bossler, *Policing Cybercrime and Cyberterror* (Durham: Carolina Academic Press, 2015), 8–9.

5 Justin Jouvenal, "Hackers Tried to Change Grades at Virginia High School, Police Say," *Washington Post*, April 4, 2018, www.washingtonpost .com/local/public-safety/hackers-tried-to-changegrades-at-virginia-high-school-police-say/2018/04/03/924ecf82-376511e8-acd5-35eac230e514 _story.html.

6 Claes Bell, "Typosquatting: Identity Theft Built on Spelling Errors," *Bankrate*, August 15, 2015, www.bankrate.com/finance/credit/typosquat ting-identity-theft.aspx.

7 Ionut Ilascu, "Amazon Customers Tricked with Verification Number Phishing Email," February 17, 2015, https://news.softpedia.com/news /Amazon-Customers-Tricked-with-Ticket-Verification-Number-Phishing -Email-473445.shtml#sgal_0.

8 Shu et al., "Breaking the Target."

9 Hawkins, "Case Study: The Home Depot Data Breach."

10 Goodman, *Future Crimes*.

11 Beehner et al., *A Contemporary Battlefield Assessment*.

12 Brett Stone-Gross et al., "Analysis of a Botnet Tracker," *IEEE Security & Privacy* 9/1 (2011): 64–72.

13 Shayan Eskandari et al., "A First Look at Browser-Based Cryptojacking," arXiv (March 2018), https://arxiv.org/pdf/1803.02887.

14 Joe Tidy, "Ronin Network: What a $600m Hack Says about the State of Crypto," *BBC News*, March 30, 2022, www.bbc.com/news/technology-60 933174.

15 Jeff Guo et al., "How to Launder $600 Million on the Internet," NPR Planet Money, September 23, 2023, www.npr.org/2023/09/15/11979540 55/axie-infinity-north-korea-ronin.

16 Guo et al., "How to Launder $600 Million on the Internet."

17 Michael Kan, "Law Enforcement Seizes $30M Stolen in North Korea's Hack of Ronin Network," *PC Mag*, September 9, 2022, www.pcmag.com /news/law-enforcement-seizes-30m-stolen-in-north-koreas-hack-of-ronin -network.

18 John Leyden, "Polish Teen Derails Tram after Hacking Train Network," *Register*, January 11, 2008, www.theregister.co.uk/2008/01/11/tram_ hack.

19 Sameer Hinduja and Justin W. Patchin, "Bullying, Cyberbullying, and Suicide," *Archives of Suicide Research* 14 (2010): 206–21.

20 James H. Price and Jagdish Khubchandani, "Adolescent Homicides,

Suicides, and the Role of Firearms: A Narrative Review," *American Journal of Health Education* 48/2 (2017): 67–79.

21 Justin W. Patchin, "Summary of Our Cyberbullying Research (2004–2016)," Cyberbullying Research Center, November 26, 2016, https://cyberbullying.org/summary-of-our-cyberbullying-research.

22 Robert D'Ovidio and James Doyle, "Study on Cyberstalking: Understanding Investigative Hurdles," *FBI Law Enforcement Bulletin* 72/3 (2003): 10–17.

23 Brian H. Spitzberg and Gregory Hoobler, "Cyberstalking and the Technologies of Interpersonal Terrorism," *New Media and Society* 4/1 (2002): 67–88.

24 Lauren Walker, "Three Family Members Received Life Sentences for the First-Ever Cyberstalking-to-Death Conviction," *Newsweek*, February 26, 2016, www.newsweek.com/familyreceives-life-prison-first-ever-cyberstalking-conviction-430833.

25 US District Court, Southern District of New York, *United States of America v. Ross William Ulbricht*, Indictment, February 4, 2014.

26 Kim Zetter, "How the Feds Took Down the Silk Road Drug Wonderland," *Wired*, November 18, 2013, www.wired.com/2013/11/silk-road.

27 Allesandro Mascellino, "Dark Web Actors Fight for Drug Trafficking and Illegal Pharmacy Supremacy," *Infosecurity Magazine*, January 9, 2023, www.infosecurity-magazine.com/news/dark-web-fights-for-drug.

28 Holt, Burruss and Bossler, *Policing Cybercrime and Terror*.

29 Federal Bureau of Investigation, "The Scourge of Child Pornography: Working to Stop the Sexual Exploitation of Children," April 25, 2017, www.fbi.gov/news/stories/the-scourge-of-child-pornography.

30 Ibid.

31 Ibid.

32 Lexi Lonas, "Sharp Rise in Online Child Pornography," *The Hill*, March 19, 2022, https://thehill.com/policy/technology/598872-sharp-rise-in-online-child-pornography-study.

33 Lizzie Dearden, "Sadistic Paedophile Jailed for 32 Years after Blackmail Campaign on the Dark Web," *Independent*, February 20, 2018, 18–19.

34 Ibid.

35 Luke Goode, "Anonymous and the Political Ethos of Hacktivism," *Popular Communication* 13/1 (2015): 74–86.

36 Marco Deseriis, "Hacktivism: On the Use of Botnets in Cyberattacks," *Theory, Culture & Society* 34/4 (2017): 131–52.

37 Cross-site scripting is a type of computer security vulnerability typically found in web applications. XSS enables attackers to inject client-side scripts into web pages viewed by other users.

38 SQL injection is a code injection technique, used to attack data-driven

applications, in which nefarious SQL statements are inserted into an entry field for execution (e.g. to dump the database contents to the attacker).

39 Parmy Olson, *We Are Anonymous: Inside the Hacker World of LulzSec, Anonymous, and the Global Cyber Insurgency* (New York: Back Bay Books, 2013).

40 Ibid.

41 Burcu S. Bakioğlu, "The Gray Zone: Networks of Piracy, Control, and Resistance," *The Information Society* 32/1 (2015): 40–50.

42 Keely Lockhard and Myles Burke, "Video: #OpISIS: Why Anonymous Has Declared an Online War against Isil – in 90 Seconds – Telegraph," *Telegraph*, December 11, 2015, www.telegraph.co.uk/news/worldnews/is lamic-state/12003242/OpISIS-Why-Anonymous-has-declared-an online-war-against-Isil-in-90-seconds.html.

43 Emerson T. Brooking, "Anonymous vs. the Islamic State," *Foreign Policy*, November 13, 2015, https://foreignpolicy.com/2015/11/13/anonymous-h ackers-islamic-state-isis-chan-online-war.

44 Alexander Klimburg, "Mobilising Cyber Power," *Survival* 53/1 (2011): 41–60.

45 Beehner et al., *A Contemporary Battlefield Assessment*.

46 Scott J. Shapiro, *Fancy Bear Goes Phishing: The Dark History of the Information Age, in Five Extraordinary Hacks* (New York: Farrar, Straus and Giroux, 2023).

47 Orly Turgeman-Goldschmidt, "Identity Construction among Hackers," in *Cyber Criminology: Exploring Internet Crimes and Criminal Behavior*, ed. K. Jaishankar (Boca Raton, FL: CRC Press, 2011).

48 Holt, Burruss and Bossler, *Policing Cybercrime and Terror*.

49 Ibid.

50 Gabriel Weimann, *Terrorism in Cyberspace: The Next Generation* (New York: Columbia University Press, 2015), 6.

51 Bruce Hoffman, *Inside Terrorism* (New York: Columbia University Press, 2006), 2.

52 Helene Cooper, "U.S. Military Social Media Feeds Are Seized by ISIS Sympathizers," *New York Times*, January 13, 2015, A4.

53 Ibid.

54 David C. Gompert and Martin C. Libicki, "Decoding the Breach: The Truth about the CENTCOM Hack," The RAND Blog, February 3, 2015, www.rand.org/blog/2015/02/decoding-the-breach-the-truthabout-the-cen tcom-hack.html.

55 John Scott-Railton and Seth Hardy, "Malware Attacks Targeting Syrian ISIS Critics," Citizen Lab, December 18, 2014, https://citizenlab.ca/2014 /12/malware-attack-targeting-syrian-isis-critics.

56 Recorded Future Special Intelligence Desk (RFSID), "Cyber Caliphate:

ISIS Plays Offense on the Web," Recorded Future, April 2, 2015, www. recordedfuture.com/cyber-caliphateanalysis.

57 Ibid.

58 Editor, "UK Jihadist 'Killed in Drone Strike,'" *BBC News*, August 27, 2015, www.bbc.co.uk/news/uk-34078900.

59 Christopher Heffelfinger, "The Risks Posed by Jihadist Hackers," *CTC Sentinel* 6/7 (2013): 1–5.

60 Jytte Klausen, "Tweeting the Jihad: Social Media Networks of Western Foreign Fighters in Syria and Iraq," *Studies in Conflict & Terrorism* 38/1 (2014): 1–22; Gabriel Weimann, "Cyberterrorism: The Sum of All Fears?" *Studies in Conflict & Terrorism* 28/2 (2005): 129–49.

61 J. M. Berger and Jonathon Morgan, *The ISIS Twitter Census: Defining and Describing the Population of ISIS Supporters on Twitter* (Washington, DC: Center for Middle East Policy at Brookings, 2015).

62 Brantly, "Innovation and Adaptation in Jihadist Digital Security."

63 Aaron F. Brantly, "Financing Terror Bit by Bit," *CTC Sentinel* 7/10 (2014): 1–5; Joshua Baron et al., *National Security Implications of Virtual Currency* (Santa Monica, CA: RAND, 2015).

64 Sanger, *The Perfect Weapon*.

65 Ibid.

66 Hsinchun Chen et al., "Uncovering the Dark Web: A Case Study of Jihad on the Web," *Journal of the American Society for Information Science and Technology* 59/8 (2008): 1347–59; Gabriel Weimann, *Going Darker? The Challenge of Dark Net Terrorism* (Washington, DC: Wilson Center, 2018).

67 T. Maurer, "'Proxies' and Cyberspace," *Journal of Conflict and Security Law* 21 (2016): 383–403.

68 Tim Maurer, *Cyber Mercenaries: The State, Hackers, and Power* (Cambridge University Press, 2018).

69 Justin K. Canfil, "The Illogic of Plausible Deniability: Why Proxy Conflict in Cyberspace May No Longer Pay," *Journal of Cybersecurity* 8/1 (2022): 1–16.

70 Florian J. Egloff, *Semi-state Actors in Cybersecurity* (New York: Oxford University Press, 2022).

71 Ibid.

72 Ibid.

73 E. D. Borghard and S. W. Lonergan "Can States Calculate the Risks of Using Cyber Proxies?" *Orbis* 60/3 (2016): 395–416.

74 Ibid.

75 Jon R. Lindsay, "The Impact of China on Cybersecurity: Fiction and Friction," *International Security* 39/3 (2015): 7–47.

76 Soldatov and Borogan, *The Red Web*.

9 Cybersecurity and democracy

1 Aaron F. Brantly, "From Cyberspace to Independence Square: Understanding the Impact of Social Media on Physical Protest Mobilization during Ukraine's Euromaidan Revolution," *Journal of Information Technology and Politics* 16/4 (2019): 1–19.

2 Miranda Patrucic and Kelly Bloss, "Life in Azerbaijan's Digital Autocracy: 'They Want to be in Control of Everything,'" Organized Crime and Corruption Reporting Project, July 18, 2021, www.occrp.org/en/the-pegas us-project/life-in-azerbaijans-digital-autocracy-they-want-to-be-in-control -of-everything.

3 Ronald J. Deibert and Rafal Rohozinski, "Liberation vs. Control: The Future of Cyberspace," *Journal of Democracy* 21/4 (2010): 48.

4 Chung-pin Lee, Kaiju Chang and Frances Stokes Berry, "Testing the Development and Diffusion of E-government and E-democracy: A Global Perspective," *Public Administration Review* 71/3 (2011): 444–5.

5 Donald F. Norris, "E-government 2020: Plus ça change, plus c'est la meme chose," *Public Administration Review* 70/1 (2010): 180.

6 Michael Margolis, "E-government and Democracy," in *The Oxford Handbook of Political Behavior*, ed. Russel J. Dalton and Hans-Dieter Klingemann (Oxford University Press, 2009, online).

7 See, for example, the Church Committee report: US Senate, Select Committee to Study Governmental Operations with Respect to Intelligence Activities, "Intelligence Activities and the Rights of Americans," Book II, April 26, 1976.

8 Aaron F. Brantly, "Utopia Lost – Human Rights in a Digital World," *Applied Cybersecurity and Internet Governance* 1/1 (2022): 25–43.

9 This can be tested at home by accessing the website whatismyipaddress .com.

10 National Security Agency, "PRISM/US-984XN Overview," April 2013, www.washingtonpost.com/wp-srv/special/politics/prism-collection-docu ments/?noredirect=on.

11 See, for example, Zygmunt Bauman et al., "After Snowden: Rethinking the Impact of Surveillance," *International Political Sociology* 8/2 (2014): 122.

12 Singer and Friedman, *Cybersecurity and Cyberwar*, 34.

13 Matt Burgess, "That Yahoo Data Breach Actually Hit Three Billion Accounts," *Wired*, October 4, 2017, www.wired.co.uk/article/hacks-data -breaches-2017.

14 For a summary on GDPR, see Michael Nadeau, "General Data Protection Regulation (GDPR): What You Need to Know to Stay Compliant," CSO Online, April 23, 2018, www.csoonline.com/article/3202771/data-protec tion/general-data-protection-regulation-gdpr-requirementsdeadlines-and -facts.html.

15 Larry Diamond, "Liberation Technology," *Journal of Democracy* 21/3 (2010): 70.

16 Tom Sorell, "Human Rights and Hacktivism: The Cases of Wikileaks and Anonymous," *Journal of Human Rights Practice* 7/3 (2015): 393.

17 Diamond, "Liberation Technology," 73–5.

18 Ibid., 69–70.

19 Thomas Rid and Daniel Moore, "Cryptopolitik and the Darknet," *Survival* 58/1 (2016): 17.

20 Tetyana Bohdanova, "Unexpected Revolution: The Role of Social Media in Ukraine's Euromaidan Uprising," *European View* 13/1 (2014): 136.

21 Lena Surzhko-Harned and Andrew J. Zahuranec, "Framing the Revolution: The Role of Social Media in Ukraine's Euromaidan Movement," *Nationalities Papers* 45/5 (2017): 758–9.

22 Olga Onuch, "EuroMaidan Protests in Ukraine: Social Media versus Social Networks," *Problems of Post-Communism* 62/4 (2015): 233.

23 Bohdanova, "Unexpected Revolution," 139–40; Megan MacDuffee Metzger and Joshua A. Tucker, "Social Media and EuroMaidan: A Review Essay," *Slavic Review* 76/1 (2017): 187–91.

24 White House, "International Strategy for Cyberspace: Prosperity, Security, and Openness in a Networked World," May 2011, 23–4, https:// obamaw hitehouse.archives.gov/sites/default/files/rss_viewer/international_strategy _for_cyberspace.pdf.

25 Hillary Rodham Clinton, "Internet Freedom," speech delivered at Newseum, Washington, DC, January 21, 2010, https://foreignpolicy.com /2010/01/21/internet-freedom.

26 Singer and Friedman, *Cybersecurity and Cyberwar*, 106.

27 Sanja Kelly et al., "Silencing the Messenger: Communications Apps under Pressure," in Freedom House, *Freedom on the Net 2016*, 2, https://freedom house.org/sites/ default/files/FOTN_2016_Full_Report.pdf.

28 Singer and Friedman, *Cybersecurity and Cyberwar*, 108.

29 Brantly, "The Cyber Losers," 142–3.

30 Deibert and Rohozinski, "Liberation vs. Control," 50.

31 Aaron F. Brantly, "A Brief History of Fake: Surveying Russian Dis-information from the Russian Empire through the Cold War to the Present," in *Information Warfare in the Age of Cyber Conflict*, ed. Christopher Whyte, Trevor Thrall and Bryan Mazanec (Abingdon: Routledge, 2020), 27–41.

32 Chad Fitzgerald and Aaron Brantly, "Subverting Reality: The Role of Propaganda in 21st Century Intelligence," *Journal of Intelligence and CounterIntelligence* 30/2 (2017): 215–40.

33 Diamond, "Liberation Technology," 80.

34 Ibid., 71.

35 Brantly, "The Cyber Losers," 142.
36 Nick Hopkins and Jake Morris, "UK Firm's Surveillance Kit 'Used to Crush Uganda Opposition,'" *BBC News*, October 15, 2015, www.bbc.co.uk/news/uk-34529237; Morgan Marquis-Boire and Bill Marczak, "From Bahrain with Love: FinFisher's Spy Kit Exposed?" Citizen Lab, July 25, 2012, https://citizenlab.ca/2012/07/from-bahrain-with-love-finfishers-spy-kit-exposed.
37 Deibert and Rohozinski, "Liberation vs. Control," 47.
38 Brantly, "The Cyber Losers," 142.
39 Kim Zetter, "Pegasus Spyware: How It Works and What It Collects," August 4, 2021, https://zetter.substack.com/p/pegasus-spyware-how-it-works-and 2021.
40 Laurent Richard and Sandrine Rigaud, *Pegasus: How the Spy in Your Pocket Threatens the End of Privacy, Dignity, and Democracy* (New York: Henry Holt and Company, 2023).
41 Emma Szczesniak and Ahissa Rice, "Issues of Government Surveillance and Spyware Use in India," Tech4Humanity Lab, 2023, https://tech4humanitylab.org/blog/2023/11/5/issues-of-government-surveillance-and-spyware-use-in-india.
42 Aaron F. Brantly and Brooke Spens, "Hacking the Fourth Estate: Spyware, Assassination, and Harassment in Latin America," paper presented at the Political Economy of Cyber Conflict conference, Zurich, October 27, 2023.
43 Ronald Deibert and Rafal Rohozinski, "Tracking GhostNet: Investigating a Cyber Espionage Network," *Information Warfare Monitor*, March 29, 2009, 17–45.
44 Ibid., 41.
45 Ibid., 46.
46 Ibid., 48.
47 See, for example, the security planners developed by the Citizen Lab at https://securityplanner.org, and the EFF at https://ssd.eff.org/en.
48 Brantly, "The Cyber Losers," 153.
49 Ellen Nakashima and Barton Gellman, "As Encryption Spreads, U.S. Grapples with Clash between Privacy, Security," *Washington Post*, April 10, 2015.
50 Rid and Moore, "Cryptopolitik and the Darknet," 7. On terrorist use of digital security tools, see Brantly, "Innovation and Adaptation in Jihadist Digital Security," 92–3.
51 Rid and Moore, "Cryptopolitik and the Darknet," 9.
52 Gregory T. Nojeim, "Cybersecurity and Freedom on the Internet," *Journal of National Security Law & Policy* 4/1 (2010): 120.
53 For a summary, see: Editor, "Breaking Down Apple's iPhone Fight with

the U.S. Government," *New York Times*, March 21, 2016, www.nytimes
.com/interactive/2016/03/03/technology/apple-iphone-fbi-fightexplained
.html.

54 David Shammah, "Gov't contract a strong sign FBI used Israeli tech
to crack San Bernardino iPhone," *Times of Israel*, April 4, 2016, www
.timesofisrael.com/fbi-contract-a-strong-sign-fbi-used-israeli-tech-to
crack-san-bernardino-iphone.

55 Emily A. Vogels, "Some digital divides persist between rural, urban and
suburban America," Pew Research Center, August 19, 2021, www.pewrese
arch.org/short-reads/2021/08/19/some-digital-divides-persist-between-ru
ral-urban-and-suburban-america.

56 White House, Office of Science and Technology Policy, "Blueprint for
an AI Bill of Rights: Making Automated Systems Work for the American
People," October 2022, 5, www.whitehouse.gov/ostp/ai-bill-of-rights/algo
rithmic-discrimination-protections-2.

57 Mary Manjikian, *Cybersecurity Ethics: An Introduction* (Abingdon:
Routledge, 2023).

58 Ibid.

59 Brantly, "Battling the Bear," 157–71.

60 Kostyuk and Brantly, "War in the Borderland through Cyberspace,"
498–515.

61 Graham Cluley, "Ukraine Calls For Volunteer Hackers to Protect Its
Critical Infrastructure and Spy on Russian Forces," Bitdefender, February
25, 2022, www.bitdefender.com/blog/hotforsecurity/ukraine-calls-for-vo
lunteer-hackers-to-protect-its-critical-infrastructure-and-spy-on-russian
-forces.

62 Monica Pitrelli, "Hacktivist Group Anonymous Is Using Six Top
Techniques to 'Embarrass' Russia," CNBC, July 28, 2022, www.cnbc.com
/2022/07/28/how-is-anonymous-attacking-russia-the-top-six-ways-ranked
-.html.

63 Monica Pitrelli, "Anonymous Declared a 'Cyber War' against Russia. Here
Are the Results," CNBC, March 16, 2022, www.cnbc.com/2022/03/16
/what-has-anonymous-done-to-russia-here-are-the-results-.html.

64 Egloff, *Semi-state Actors in Cybersecurity*, 91–125.

65 Rid and Moore, "Cryptopolitik and the Darknet," 9.

10 The futures of cybersecurity

1 Center for Long-Term Cybersecurity, *Cybersecurity Futures 2020* (San
Francisco: University of California, Berkeley, 2016), 2–3.

2 See, for example, Jason Healey, "The Five Futures of Cyber Conflict and
Cooperation," Atlantic Council Issue Brief, 2011. For a synthesis of existing
scenarios, see Meredydd Williams et al., "Future Scenarios and Challenges

for Security and Privacy," paper presented at the IEEE International Forum on Research and Technologies for Society and Industry, Leveraging a Better Tomorrow (2016), https://ieeexplore.ieee.org/document/7740625.

3 Roey Tzezana, "High-Probability and Wild-Card Scenarios for Future Crimes and Terror Attacks Using the Internet of Things," *Foresight* 19/1 (2017): 1.

4 Leonie Maria Tanczer et al., "Emerging Risks in the IoT Ecosystem: Who's Afraid of the Big Bad Smart Fridge?" paper presented at the IEEE Conference on Living in the Internet of Things: Cybersecurity of the IoT, London (2018), https://ieeexplore.ieee.org/document/8379720.

5 Satyajit Sinha, "State of IoT 2023: Numbers of Connected IoT Devices Growing 16% to 16.7 Billion Globally," IoT Analytics, May 24, 2023, https://iot-analytics.com/number-connected-iot-devices.

6 Edward Skoudis, "Evolutionary Trends in Cyberspace," 160–1.

7 Jeremy Hsu, "The Strava Heat Map and the End of Secrets," *Wired*, January 29, 2018, www.wired.com/story/strava-heat-map-military-bases -fitness-trackers-privacy.

8 Spencer Ackerman and Sam Thielman, "US Intelligence Chief: We Might Use the Internet of Things to Spy on You," *Guardian*, February 9, 2016.

9 Singer and Friedman, *Cybersecurity and Cyberwar*, 251–2.

10 Center for Long-Term Cybersecurity, *Cybersecurity Futures 2020*, 6.

11 Tanczer et al., "Emerging Risks in the IoT Ecosystem," 1.

12 Aaron F. Brantly, "When Everything Becomes Intelligence: Machine Learning and the Connected World," *Intelligence and National Security* 33/4 (2018): 562.

13 Kevin Bartley, "Big Data Statistics: How Much Data Is There in the World?" Rivery, August 27, 2023, https://rivery.io/blog/big-data-statistics -how-much-data-is-there-in-the-world.

14 Andrea De Mauro, Marco Greco and Michele Grimaldi, "What Is Big Data? A Consensual Definition and a Review of Key Research Topics," in *American Institute of Physics Conference Proceedings*, ed. Georgios Giannakopoulos, Damianos P. Sakas and Daphne Kyriaki-Manessi, 1644/1 (2015): 103.

15 Brantly, "When Everything Becomes Intelligence," 566; Damien Van Puyvelde, Stephen Coulthart and Shahriar Hossain, "Beyond the Buzzword: Big Data and National Security Decision-Making," *International Affairs* 93/6 (2017): 1397.

16 Office of the Director of National Intelligence, "The AIM Initiative: A Strategy for Augmenting Intelligence Using Machines," 2019, www.dni .gov/files/ODNI/documents/AIM-Strategy.pdf.

17 Webroot, *Game Changers: AI and Machine Learning in Cybersecurity* (Broomfield, CO: Webroot, 2017), 2, www.webroot.com/us/en/about

/press-room/releases/cybercriminals-using-ai-in-attacks?sc=7016100000 0Trru&rc=8200.

18 Van Puyvelde, Coulthart and Hossain, "Beyond the Buzzword," 1404.

19 Janine Hiller, Gerlinde Berger-Walliser and Aaron F. Brantly, "Critical Protection for the Network of Persons," *Journal of Law and Social Change* 25/2 (2021):117–52.

20 Tanczer et al., "Emerging Risks in the IoT Ecosystem," 4–6.

21 Kristian Lum and William Isaac, "To Predict and Serve?" *Significance* 13/5 (2016): 14–19.

22 Jennifer L. Collinger et al., "High-Performance Neuroprosthetic Control by an Individual with Tetraplegia," *Lancet* 381 (2013): 557–64; Benoit Dupont, "Cybersecurity Futures: How Can We Regulate Emergent Risks?" *Technology Innovation Management Review* (2013): 6–118.

23 Nataliya Brantly, "Automating Health: The Promises and Perils of Biomedical Technologies for Diabetes Management," doctoral dissertation, Virginia Tech, May 15, 2023, https://vtechworks.lib.vt.edu/bitstrea ms/d8f8f7ea-f071-463d-b9c2-4e28371c8763/download.

24 Hiller et al., "Critical Protection for the Network of Persons."

25 Nataliya Brantly, "Homefront to Battlefield: Why the U.S. Military Should Care about Biomedical Cybersecurity," *Cyber Defense Review* 6/2 (2021): 93–110.

26 Center for Long-Term Cybersecurity, *Cybersecurity Futures 2020*, 7.

27 Internet Society, "Paths to Our Digital Future, 2017: Executive Summary," https://future.internetsociety.org/introduction/executive-summary.

28 Amitai Etzioni and Oren Etzioni, "Designing AI Systems That Obey Our Laws and Values," *Communications of the ACM* 59/9 (2016): 29–31.

29 John Timmer, "IBM Releases 1,000+ Qubit Processor, Roadmap to Error Correction," *Ars Technica*, December 4, 2023, https://arstechnica.com /science/2023/12/ibm-adds-error-correction-to-updated-quantum-compu ting-roadmap.

30 David Nield, "Google Quantum Computer Is '47 Years' Faster than #1 Supercomputer," *Science Alert*, July 05, 2023, www.sciencealert.com/goog le-quantum-computer-is-47-years-faster-than-1-supercomputer.

31 Tanczer et al., "Emerging Risks in the IoT Ecosystem," 4–5.

32 Brantly, "When Everything Becomes Intelligence," 569.

33 Williams et al., "Future Scenarios and Challenges for Security and Privacy."

34 Dupont, "Cybersecurity Futures," 9.

35 Internet Society, "Paths to Our Digital Future."

36 Alec Ross, "Want Job Security? Try Online Security," *Wired*, April 25, 2016, www.wired.co.uk/article/job-security-cybersecurity-alec-ross.

37 Internet Society, "Paths to Our Digital Future."

Select bibliography

"A Brief History of Wi-Fi," *The Economist*, June 10, 2004, 26.

Abbate, Janet, *Inventing the Internet* (Cambridge, MA: MIT Press, 2000).

Adamsky, Dmitry, "From Moscow with Coercion: Russian Deterrence Theory and Strategic Culture," *Journal of Strategic Studies* 41/1–2 (2018): 33–66.

Anderson, Julie, "The Chekist Takeover of the Russian State," *International Journal of Intelligence and CounterIntelligence* 19/2 (2006): 237–88.

Arquilla, John, "Cyberwar Is Already upon Us," *Foreign Policy* 192 (2012): 84–5.

Arquilla, John, and David Ronfeldt, "Cyber War Is Coming!" *Comparative Strategy* 12/2 (1993): 141–65.

Arquilla, John, and David F. Ronfeldt, *Cyberwar Is Coming!* (Santa Monica, CA: RAND, 1992).

Austin, Greg, *Cyber Policy in China* (New York: Polity, 2014).

Bakioğlu, Burcu S., "The Gray Zone: Networks of Piracy, Control, and Resistance," *The Information Society* 32/1 (2015): 40–50.

Baron, Joshua, Angela O'Mahony, David Manheim and Cynthia Dion-Schwarz, *National Security Implications of Virtual Currency* (Santa Monica, CA: RAND, 2015).

Bauman, Zygmunt, Didier Bigo, Paulo Esteves, et al., "After Snowden: Rethinking the Impact of Surveillance," *International Political Sociology* 8/2 (2014): 121–44.

Beehner, Lionel, Liam Collins, Steve Ferenzi, Robert Person and Aaron Brantly, *A Contemporary Battlefield Assessment* (West Point, NY: Modern War Institute, 2018).

Benjamin, Jacob, and Michael Haney, "Nonproliferation of Cyber Weapons," in *2020 International Conference on Computational Science and Computational Intelligence* (Las Vegas: IEEE Explore, 2020), 105–8.

Berger, J. M., and Jonathon Morgan, *The ISIS Twitter Census: Defining and Describing the Population of ISIS Supporters on Twitter* (Washington, DC: Center for Middle East Policy at Brookings, 2015).

Betz, David, "The Mystique of 'Cyberwar' and the Strategic Latency of Networked Social Movements," *Strategic Insights* 10 (2011): 61–77.

Biden, Joseph R., "National Cybersecurity Strategy 2023," Washington, DC: The White House, March 2023, www.whitehouse.gov/wp-content/uploads/2023/03/National-Cybersecurity-Strategy-2023.pdf.

Bizeul, David, "Russian Business Network Study," 2007, www.bizeul.org/files/RBN_study.pdf.

Bohdanova, Tetyana, "Unexpected Revolution: The Role of Social Media in Ukraine's Euromaidan Uprising," *European View* 13/1 (2014): 133–42.

Borghard, Erica D., and Shawn W. Lonergan, "Can States Calculate the Risks of Using Cyber Proxies?" *Orbis* 60/3 (2016): 395–416.

Borghard, Erica D., and Shawn W. Lonergan, "Cyber Operations as Imperfect Tools of Escalation," *Strategic Studies Quarterly* 13/3 (2019): 122–45.

Braman, Sandra, "The Interpenetration of Technical and Legal Decision-Making for the Internet," *Information, Communication & Society* 13/3 (2010): 309–24.

Brantly, Aaron F., "A Brief History of Fake: Surveying Russian Disinformation from the Russian Empire through the Cold War to the Present," in *Information Warfare in the Age of Cyber Conflict*, ed. Christopher Whyte, Trevor Thrall and Bryan Mazanec (Abingdon: Routledge, 2020), 27–41.

Brantly, Aaron F., "Battling the Bear: Ukraine's Approach to National Cyber and Information Security," in *Cybersecurity Politics*, ed. Myriam D. Cavelty and Andreas Wenger (Abingdon: Routledge, 2022), 157–71.

Brantly, Aaron F., "Financing Terror Bit by Bit," *CTC Sentinel* 7/10 (2014): 1–5.

Brantly, Aaron F., "From Cyberspace to Independence Square: Understanding the Impact of Social Media on Physical Protest Mobilization during Ukraine's Euromaidan Revolution," *Journal of Information Technology Politics* 16/4 (2019): 1–19.

Brantly, Aaron F., "Innovation and Adaptation in Jihadist Digital Security," *Survival* 59/1 (2017): 79–102.

Brantly, Aaron F., "Public Health and Epidemiological Approaches to National Cybersecurity: A Baseline Comparison," in *US National Cybersecurity*, ed. Van Puyvelde and Brantly, 91–109.

Brantly, Aaron F., "The Cyber Deterrence Problem," in *Proceedings of the 10th International Conference on Cyber Conflict, NATO Cyber Defense Center of Excellence* (Tallinn: IEEE, 2018), 31–54.

Brantly, Aaron F., "The Cyber Losers," *Democracy and Security* 10/2 (2014): 132–55.

Brantly, Aaron F., *The Decision to Attack: Military and Intelligence Cyber Decision-Making* (Athens: University of Georgia Press, 2016).

Brantly, Aaron F., "The Most Governed Ungoverned Space: Legal and Policy Constraints on Military Operations in Cyberspace," *SAIS Review of International Affairs* 36/2 (2016): 29–39.

Brantly, Aaron F., "The Violence of Hacking: State Violence and Cyberspace," *Cyber Defense Review* 2/1 (2017): 1–19.

Brantly, Aaron F., "Utopia Lost – Human Rights in a Digital World," *Applied Cybersecurity and Internet Governance* 1/1 (2022): 25–43.

Brantly, Aaron F., "When Everything Becomes Intelligence: Machine Learning and the Connected World," *Intelligence and National Security* 33/4 (2018): 562–73.

Brantly, Aaron F., Nerea M. Cal and Devlin P. Winkelstein, *Defending the Borderland: Ukrainian Military Experiences with IO, Cyber, and EW* (West Point, NY: US Army Cyber Institute, 2017).

Brantly, Aaron F., and Brooke Spens, "Hacking the Fourth Estate: Spyware, Assassination, and Harassment in Latin America," paper presented at the Political Economy of Cyber Conflict conference, Zurich, October 27, 2023.

Brantly, Nataliya, "Automating Health: The Promises and Perils of Biomedical Technologies for Diabetes Management," doctoral dissertation, Virginia Tech, May 15, 2023, https://vtechworks.lib.vt.edu/bitstreams/d8f8f7ea-f0 71-463d-b9c2-4e28371c8763/download.

Brantly, Nataliya, "Homefront to Battlefield: Why the U.S. Military Should Care about Biomedical Cybersecurity," *Cyber Defense Review* 6/2 (2021): 93–110.

Bronk, Chris, and Eneken Tikk-Ringas, "The Cyber Attack on Saudi Aramco," *Survival* 55/2 (2013): 81–96.

Brooking, Emerson T., "Anonymous vs. the Islamic State," *Foreign Policy*, November 13, 2015, https://foreignpolicy.com/2015/11/13/anonymous-ha ckers-islamic-state-isis-chan-online-war.

Brown, Gary, and Christopher D. Yung, "Evaluating the US–China Cybersecurity Agreement, Part 1: The US Approach to Cyberspace," *Diplomat*, January 19, 2017, https://thediplomat.com/2017/01/evaluating-the-us-china-cybersecurity-agreement-part-1-the-us-approach-to-cyberspace.

Buchanan, Ben, "Cyber Deterrence Isn't MAD; It's Mosaic," *Georgetown Journal of International Affairs* 4 (2018): 130–40.

Calleja, Alejandro, and Juan Caballero, *A Look into 30 Years of Malware Development from a Software Metrics Perspective* (Cham: Springer, 2016).

Campbell-Kelly, Martin, William Aspray, Nathan Ensmenger and Jeffrey R. Yost, *Computer: A History of the Information Machine* (New York: HarperCollins, 2017).

Canfil, Justin K. "The Illogic of Plausible Deniability: Why Proxy Conflict in Cyberspace May No Longer Pay," *Journal of Cybersecurity* 8/1 (2022): 1–16.

Cartwright, James E., "Memorandum: Joint Terminology for Cyberspace Operations," November 2010.

Center for Long-Term Cybersecurity, *Cybersecurity Futures 2020* (San Francisco: University of California, Berkeley, 2016).

Cerf, Vinton G., and Robert E. Kahn, "A Protocol for Packet Network

Intercommunication," *Data Communications of the IEEE Communications Society* 22/5 (1974): 1–13.

Ceruzzi, Paul E., *Computing: A Concise History* (Cambridge, MA: MIT Press, 2012).

Chairman of the Joint Chiefs of Staff, "National Military Strategy for Cyberspace Operations," December 2006, www.hsdl.org/?view&did=3 5693.

Chen, Hsinchun, et al., "Uncovering the Dark Web: A Case Study of Jihad on the Web," *Journal of the American Society for Information Science and Technology* 59/8 (2008): 1347–59.

Clarke, Richard A., and Robert K. Knake, *Cyber War: The Next Threat to National Security and What to Do about It* (New York: Ecco, 2010).

Clausewitz, Carl von, *On War*, ed. Michael Howard and Peter Part (Princeton University Press, 2008).

Cohen, Eliot, "Changes and Transformation in Military Affairs," *Journal of Strategic Studies* 27/3 (2004): 395–407.

Collinger, Jennifer L., B. Wodlinger, J. E. Downey et al., "High-Performance Neuroprosthetic Control by an Individual with Tetraplegia," *Lancet* 381 (2013): 557–64.

Conti, Greg, and David Raymond, *On Cyber: Towards an Operational Art for Cyber Conflict* (n.p.: Kopidion Press, 2017).

Corradini, Isabella, Enrico Nardelli and Tareq Ahram, *Advances in Human Factors in Cybersecurity, AHFE Virtual Conference on Human Factors in Cybersecurity* (Cham: Springer, 2020

Council of Europe, Convention on Cybercrime, Budapest, November 23, 2001, www.coe.int/en/web/conventions/full-list/-/conventions/rms/090000 1680081561.

Council of the Executive Office of the President of the United States, Select Committee on Artificial Intelligence of the National Science and Technology Council, "National Artificial Intelligence Research and Development Strategic Plan 2023 Update," May 2023, www.whitehouse.gov/wp-content /uploads/2023/05/National-Artificial-Intelligence-Research-and-Develop ment-Strategic-Plan-2023-Update.pdf.

D'Ovidio, Robert, and James Doyle, "Study on Cyberstalking: Understanding Investigative Hurdles," *FBI Law Enforcement Bulletin* 72/3 (2003): 10–17.

De Mauro, Andrea, Marco Greco and Michele Grimaldi, "What Is Big Data? A Consensual Definition and a Review of Key Research Topics," in *American Institute of Physics Conference Proceedings*, ed. Georgios Giannakopoulos, Damianos P. Sakas and Daphne Kyriaki-Manessi, 1644/1 (2015): 97–104.

Deibert, Ronald J., *Black Code: Surveillance, Privacy, and the Dark Side of the Internet* (Toronto: McClelland & Stewart, 2013).

Deibert, Ronald J., and Rafal Rohozinski, "Liberation vs. Control: The Future of Cyberspace," *Journal of Democracy* 21/4 (2010): 43–57.

Deibert, Ronald J., and Rafal Rohozinski, "Tracking GhostNet: Investigating a Cyber Espionage Network," *Information Warfare Monitor*, March 29, 2009, 17–45.

Deibert, Ronald J., Rafal Rohozinski and Masashi Crete-Nishihata, "Cyclones in Cyberspace: Information Shaping and Denial in the 2008 Russia–Georgia War," *Security Dialogue* 43/1 (2012): 3–24.

Demchak, Chris, *Wars of Disruption and Resilience: Cybered Conflict, Power, and National Security* (Athens: University of Georgia Press, 2011).

Demchak, Chris, and Peter Dombrowski, "Cyber Westphalia: Asserting State Prerogatives in Cyberspace," *Georgetown Journal of International Affairs* (2013): 29–38.

Demchak, Chris, and Peter Dombrowski, "Rise of a Cybered Westphalian Age," *Strategic Studies Quarterly* 5/1 (2011): 32–61.

DeNardis, Laura, *Protocol Politics: The Globalization of Internet Governance* (Cambridge, MA: MIT Press, 2009).

DeNardis, Laura, *The Global War for Internet Governance* (New Haven, CT: Yale University Press, 2014).

Department of the Treasury, "Potential Federal Insurance Response to Catastrophic Cyber Incidents," *Federal Register* 87/188, September 29, 2022, 59161-3.

Deseriis, Marco, "Hacktivism: On the Use of Botnets in Cyberattacks," *Theory, Culture & Society* 34/4 (2017): 131–52.

Diamond, Larry, "Liberation Technology," *Journal of Democracy* 21/3 (2010): 69–83.

Dinniss, Heather Harrison, *Cyber Warfare and the Laws of War* (New York: Cambridge University Press, 2012).

DiNucci, Darcy, "Fragmented Future," *Print* 53/4 (1999): 32, 221–2.

Dobbs, Michael, *One Minute to Midnight: Kennedy, Khrushchev, and Castro on the Brink of Nuclear War* (New York: Vintage Books, 2009).

Dombrowski, Peter, and Chris C. Demchak, "Cyber War, Cybered Conflict, and the Maritime Domain," *Naval War College Review* 67/2 (2014): 71–96.

Dunn Cavelty, Myriam, *Cyber-Security and Threat Politics: US Efforts to Secure the Information Age* (London: Routledge, 2008).

Dupont, Benoit, "Cybersecurity Futures: How Can We Regulate Emergent Risks?" *Technology Innovation Management Review* (2013): 6–11.

Durairajan, Ramakrishnan, Paul Barford, Joel Sommers and Walter Willinger, *InterTubes* (New York: ACM Press, 2015).

Egloff, Florian J., *Semi-state Actors in Cybersecurity* (New York: Oxford University Press, 2022).

Etzioni, Amitai, and Oren Etzioni, "Designing AI Systems That Obey Our Laws and Values," *Communications of the ACM* 59/9 (2016): 29–31.

European Union Agency for Cybersecurity, "A Governance Framework for National Cybersecurity Strategies," February 2023, www.enisa.europa.eu /publications/a-governance-framework-for-national-cybersecurity-strategies.

European Union Agency for Cybersecurity, "Cyber Insurance: Fitting the Needs of Operators of Essential Services?" February 23, 2023, www.enisa .europa.eu/news/cyber-insurance-fitting-the-needs-of-operators-of-essential -services.

Federal Trade Commission, "Cyber Insurance," www.ftc.gov/business-guidan ce/small-businesses/cybersecurity/cyber-insurance.

Ferris, John, "A New American Way of War? C4ISR, Intelligence and Information Operations in Operation 'Iraqi Freedom': A Provisional Assessment," *Intelligence and National Security* 81/3 (2003): 155–74.

Fischerkeller, Michael P., Emily O. Goldman and Richard J. Harknett, *Cyber Persistence Theory: Redefining National Security in Cyberspace* (Oxford University Press, 2022).

Fitzgerald, Chad, and Aaron Brantly, "Subverting Reality: The Role of Propaganda in 21st Century Intelligence," *Journal of Intelligence and Counterintelligence* 30/2 (2017): 215–40.

Folsom, Thomas C., "Defining Cyberspace (Finding Real Virtue in the Place of Virtual Reality)," *Tulane Journal of Technology and Intellectual Property* 9/1 (2007): 75–121.

Futter, A., *Hacking the Bomb: Cyber Threats and Nuclear Weapons* (Washington, DC: Georgetown University Press, 2018).

Gartzke, Erik, "The Myth of Cyberwar: Bringing War in Cyberspace Back Down to Earth," *International Security* 38/2 (2013): 41–73.

Gartzke, Erik, and Jon R. Lindsay, "Weaving Tangled Webs: Offense, Defense, and Deception in Cyberspace," *Security Studies* 24/2 (2015): 316–48.

George, Alexander L., and Richard Smoke, *Deterrence in American Foreign Policy: Theory and Practice* (New York: Columbia University Press, 1974).

Gibson, William, *Neuromancer* (New York: Ace Books, 1984).

Goode, Luke, "Anonymous and the Political Ethos of Hacktivism," *Popular Communication* 13/1 (2015): 74–86.

Goodman, Marc, *Future Crimes: Everything Is Connected, Everyone Is Vulnerable and What We Can Do about It* (New York: Doubleday, 2015).

Goodman, Will, "Cyber Deterrence: Tougher in Theory than in Practice?" *Strategic Studies Quarterly* 4/3 (2010): 102–35.

Gray, Colin, *Another Bloody Century: Future Warfare* (London: Orion Books, 2006).

Guerrero-Saade, Juan Andres, "AcidRain: A Modem Wiper Rains Down on

Europe," *Sentinel One*, March 31, 2022, www.sentinelone.com/labs/acidra in-a-modem-wiper-rains-down-on-europe.

Gvodsev, Nicholas, "The Bear Goes Digital: Russia and Its Cyber Capabilities," in *Cyberspace and National Security*, ed. Reveron, 173–89.

Haddad, Saïd, "Le Cyberespace ou la construction d'un 'champ de confrontation à part entière,'" in *La Cyberdéfense. Politique de l'espace numérique*, ed. Amaël Cattaruzza, Didier Danet and Stéphane Taillat (Paris: Armand Collin, 2018), 44–51.

Hafner, Katie, and Matthew Lyon, *Where Wizards Stay Up Late: The Origins of the Internet* (New York: Simon & Schuster, 1996).

Hanson, Fergus, *Revolution @State: The Spread of EDiplomacy* (Sydney: Lowy Institute for International Affairs, 2012).

Harnett, Eric, "Welcome to Hyperwar," *Bulletin of the Atomic Scientists* 48/7 (1992): 14–21.

Healey, Jason, *A Fierce Domain: Conflict in Cyberspace, 1986 to 2012* (Arlington, VA: Cyber Conflict Studies Association, 2013).

Healey, Jason, "The Five Futures of Cyber Conflict and Cooperation," Atlantic Council Issue Brief, 2011, www.atlanticcouncil.org/wp-content/uploads/20 11/12/121311_ACUS_FiveCyberFutures.pdf.

Heffelfinger, Christopher, "The Risks Posed by Jihadist Hackers," *CTC Sentinel* 6/7 (2013): 1–5.

Highfill, Tina, and Christopher Surfield, "New and Revised Statistics of the U.S. Digital Economy 2005–2021," Bureau of Economic Analysis, US Department of Commerce, November 2022, www.bea.gov/system/files/20 22-11/new-and-revised-statistics-of-the-us-digital-economy-2005-2021.pdf.

Hiller, Janine, Gerlinde Berger-Walliser and Aaron Brantly, "Critical Protection for the Network of Persons," *Journal of Law and Social Change* 25/2 (2021): 117–52.

Hinduja, Sameer, and Justin W. Patchin, "Bullying, Cyberbullying, and Suicide," *Archives of Suicide Research* 14 (2010): 206–21.

Hoffman, Bruce, *Inside Terrorism* (New York: Columbia University Press, 2006).

Holt, Thomas J., George W. Burruss and Adam M. Bossler, *Policing Cybercrime and Cyberterror* (Durham: Carolina Academic Press, 2015).

Homer, *The Iliad & the Odyssey* (New York: Barnes & Noble Books, 2008).

IBM Global Technology Services, "IBM Security Services 2014 Cyber Security Intelligence Index," https://media.scmagazine.com/documents/82/ibm_cyb er_security_intelligenc_20450.pdf.

Inkster, Nigel, *China's Cyber Power* (Abingdon: Routledge, 2016).

Inkster, Nigel, "The Chinese Intelligence Agencies: Evolution and Empowerment," in *China and Cybersecurity*, ed. Lindsay, Cheung and Reveron, 29–50.

Internet Society, "Paths to Our Digital Future, 2017: Executive Summary," https://future.internetsociety.org/introduction/executive-summary.

Jarmon, Jack, and Pano Yannakogeorgos, *The Cyber Threat and Globalization: The Impact on U.S. National and International Security* (New York: Rowman and Littlefield, 2018).

Jasper, Scott, "U.S. Cyber Threat Intelligence Sharing Frameworks," *International Journal of Intelligence and CounterIntelligence* 30/1 (2016): 53–65.

Jeangène Vilmer, Jean-Baptiste, "Successfully Countering Russian Electoral Interference: 15 Lessons Learned from the Macron Leaks," *CSIS Brief*, 2018.

Jianwei, Zhuge, Gu Lion, Duan Haixin and Taylor Roberts, "Investigating the Chinese Online Underground Economy," in *China and Cybersecurity*, ed. Lindsay, Cheung and Reveron, 87–120.

Johnston, Alastair Iain, "Thinking about Strategic Culture," *International Security* 19/4 (1995): 32–64.

Johnston, Jessica, *Technological Turf Wars: A Case Study of the Computer Antivirus Industry* (Philadelphia: Temple University Press, 2009).

Jones, Jeffrey B., "Confronting China's Efforts to Steal Defense Information," The Belfer Center for Science and International Affairs, May 2020, www.belfercenter.org/sites/default/files/2020-05/ChinaStealing.pdf.

Junio, Timothy J., "How Probable Is Cyber War? Bringing IR Theory Back into the Cyber Conflict Debate," *Journal of Strategic Studies* 36/1 (2013): 125–33.

Kan, Michael, "Law Enforcement Seizes $30M Stolen in North Korea's Hack of Ronin Network," *PC Mag*, September 9, 2022, www.pcmag.com/news/law-enforcement-seizes-30m-stolen-in-north-koreas-hack-of-ronin-network.

Kaplan, Fred M., *Dark Territory: The Secret History of Cyber War* (New York: Simon & Schuster, 2017).

Kello, Lucas, *The Virtual Weapon and International Order* (New Haven, CT: Yale University Press, 2017).

Kelly, Sanja, Mai Tuong, Adrian Shahba and Madeline Earp, "Silencing the Messenger: Communications Apps under Pressure," in Freedom House, *Freedom on the Net 2016*, 2, https://freedomhouse.org/sites/default/files/FOTN_2016_Full_Report.pdf.

Keohane, Robert O., and Joseph S. Nye, *Power and Interdependence: World Politics in Transition* (Boston: Little, Brown, 1977).

Kim, Choong Nyoung, Kyung Hoon Yang and Jaekyung Kim, "Human Decision-Making Behavior and Modeling Effects," *Decision Support Systems* 45/3 (2008): 517–27.

King, Gary, Jennifer Pan and Margaret E. Roberts, "How Censorship in China

Allows Government Criticism but Silences Collective Expression," *American Political Science Review* 107/2 (2013): 326–43.

Klausen, Jytte, "Tweeting the Jihad: Social Media Networks of Western Foreign Fighters in Syria and Iraq," *Studies in Conflict & Terrorism* 38/1 (2014): 1–22.

Klimburg, Alexander, "Mobilising Cyber Power," *Survival* 53/1 (2011): 41–60.

Klimburg, Alexander, *The Darkening: The War for Cyberspace* (New York: Penguin Books, 2017).

Kock, Ned, "E-Collaboration and E-Commerce in Virtual Worlds," *International Journal of E-Collaboration* 4/3 (2008): 1–13.

Kostyuk, Nadiya, "Allies and Diffusion of State Military Capacity," *Journal of Peace Research* 61/1 (2024): 44–58.

Kostyuk, Nadyia, and Aaron F. Brantly, "War in the Borderland through Cyberspace: Limits of Defending Ukraine through Interstate Cooperation," *Contemporary Security Policy* 43/3 (2022): 498–515.

Kramer, Franklin D., "Cyberpower and National Security: Policy Recommendations for a Strategic Framework," in *Cyberpower and National Security*, ed. Kramer, Starr and Wentz, 3–23.

Kramer, Franklin D., Stuart H. Starr and Larry K. Wentz (eds.), *Cyberpower and National Security* (Washington, DC: National Defense University, 2009).

Kshetri, Nir. "The Economics of Cyber-Insurance," *IEEE IT Professional* 20/6 (2019): 9–14.

Kuehl, Daniel T., "From Cyberspace to Cyberpower: Defining the Problem," in *Cyberpower and National Security*, ed. Kramer, Starr and Wentz, 24–42.

Kurbalija, Jovan, *An Introduction to Internet Governance*, 7th edn. (Geneva: DiploFoundation, 2016).

Lee, Chung-pin, Kaiju Chang and Frances Stokes Berry, "Testing the Development and Diffusion of E-government and E-democracy: A Global Perspective," *Public Administration Review* 71/3 (2011): 444–54.

Leiner, Barry M., Vincton G. Cerf, David D. Clark et al., "The Past and Future History of the Internet," *Communications of the ACM* 40/2 (1997): 102–8.

Levy, Steven, *Hackers: Heroes of the Computer Revolution* (Sebastopol, CA: O'Reilly Media, 2010).

Lewis, James, Hannah L. Malekos Smith and Eugenie Lostri, "The Hidden Cost of Cybercrime," CSIS/McAfee, 2020, www.csis.org/analysis/hidden-co sts-cybercrime.

Libicki, Martin C., *Cyberdeterrence and Cyberwar* (Santa Monica, CA: RAND, 2009).

Libicki, Martin C., *Cyberspace in Peace and War* (Annapolis: Naval Institute Press, 2016).

Libicki, Martin C., "Why Cyber War Will Not and Should Not Have Its Grand Strategist," *Strategic Studies Quarterly* 8/1 (2014): 23–39.

Lin, Herbert, *Cyber Threats and Nuclear Weapons* (Redwood City, CA: Stanford University Press, 2021).

Lin, Herbert, "Operational Considerations in Cyber Attack and Cyber Exploitation," in *Cyberspace and National Security*, ed. Reveron, 37–56.

Lindsay, Jon R., "Introduction: China and Cybersecurity – Controversy and Context," in *China and Cybersecurity*, ed. Lindsay, Cheung and Reveron, 1–26.

Lindsay, Jon R., "Stuxnet and the Limits of Cyber Warfare," *Security Studies* 22/3 (2013): 365–404.

Lindsay, Jon R., "The Impact of China on Cybersecurity: Fiction and Friction," *International Security* 39/3 (2015): 7–47.

Lindsay, Jon R., "Tipping the Scales: The Attribution Problem and the Feasibility of Deterrence against Cyberattack," *Journal of Cybersecurity* 1/1 (2015): 53–67.

Lindsay, Jon R., and Tai Ming Cheung, "From Exploitation to Innovation: Acquisition, Absorption, and Application," in *China and Cybersecurity*, ed. Lindsay, Cheung and Reveron, 51–86.

Lindsay, Jon R., Tai Ming Cheung and Derek S. Reveron (eds.), *China and Cybersecurity: Espionage, Strategy, and Politics in the Digital Domain* (Oxford University Press, 2015).

Lindsay, Jon R., and Derek S. Reveron, "Conclusion: The Rise of China and the Future of Cybersecurity," in *China and Cybersecurity*, ed. Lindsay, Cheung and Reveron, 333–54.

Lockheed Martin, "The Cyber Kill Chain," www.lockheedmartin.com/en-us /capabilities/cyber/cyber-kill-chain.html.

Lotrionte, Catherine, "A Better Defense: Examining the United States' New Norms-Based Approach to Cyber Deterrence," *Georgetown Journal of International Affairs* (2016): 75–88.

Lum, Kristian, and William Isaac, "To Predict and Serve?" *Significance* 13/5 (2016): 14–19.

MacDuffee Metzger, Megan, and Joshua A. Tucker, "Social Media and EuroMaidan: A Review Essay," *Slavic Review* 76/1 (2017): 187–91.

Madsen, Wayne, "Intelligence Agency Threats to Computer Security," *International Journal of Intelligence and CounterIntelligence* 6/4 (1993): 413–88.

Mandiant Threat Intelligence Center, "APT1 Exposing One of China's Cyber Espionage Units," www.fireeye.com/content/dam/fireeye-www/services/ pdfs/mandiant-apt1-report.pdf.

Manjikian, Mary, *Cybersecurity Ethics: An Introduction* (Abingdon: Routledge, 2023).

Manjikian, Mary, "From Global Village to Virtual Battlespace: The Colonizing of the Internet and the Extension of Realpolitik," *International Studies Quarterly* 54/2 (2010): 381–401.

Marczak, Bill, and John Scott-Railton, "Keep Calm and (Don't) Enable Macros: A New Threat Actor Targets UAE Dissidents – the Citizen Lab," Citizen Lab, May 29, 2016, https://citizenlab.ca/2016/05/stealth-falcon.

Margolis, Michael, "E-government and Democracy," in *The Oxford Handbook of Political Behavior*, ed. Russel J. Dalton and Hans-Dieter Klingemann (Oxford University Press, 2009 online), 765–82.

Marotta, Angelica, Fabio Martinelli, Stefano Nanni, Albina Orlando and Artsiom Yautsiukhin, "Cyber-Insurance Survey," *Computer Science Review* 24 (2017): 35–61.

Marquis-Boire, Morgan, and Bill Marczak, "From Bahrain with Love: FinFisher's Spy Kit Exposed?" Citizen Lab, July 25, 2012, https://citizenlab.ca/2012/07/from-bahrain-with-love-finfishers-spy-kit-exposed.

Maurer, Tim, *Cyber Mercenaries: The State, Hackers, and Power* (Cambridge University Press, 2018).

Maurer, Tim, "'Proxies' and Cyberspace," *Journal of Conflict and Security Law* 21/3 (2016): 383–403.

Mazanec, Brian, "The Outlook for Constraining International Norms for Offensive Cyber Operations", in *US National Cybersecurity*, ed. Van Puyvelde and Brantly, 40–54.

Mazarr, Michael J., Bryan Frederick and Yvonne K. Crane, *Understanding A New Era of Strategic Competition* (Santa Monica, CA: RAND Corporation, 2022).

McGraw, Gary, "Cyber War Is Inevitable (unless We Build Security In)," *Journal of Strategic Studies* 36/1 (2013): 109–19.

Medvedev, Sergey, "Data Protection in the Russian Federation: Overview," *Thomson Reuters Practical Law*, December 1, 2017, https://uk.practicallaw. thomsonreuters.com/2-502-2227.

Miller, Chris, *Chip War: The Fight for the World's Most Critical Technology* (New York: Simon & Schuster, 2022).

Mitnick, Kevin, and William L. Simon, *Ghost in the Wires: My Adventures as the World's Most Wanted Hacker* (New York: Little, Brown and Company, 2011).

Mowery, David C., and Timothy Simcoe, "Is the Internet a US Invention? An Economic and Technological History of Computer Networking," *Research Policy* 31 (2002): 1369–87.

Mueller, Milton, *Networks and States: The Global Politics of Internet Governance* (Cambridge, MA: MIT Press, 2010).

Mueller, Milton, *Will the Internet Fragment? Sovereignty, Globalization and Cyberspace* (Malden, MA: Polity, 2017).

Murray, Andrew, *Information Technology Law: The Law and Society* (Oxford University Press, 2016).

Myers, Brad A., "A Brief History of Human–Computer Interaction Technology," *ACM Interactions* (1998): 44–54.

National Audit Office, "Investigation: WannaCry Cyber Attack and the NHS," October 27, 2017, www.nao.org.uk/report/investigation-wannacry -cyber-attack-and-the-nhs.

National Security Agency, "PRISM/US-984XN Overview," April 2013, www .washingtonpost.com/wp-srv/special/politics/prism-collection-documents/ ?noredirect=on.

NATO Cooperative Cyber Defence Centre of Excellence, "Cyber Security Strategy Documents," October 18, 2018, https://ccdcoe.org/cybersecurity-st rategy-documents.html.

NATO Cooperative Cyber Defence Centre of Excellence, "Incyder: International Cyber Developments Review," https://ccdcoe.org/incyder .html.

NATO Cooperative Cyber Defence Centre of Excellence, "National Cyber Security Organisation," https://ccdcoe.org/national-cyber-security-organisa tion.html.

Naugle, Matthew G., *Network Protocols* (New York: McGraw-Hill Professional, 1999).

Netmundial, "NetMundial Multistakeholder Statement," Sao Paulo, Brazil, April 24, 2014, http://netmundial.br/netmundial-multistakeholder-sta tement.

Nojeim, Gregory T., "Cybersecurity and Freedom on the Internet," *Journal of National Security Law & Policy* 4/1 (2010): 119–37.

Nordrum, Amy, "Popular Internet of Things Forecast of 50 Billion Devices by 2020 Is Outdated," *IEEE Spectrum*, August 18, 2016, https://spectrum.ieee .org/tech-talk/telecom/internet/popular-internet-ofthings-forecast-of-50-bil lion-devices-by-2020-is-outdated.

Norris, Donald F., "E-government 2020: plus ça change, plus c'est la meme chose," *Public Administration Review* 70/1 (2010): 180–1.

Nye, Joseph S., "Get Smart: Combining Hard and Soft Power," *Foreign Affairs* 88/4 (2009): 160–3.

Nye, Joseph S., "Hard, Soft, and Smart Power," in *The Oxford Handbook of Modern Diplomacy*, ed. Andrew F. Cooper, Jorge Heine and Ramesh Thakur (Oxford University Press, 2013).

Obama, Barack, "Cyber-Insurance Metrics and Impact on Cyber-Security," Washington, DC: The White House, https://obamawhitehouse.archives.gov /files/documents/cyber/ISA%20-%20Cyber-Insurance%20Metrics%20and %20Impact%20on%20Cyber-Security.pdf.

Office of the Director of National Intelligence, "The AIM Initiative: A Strategy for Augmenting Intelligence Using Machines," 2019, www.dni.gov/files /ODNI/documents/AIM-Strategy.pdf.

Office of the Director of National Intelligence, Background to "Assessing Russian Activities and Intentions in Recent US Elections: The Analytic Process and Cyber Incident Attribution," January 6, 2017.

Office of the President of the United States, "National Strategy for Global Supply Chain Security," Washington, DC, 2012, https://obamawhiteh ouse.archives.gov/sites/default/files/docs/national_strategy_for_global_sup ply_chain_security_implementation_update_public_version_final2-26-131 .pdf.

Olson, Parmy, *We Are Anonymous: Inside the Hacker World of LulzSec, Anonymous, and the Global Cyber Insurgency* (New York: Back Bay Books, 2013).

Onuch, Olga, "EuroMaidan Protests in Ukraine: Social Media versus Social Networks," *Problems of Post-Communism* 62/4 (2015): 217–35.

Pal, Ranjan, Leana Golubchik, Konstantinos Psounis and Pan Hui, "Will Cyber-Insurance Improve Network Security? A Market Analysis," in *IEEE INFOCOM 2014 – IEEE Conference on Computer Communications* (2014): 235–43.

Patchin, Justin W., "Summary of Our Cyberbullying Research (2004–2016)," Cyberbullying Research Center, November 26, 2016, https://cyberbullying .org/summary-of-our-cyberbullying-research.

Patrucic, Miranda, and Kelly Bloss, "Life in Azerbaijan's Digital Autocracy: 'They Want to Be in Control of Everything,'" Organized Crime and Corruption Reporting Project, July 18, 2021, www.occrp.org/en/the-pega sus-project/life-in-azerbaijans-digital-autocracy-they-want-to-be-in-control -of-everything.

Philipson, Graeme, "A Short History of Software," in *Management, Labour Process and Software Development: Reality Bites*, ed. Rowena Barrett (New York: Routledge, 2005), 13–44.

Ponemon Institute, "2017 Cost of Data Breach Study," research report, June 2017.

Price, James H., and Jagdish Khubchandani, "Adolescent Homicides, Suicides, and the Role of Firearms: A Narrative Review," *American Journal of Health Education* 48/2 (2017): 67–79.

Rashid, Fahmida Y., "Inside the Aftermath of the Saudi Aramco Breach," DarkReading, August 8, 2015, www.darkreading.com/attacks-breaches/insi de-the-aftermath-of-the-saudi-aramco-breach.

Rattray, Gregory J., *Strategic Warfare in Cyberspace* (Cambridge, MA: MIT Press, 2001).

Raymond, Mark, and Laura DeNardis, "Multistakeholderism: Anatomy of an Inchoate Global Institution," *International Theory* 7/3 (2015): 572–616.

Reinhold, Thomas, and Christian Reuter, "Toward a Cyber Weapons Assessment Model – Assessment of the Technical Features of Malicious Software," *IEEE Transactions on Technology and Society* 3/3 (2022): 226–39.

Reveron, Derek S., "An Introduction to National Security and Cyberspace," in *Cyberspace and National Security*, ed. Reveron, 3–19.

Reveron, Derek S. (ed.), *Cyberspace and National Security: Threats, Opportunities, and Power in a Virtual World* (Washington, DC: Georgetown University Press, 2012).

Richard, Laurent, and Sandrine Rigaud, *Pegasus: How the Spy in your Pocket Threatens the End of Privacy, Dignity, and Democracy* (New York: Henry Holt and Company, 2023).

Rid, Thomas, "Cyber War Will Not Take Place," *Journal of Strategic Studies* 35/1 (2012): 5–32.

Rid, Thomas, *Cyber War Will Not Take Place* (London: Hurst, 2013).

Rid, Thomas, *Rise of the Machines: A Cybernetic History* (London: Scribe, 2016).

Rid, Thomas, and Ben Buchanan, "Attributing Cyber Attacks," *Journal of Strategic Studies* 38/1–2 (2015): 4–37.

Rid, Thomas, and Daniel Moore, "Cryptopolitik and the Darknet," *Survival* 58/1 (2016): 7–38.

Roberts, Lawrence G., "The Evolution of Packet Switching," *Proceedings of the IEEE* 66/11 (1978): 1307–13.

Rogin, Josh, "NSA Chief: Cybercrime Constitutes the 'Greatest Transfer of Wealth in History,'" *Foreign Policy*, July 9, 2012, https://foreignpolicy.com/2012/07/09/nsa-chief-cybercrime-constitutes-the-greatest-transfer-ofwealth-in-history.

Rollins, John, "U.S.–China Cyber Agreement," CRS Insight, October 16, 2016, https://fas.org/sgp/crs/row/IN10376.pdf.

Romanosky, Sasha, Lillian Ablon, Andreas Kuehn and Therese Jones, "Content Analysis of Cyber Insurance Policies: How Do Carriers Price Cyber Risk?" *Journal of Cybersecurity* 5/1 (2019): 1–19.

Ross, Ron, Michael McEvilley and Janey Carrier Oren, *Systems Security Engineering* (Gaithersburg, MD: National Institute of Standards and Technology, 2016).

Rumsfeld, Donald, "Transforming the Military," *Foreign Affairs* 81/3 (2002): 20–32.

Ryan, Camille, and Jamie M. Lewis, *Computer and Internet Use in the United States: 2015* (Washington, DC: US Census Bureau, 2017).

Sandler, Stanley, *World War II in the Pacific: An Encyclopedia* (New York: Routledge, 2015).

Sanger, David E., *The Perfect Weapon: War, Sabotage, and Fear in the Cyber Age* (New York: Crown Publishers, 2018).

Schmitt, Michael N., "Classification of Cyber Conflict," *Journal of Conflict & Security Law* 17/2 (2012): 245–60.

Schmitt, Michael N., *Tallinn Manual on the International Law Applicable to Cyber Warfare: Prepared by the International Group of Experts at the Invitation of the NATO Cooperative Cyber Defence Centre of Excellence* (Cambridge University Press, 2013).

Schmitt, Michael N., and Liis Vihul, *Tallinn Manual 2.0 on the International Law Applicable to Cyber Operations* (Cambridge University Press, 2017).

Scott-Railton, John, and Seth Hardy, "Malware Attacks Targeting Syrian ISIS Critics," Citizen Lab, December 18, 2014, https://citizenlab.ca/2014/12/malware-attack-targeting-syrian-isis-critics.

Searle, Loyd, "The Bombsight War: Nordern vs. Sperry," *IEEE Spectrum* (1989): 60–4.

Segal, Adam, "Holding the Multistakeholder Line at the ITU," Council on Foreign Relations, October 21, 2014, www.cfr.org/report/holding-multistakeholder-line-itu.

Shadow Server Foundation, "AS40989 RBN as RBusiness Network," www.shadowserver.org/wiki/uploads/Information/RBN-AS40989.pdf.

Shapiro, Scott J., *Fancy Bear Goes Phishing: The Dark History of the Information Age, in Five Extraordinary Hacks* (New York: Farrar, Straus and Giroux, 2023).

Sheldon, John, "The Rise of Cyberpower," in *Strategy in the Contemporary World*, ed. John Baylis, James J. Wirtz and Colin S. Gray (Oxford University Press, 2013), 303–19.

Sheldon, Robert, and Joe McReynolds, "Civil–Military Integration and Cybersecurity: A Study of Chinese Information Warfare Militias," in *China and Cybersecurity*, ed. Lindsay, Cheung and Reveron, 188–222.

Shu, Xiaokui, Ke Tian, Andrew Ciambrone and Danfeng Yao, "Breaking the Target: An Analysis of Target Data Breach and Lessons Learned," arXiv (January 2017), 1–10, https://arxiv.org/pdf/1701.04940.

Singer, Peter W., and Allan Friedman, *Cybersecurity and Cyberwar: What Everyone Needs to Know* (Oxford University Press, 2014).

Skoudis, Edward, "Evolutionary Trends in Cyberspace," in *Cyberpower and National Security*, ed. Kramer, Starr and Wentz, 147–70.

Slayton, Rebecca, "What Is the Cyber Offense–Defense Balance? Conceptions, Causes, and Assessment," *International Security* 41/3 (2017): 72–109.

Soldatov, Andrei, and Irina Borogan, *The Red Web: The Struggle between Russia's Digital Dictators and the New Online Revolutionaries* (New York: Public Affairs, 2015).

Sorell, Tom, "Human Rights and Hacktivism: The Cases of Wikileaks and Anonymous," *Journal of Human Rights Practice* 7/3 (2015): 391–410.

Spitzberg, Brian H., and Gregory Hoobler, "Cyberstalking and the

Technologies of Interpersonal Terrorism," *New Media and Society* 4/1 (2002): 67–88.

Staeder, Tracy, "Why Russia Is Building Its Own Internet," *IEEE Spectrum*, January 17, 2018, https://spectrum.ieee.org/tech-talk/telecom/internet/cou ld-russia-really-build-its-own-alternate-internet.

Stolberg, Alan G., "Crafting National Interests in the 21st Century," in *U.S. Army War College Guide to National Security Issues*, vol. II: *National Security Policy and Strategy*, ed. J. Boone Bartholomees Jr. (Carlisle, PA: Strategic Studies Institute, 2012), 13–25.

Stoll, Clifford, "Stalking the Wily Hacker," *Communications of the ACM* 31/5 (1988): 484–97.

Stoll, Clifford, *The Cuckoo's Egg: Tracking a Spy through the Maze of Computer Espionage* (New York: Doubleday, 1989).

Stone, John, "Cyber War Will Take Place!" *Journal of Strategic Studies* 36/1 (2013): 101–8.

Stone-Gross, Brett, Marco Cova, Bob Gilbert, Richard Kemmerer, Christopher Kruegel and Giovanni Vigna, "Analysis of a Botnet Tracker," *IEEE Security & Privacy* 9/1 (2011): 64–72.

Stone-Gross, Brett, Ryan Abman, Richard A. Kemmerer, Christopher Kruegel, Douglas G. Steigerwald and Giovanni Vigna, "The Underground Economy of Fake Antivirus Software," in *Economics of Information Security and Privacy III*, ed. Bruce Schneier (New York: Springer, 2013), 55–78.

Surzhko-Harned, Lena, and Andrew J. Zahuranec, "Framing the Revolution: The Role of Social Media in Ukraine's Euromaidan Movement," *Nationalities Papers* 45/5 (2017): 758–79.

Syverson, Paul, "A Peel of Onion," in *Proceedings of the 27th Annual Computer Security Applications Conference, Orlando, FL* (New York: Association for Computing Machinery, 2011), 123–37.

Tanczer, Leonie Maria, Ine Steenmans, Miles Elsden, Jason Blackstock and Madeline Carr, "Emerging Risks in the IoT Ecosystem: Who's Afraid of the Big Bad Smart Fridge?" paper presented at Living in the Internet of Things: Cybersecurity of the IoT Conference, London, 2018, https://ieeexplore.ieee .org/document/8379720.

Thomas, Timothy L., "Nation-State Cyber Strategies: Examples from China and Russia," in *Cyberpower and National Security*, ed. Kramer, Starr and Wentz, 468–75.

Thomas, Timothy L., "Russian Reflexive Control, Theory and the Military," *Journal of Slavic Military Studies* 17/2 (2004): 237–56.

Timmer, John, "IBM Releases 1,000+ Qubit Processor, Roadmap to Error Correction," *Ars Technica*, December 4, 2023, https://arstechnica.com/sci ence/2023/12/ibm-adds-error-correction-to-updated-quantum-computing -roadmap.

Turgeman-Goldschmidt, Orly, "Identity Construction among Hackers," in *Cyber Criminology: Exploring Internet Crimes and Criminal Behavior* ed. K. Jaishankar (Boca Raton, FL: CRC Press, 2011).

Tzezana, Roey, "High-Probability and Wild-Card Scenarios for Future Crimes and Terror Attacks Using the Internet of Things," *Foresight* 19/1 (2017): 1–14.

UK Government, "National Cyber Security Strategy 2016 to 2021," November 2016, www.gov.uk/government/publications/national-cyber-security-strategy-2016-to-2021.

United States Army Training and Doctrine Command, "Multi-domain Battle: Evolution of Combined Arms for the 21st Century, 2025–2040," December 2017, i, www.tradoc.army.mil/wp-content/uploads/2020/10/MDB_Evolutionfor21st.pdf.

US Army War College, "Strategic Cyberspace Operations Guide," June 1, 2016, archive.org/details/USAWCStrategicCyberOpsGuide.

US Cyber Command, "Achieve and Maintain Cyberspace Superiority: Command Vision for US Cyber Command," 2018, www.hsdl.org/?view&did=812923.

US Department of Commerce, Bureau of Industry and Security, "Commerce Implements New Export Controls on Advanced Computing and Semiconductor Manufacturing Items to the People's Republic of China (PRC)," October 7, 2022, www.bis.doc.gov/index.php/documents/about-bis/newsroom/press-releases/3158-2022-10-07-bis-press-release-advanced-computing-and-semiconductor-manufacturing-controls-final/file.

US Department of Defense, "The DoD Cyber Strategy," April 2015, http://archive.defense.gov/home/features/2015/0415_cyber-strategy/final_2015_dod_cyber_strategy_for_web.pdf.

US Department of State, "A Declaration for the Future of the Internet," April 2022, www.state.gov/wp-content/uploads/2022/04/Declaration-for-the-Future-for-the-Internet.pdf.

US Government, "Improvement of Technical Management of Internet Names and Addresses; Proposed Rule," in *Federal Register*, vol. LXIII (Washington, DC: Office of the Federal Register, 1998).

US Government, "National Military Strategy for Cyberspace Operations," December 2006, www.hsdl.org/?view&did=35693.

US House of Representatives, Committee on Oversight and Government Reform, Subcommittee on Information Technology, "Wassenaar: Cybersecurity and ExportControl," 114th Congress, 2nd sess., January 12, 2016, https://oversight.house.gov/hearing/wassenaar-cybersecurity-and-export-control.

US House of Representatives, Committee on Science, Space, and Technology, Subcommittee on Technology and Competitiveness, Hearing: Computer

Security, "Statement of Winn Schwartau," 102nd Congress, 1st sess., June 27, 1991.

US Joint Chiefs of Staff, Joint Publication 3-0, "Joint Operations," Washington, DC, January 17, 2017, http://irp.fas.org/doddir/dod/jp3_0.pdf.

US Joint Chiefs of Staff, Joint Publication 3-12 (R), "Cyberspace Operations," Washington, DC, 2013, https://irp.fas.org/doddir/dod/jp3_12r.pdf.

US Senate, Select Committee to Study Governmental Operations with Respect to Intelligence Activities, "Intelligence Activities and the Rights of Americans," Book II, April 26, 1976.

Vacca, W. Alexander, "Military Culture and Cyber Security," *Survival* 53/6 (2011): 159–76.

Valeriano, Brandon, Benjamin Jensen and Ryan C. Maness, *Cyber Strategy: The Evolving Character of Power and Coercion* (Oxford University Press, 2018).

Valeriano, Brandon, and Ryan C. Maness, *Cyber War versus Cyber Realities: Cyber Conflict in the International System* (New York: Oxford University Press, 2015).

Valeriano, Brandon, and Ryan C. Maness, "The Coming Cyberpeace," *Foreign Affairs*, May 13, 2015, www.foreignaffairs.com/articles/2015-05-13/coming -cyberpeace.

Valeriano, Brandon, and Ryan Maness, "The Fog of CyberWar," *Foreign Affairs*, November 21, 2012, www.foreignaffairs.com/articles/2012-11-21 /fog-cyberwar.

Van Puyvelde, Damien, "From Information to Cybersecurity: Bridging the Public–Private Divide," in *US National Cybersecurity*, ed. Van Puyvelde and Brantly, 177–94.

Van Puyvelde, Damien, and Aaron F. Brantly (eds.), *US National Cybersecurity: International Politics, Concepts and Organization* (New York: Routledge, 2017).

Van Puyvelde, Damien, Stephen Coulthart and Shahriar Hossain, "Beyond the Buzzword: Big Data and National Security Decision-Making," *International Affairs* 93/6 (2017): 1397–1416.

Vogels, Emily A., "Some Digital Divides Persist between Rural, Urban and Suburban America," Pew Research Center, August 19, 2021, www.pewrese arch.org/short-reads/2021/08/19/some-digital-divides-persist-between-rural -urban-and-suburban-america.

Warner, Michael, "Cybersecurity: A Pre-history," *Intelligence and National Security* 27/5 (2012): 781–99.

Warner, Michael, "Intelligence in Cyber – and Cyber in Intelligence," in *Understanding Cyber Conflict*, ed. George Perkovich and Ariel E. Levite (Washington, DC: Georgetown University Press, 2018), 17–29.

Webroot, *Game Changers: AI and Machine Learning in Cybersecurity* (Broomfield, CO: Webroot, 2017).

Weimann, Gabriel, "Cyberterrorism: The Sum of All Fears?" *Studies in Conflict & Terrorism* 28/2 (2005): 129–49.

Weimann, Gabriel, *Going Darker? The Challenge of Dark Net Terrorism* (Washington, DC: Wilson Center, 2018).

Weimann, Gabriel, *Terrorism in Cyberspace: The Next Generation* (New York: Columbia University Press, 2015).

Wendt, Alexander, "Anarchy Is What States Make of It," *International Organization* 46/2 (1992): 391–425.

White, Sarah P., *Understanding Cyberwarfare: Lessons from the Russia–Georgia War* (West Point, NY: Modern War Institute, 2018).

White House, "International Strategy for Cyberspace: Prosperity, Security, and Openness in a Networked World," May 2011, https:// obamawhitehouse.ar chives.gov/sites/default/files/rss_viewer/international_strategy_for_cyberspa ce.pdf.

White House, "National Defense Strategy of the United States of America," March 2005.

White House, "National Defense Strategy of the United States of America," June 2008.

White House, "National Defense Strategy of the United States of America," 2011.

White House, "National Defense Strategy of the United States of America: Sharpening the American Military's Competitive Edge," 2018.

White House, National Security Decision Directive 145, "National Policy on Telecommunications and Automated Information Systems Security," September 17, 1984, https://fas.org/irp/offdocs/nsdd145.htm.

White House, "National Security Strategy of the United States of America," December 2017.

White House, Office of Science and Technology Policy, "Blueprint for an AI Bill of Rights: Making Automated Systems Work for the American People," October 2022, 5, www.whitehouse.gov/ostp/ai-bill-of-rights/algorithmic -discrimination-protections-2.

White House, Presidential Decision Directive/NSC-63, "Critical Infrastructure Protection," May 22, 1998, https://fas.org/irp/offdocs/pdd/pdd-63.htm.

White House, "Presidential Policy Directive 41 – United States Cyber Incident Coordination," July 26, 2016, https://obamawhitehouse.archives .gov/the-press-office/2016/07/26/presidentialpolicy-directive-united-states -cyber-incident.

White House, "The National Strategy to Secure Cyberspace," February 2003, https://georgewbush-whitehouse.archives.gov/pcipb.

Wiener, Norbert, *Cybernetics: Or, Control and Communication in the Animal and the Machine* (New York: MIT Press, 1961).

Williams, Meredydd, et al., "Future Scenarios and Challenges for Security and

Privacy," paper presented at the IEEE International Forum on Research and Technologies for Society and Industry, Leveraging a Better Tomorrow (2016), https://ieeexplore.ieee.org/document/7740625.

Wirtz, James J., "Cyber War and Strategic Culture: The Russian Integration of Cyber Power into Grand Strategy," in *Cyber War in Perspective: Russian Aggression against Ukraine*, ed. Kenneth Geers (Tallinn: NATO Cooperative Cyber Defence Centre of Excellence, 2015), 29–37.

Wolfers, Arnold, "National Security as an Ambiguous Symbol," *Political Science Quarterly* 67/4 (1952): 481–502.

Wolff, Josephine, *Cyberinsurance Policy: Rethinking Risk in an Age of Ransomware, Computer Fraud, Data Breaches, and Cyberattacks* (Cambridge, MA: MIT Press 2022).

Yossman, K. J., "Russia Passes Censorship Law Threatening Imprisonment, Forced Labor over 'Fake News,'" *Variety*, March 4, 2022, https://variety.com/2022/politics/news/russia-censorship-law-fake-news-1235196208.

Zaman, R. Uz, "Strategic Culture: A 'Cultural' Understanding of War," *Comparative Strategy* 28/1 (2009): 68–88.

Zatko, Peiter, "If You Don't Like the Game, Hack the Playbook," presentation at DARPA Cyber Colloquium, November 7, 2011, Arlington, VA, https://apps.dtic.mil/sti/tr/pdf/ADA551945.pdf.

Zetter, Kim, "Viasat Hack 'Did Not' Have Huge Impact on Ukrainian Military Communications, Official Says," *Zero Day*, September 26, 2022, https://www.zetter-zeroday.com/p/viasat-hack-did-not-have-huge-impact?utm_source=%2Fsearch%2FViasat&utm_medium=reader2.

Zetter, Kim, *Countdown to Zero Day: Stuxnet and the Launch of the World's First Digital Weapon* (New York: Broadway Books, 2014).

Index

non-state actors, 5, 6, 24, 42, 44, 55,
60, 75, 78, 88, 90, 101, 126,
131, 132, 143–4, 152–74, 185,
188–91, 197, 205
NORAD (North American
Aerospace Defense Command),
26, 154
North Korea (DPRK), 50, 72, 84,
146, 159, 171
Norton, Nancy A., 72
Norway, 14, 179
Norwegian Seismic Array
(NORSAR), 14
NotPetya attack, 155
NSA (National Security Agency), 18,
19, 54, 72, 84, 179
nuclear weapons, 3, 73, 125–6
Nye, Joseph, 89

Obama, Barack, 62, 148, 168
Odysseus, 66
Oliver, John, 59
Open-Ended Working Group
(OEWG), 61
Open Systems Interconnection
model (OSI model), 37–8
OpenSSL, 39
Orchard, Operation, 114
Orwell, George, 179

packet-switched networks, 35–6
Pakistan, 51, 168, 183
Panetta, Leon, 115
Paris, France, 164, 169
passkeys, 139–40
patch management, 140
"Pearl Harbor," cyber, 85, 115, 129
Pentagon, the, 18
People's Liberation Army (PLA)
(China), 76, 96, 99–100, 123,
147
personal computers (PCs), 10, 14

personally identifiable information
(PII), 77, 157
personas, online, 26, 29–30, 31, 34,
38, 40–1, 42, 66, 71, 73, 80,
102, 132, 157
Philippines, 21
phishing, 71, 75, 155–7, 202
piracy, digital, 183
Plante, Erin, 159
policing, 144, 167, 201
pornography, 154, 161
Portugal, 59, 93
Postel, John, 47
privacy, 44, 51, 57, 66, 69, 95, 105,
136, 175–8, 180, 182, 185,
186, 187–8, 189, 194, 197,
200, 201, 202, 204
protocols, 12, 26, 34, 35, 37, 39, 40,
44, 47, 49, 54, 56, 57, 58, 136,
170
proxies, cyber, 74, 82, 152, 153, 155,
159, 170–2, 185
Putin, Vladimir, 102

quantum computing, 5, 194, 195,
202–3

radiation, 29, 32–3
ransomware, 61, 69, 72, 73–4,
155–6, 160, 166
Rattray, Greg, 128
Raymond, Mark, 55
Reagan, Ronald, 18, 26, 27
realism, 4, 34
Regional Internet Registry (RIR), 58
Remote Access Trojan (RAT), 185
Request for Comment (RFC), 45,
46–7, 48
retaliation, 145–7, 148, 150
Reveron, Derek, 11
Rid, Thomas, 85, 115–16, 118,
186–7

Printed and bound by CPI Group (UK) Ltd, Croydon, CR0 4YY

16/04/2025